Textbook of COMMERCE

5th EDITION

LYNDA FITZMAURICE

Heinemann is an imprint of Pearson Education Limited, a company incorporated in England and Wales, having its registered office at Edinburgh Gate, Harlow, Essex, CM20 2JE. Registered company number: 872828

www.heinemann.co.uk

Heinemann is a registered trademark of Pearson Education Ltd

First published 2008

20 19 18 17 16 15 14 13 12
IMP 11 10 9 8 7 6 5 4 3

British Library Cataloguing in Publication Data is available from the British Library on request.

ISBN 978 0 435982 25 6

Designed by Tek-Art
Typeset by Tek-Art, Crawley Down, West Sussex
Original illustrations © Pearson Education Ltd, 2008
Illustrated by Tek-Art
Cover design by Bigtop
Picture research by Christine Martin
Cover photo/illustration © Getty/Photographers choice
Printed in Malaysia, CTP-VP

The websites used in this book were correct and up to date at the time of publication. It is essential for tutors to preview each website before using it in class so as to ensure that the URL is still accurate, relevant and appropriate. We suggest that tutors bookmark useful websites and consider enabling students to access them through the school/college intranet.

Acknowledgements

The author and publisher would like to thank the following individuals and organisations for permission to reproduce photographs:

Alamy / Alex Segre p**218**; Alamy / DirectPhoto.org p**224**; Alamy / Earl Clendennen p**218**; Alamy / Jeremy Sutton-Hibbert p**43**; Alamy / Paul Thompson Images p**70**; Alamy / Peerpoint p**1**; Alamy / Photofusion Picture Library p**26**; Alamy / Powered By Light / Alan Spencer p**213**; Alamy / Steven May p**50**; **166**; Corbis / Andrew Holbrooke p**189**; Corbis / Construction Photography p**183**; Corbis / Don Mason p**44**; Corbis / Jerry Arcieri p**22**; Corbis / John and Lisa Merrill p**65**; Corbis / Jose Fuste Raya p**114**; Corbis / Lester Lefkowitz p**162**; Corbis / LWA–Sharie Kennedy p**115**; Corbis / Moodboard p**136**; Corbis / Paul Souders p**21**; Corbis / Terry Vine p**180**; Digital Vision p**167**; Getty / Photodisc p**205**, **206**; Getty / Taxi p**151**; Photoshot / Gary Lee p**235**; Rex Features / Sipa Press p**57**; Richard Smith p**225**; Shutterstock / Baloncia p**69**; Shutterstock / Harald Høiland Tjøstheim p**179**; Shutterstock / Jan van Broekhaven p**96**; Shutterstock / Kiselev Andrey Valerevich p**56**; Shutterstock / Mikael Damkier p**161**; Shutterstock / Natalia Bratslavsky p**79**; Shutterstock / Paul Maguire p**242**; Shutterstock / Yanik Chauvin p**2**.

Every effort has been made to contact copyright holders of material reproduced in this book. Any omissions will be rectified in subsequent printings if notice is given to the publishers.

Contents

Acknowledgements ii
Introduction v

Unit 1: Production 1

1.1 The chain of production and the extractive, manufacturing and construction, and tertiary industries 3
1.2 Specialisation and division of labour 8
1.3 Commerce, trade and aids to trade 11
1.4 The relationship between industry, commerce and direct services 15
Test your knowledge 18

Unit 2: Retail trade 21

2.1 The role of the retailer in the chain of distribution 23
2.2 Types of retailer 26
2.3 Selling techniques, trends in retailing and the implications of e-commerce 31
2.4 Home shopping 37
2.5 Large-scale retailing 39
Test your knowledge 41

Unit 3: Customer credit 43

3.1 The use of credit 45
3.2 Types of credit 48
Test your knowledge 54

Unit 4: Consumer protection 56

4.1 Safeguarding the consumer 58
4.2 Methods of safeguarding the consumer 60
Test your knowledge 67

Unit 5: Wholesale trade 69

5.1 The role of the wholesaler in the chain of distribution 71
5.2 Functions and services of the wholesaler 73
5.3 Intermediaries 76
Test your knowledge 77

Unit 6: Documents of trade 79

6.1 Documents of home trade 81
6.2 Terms of payment 90
Test your knowledge 94

Unit 7: International trade 96

7.1 The importance of international trade 98
7.2 Balance of trade and balance of payments 101
7.3 Customs authorities 104
7.4 Free trade and protectionism 106
7.5 Trading blocs 108
7.6 Difficulties faced by exporters 109
Test your knowledge 111

Unit 8: Advertising 114

8.1 The role of advertising 116
8.2 Advertising media 121
8.3 Methods of appeal 126
8.4 Sales promotion 129
8.5 Trends in advertising 131
Test your knowledge 134

Unit 9: Communications 136

9.1 The importance of communications in the global economy 138
9.2 Methods of communication: internal and external 140
9.3 Post Office and telecoms 156
Test your knowledge 159

Unit 10: Transport 161

10.1 Transport 163
10.2 Containerisation 171
10.3 Other trends in transport 172
10.4 Transport documents 173
10.5 International transport 175
Test your knowledge 176

Unit 11: Warehousing 179

11.1 The role of warehousing 181
11.2 Types of warehousing 185
Test your knowledge 187

Unit 12: Insurance 189

12.1 Purposes of insurance and the statistical basis of insurance 191
12.2 Business and personal risks 194
12.3 Insurance principles 197
12.4 Arranging insurance cover 199
12.5 Making a claim 201
Test your knowledge 202

Unit 13: Banking 205

13.1 Banking services 207
13.2 Means of payment for home and international trade activities 213
13.3 Trends in banking 220
Test your knowledge 222

Unit 14: The business unit 224

14.1 Location of a business 226
14.2 Public and private sector 228
14.3 The main forms of business organisation in the private sector 230
14.4 Multinationals 237
Test your knowledge 240

Unit 15: Business finance 242

15.1 Sources of finance 244
15.2 Business finance 254
Test your knowledge 259

Index 262

Introduction

Welcome to your 'Commerce' course. This book has been specifically written to help you achieve a 'GCE Ordinary Level in Commerce' qualification with the University of Cambridge International Examinations (CIE) organisation. It will also be an extremely useful resource for anyone studying commerce or business-related qualifications at Level 2 or GCSE Level.

This book aims to provide you with an overall understanding of commercial activities, both domestically and internationally, and an understanding of how activities are influenced by factors in the environment in which commercial businesses operate. Written in conjunction with specialists at CIE, this book will enable you to develop and demonstrate:

Knowledge and understanding of the:

- basic principles, techniques and ideas in commerce
- facts and terms relevant to commerce
- key features and functions of commercial activities
- main documents used in commerce.

Application of:

- commercial principles and ideas to given situations through case studies, activities and examination question practice
- data and information in written, numerical and diagrammatic form.

Analytical skills in:

- identifying and selecting significant issues in a commercial situation
- identifying the main problems that relate to a given commercial situation or scenario.

Evaluative skills in:

- distinguishing between what is presented as evidence and opinion
- presenting reasoned judgements to given commercial situations and communicating them in a relevant and logical manner.

Each unit of the book corresponds to a topic in the CIE O Level Commerce syllabus. These are as follows:

1 Production
2 Retail trade
3 Customer credit
4 Consumer protection
5 Wholesale trade

6 Documents of trade
7 International trade
8 Advertising
9 Communications
10 Transport
11 Warehousing
12 Insurance
13 Banking
14 The business unit
15 Business finance

All units are broken down in exactly the same way. Every unit is introduced with a 'What do I need to learn?' section which highlights the main learning aims of this part of the syllabus. The topic of each unit is then introduced in an interesting and stimulating way to help you to consider issues that will be investigated during the unit. Every unit has a variety of features to encourage you to apply what you have learned. These include:

- Definition boxes:
  - to help learners develop their understanding and application of commercial terminology and common vocabulary.
- Theory into practice activities:
  - to enable learners to apply what they have learned by performing or carrying out activities that allow them to test learning and understanding.
- Think it over activities:
  - to encourage learners to reflect on what they have just learned and, in many cases, to apply it to commercial activities and issues in their own country.
- Test your knowledge section
  - This is an end-of-unit selection of multiple choice and stimulus response exam questions. It is designed to check learning that has taken place and to identify gaps in knowledge and understanding that need to be addressed before the final examinations.
- Exam tips
  - This feature appears in the 'Test your knowledge' section and contains useful advice on exam technique, how to approach the questions and how to correctly interpret key examination terminology.

The layout of the book has been designed to enable you to work through each topic easily and independently. Each unit contains a range of exercises to develop understanding of the theory that is covered.

I hope everyone who uses this book – both learners and teachers alike – finds it interesting and enjoyable to read. Good luck in the examinations!

Lynda Fitzmaurice
2008

1 Production

What do I need to study?

- Define and describe the 'chain of production'.
- Identify and illustrate the extractive, manufacturing and construction, and tertiary (service) industries.
- Describe and explain the value of specialisation and division of labour.
- Explain what is meant by commerce and trade and identify what aids to trade exist.
- Describe and explain the relationship that exists between industry, commerce and direct services.

Some of these topics will be investigated in more detail later in the book.

Introduction

Needs are defined as the goods and services that we require and need to live. They include the need for food, water, clothing, and shelter.

Wants are goods or services that we do not need to live, but we still want them. For example, we all need suitable clothing but we do not necessarily need designer clothing.

Production is the process that takes place when resources, such as raw (natural, not yet processed) materials, human labour and energy are converted into goods or services that satisfy the **needs** and **wants** of consumers.

Think about what you had for breakfast this morning. Was it a nice refreshing glass of orange juice, a bread roll with butter, cereal and milk or just a cup of black coffee? Almost everything we consume whether it is food, a magazine, or a bus ride to school has to be produced. Your orange juice was squeezed from fresh oranges. These were picked and then transported from a fruit farm to a factory. At the factory they were processed using machinery and the juice was poured into cartons ready for you to drink at the breakfast table. This whole production process is aimed at satisfying your need for a healthy glass of orange juice in the morning.

1.1 The chain of production and the extractive, manufacturing and construction, and tertiary industries

There are different stages in the production process and there is a clear link from one stage to the next. Each stage relies on the stage before, so the process is often called the chain of production. Three different stages of production form separate parts of the chain of production: primary, secondary and tertiary.

Industry – This is the general term used for groups of companies and organisations that make, sell or provide a particular type of good or service. For example, the automobile industry will include the manufacturers of the parts used to make cars as well as the organisations that build the finished car and the dealers that sell them on to the final consumer.

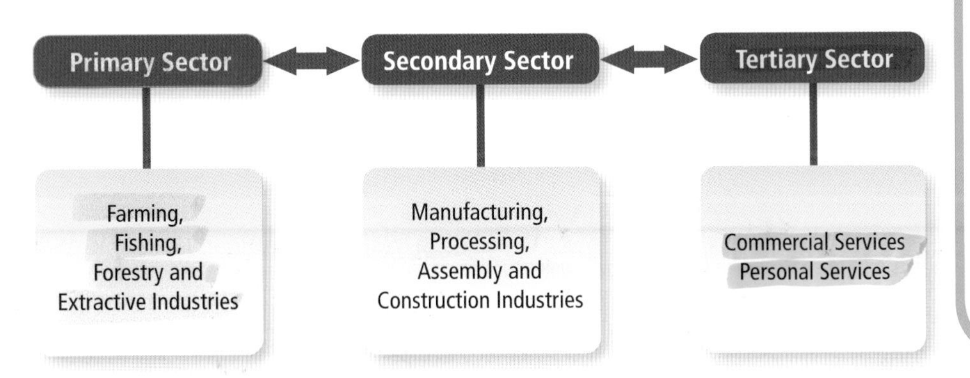

■ **Figure 1.1** *A typical chain of production*

Added value

Value is added to a product when it is transformed at each stage of the production process. In the introduction, we talked about orange juice. The fresh oranges on the trees have little value, but once they have been picked (primary stage) and taken to have the juice extracted and put into cartons (secondary stage) value has been added to them. Computer manufacturers such as Compaq or Hewlett Packard will purchase or manufacture a range of parts including circuit boards and plastic casings. These then go through an assembly process until the final product – the computer – is ready to be boxed and sold. Parts gain value when they are processed and assembled into high-quality finished products for sale. The finished products are worth a great deal more than the cost of all the parts that make them. We call this **added value**.

Added value – the extra value given to products and services as a result of production or manufacturing processes, transport or storage.

Each of the three industrial sectors are linked to form a **chain of production** (see Figure 1.1).

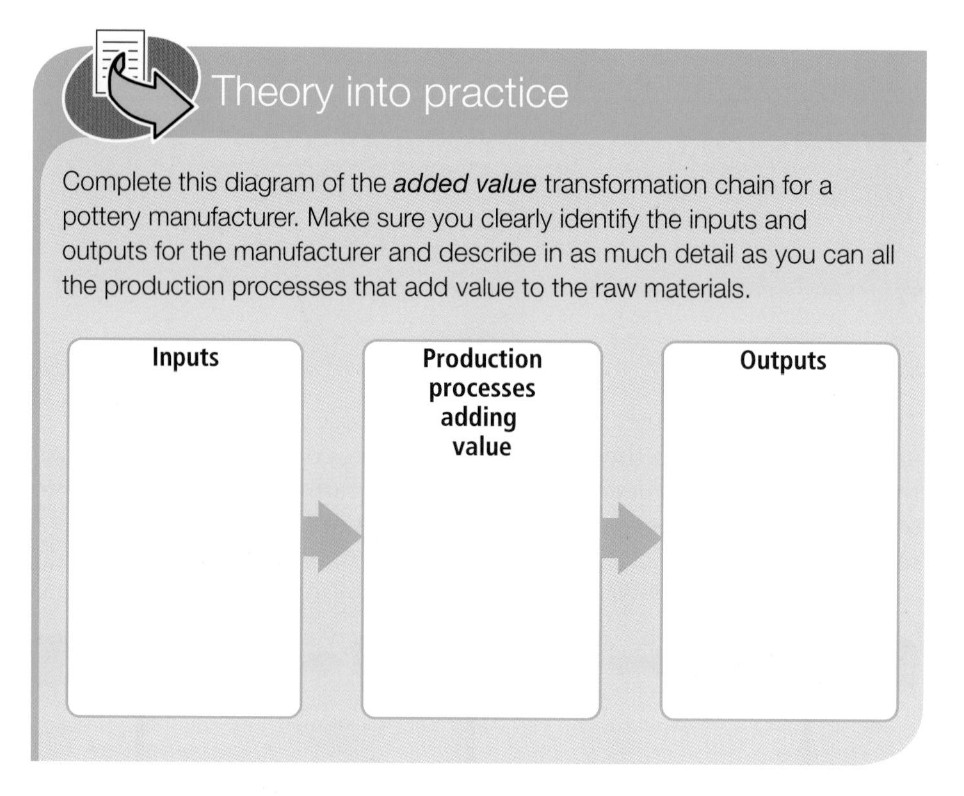

Primary sector industries are concerned with getting or growing raw materials. For example fruit, vegetable and cereal crops are farmed, animals are reared, trees are grown and felled (cut down), iron and coal are mined from the ground and oil is drilled and piped from under the sea. These are sometimes known as 'extractive production' industries.

Secondary sector industries will purchase the raw materials grown or extracted by primary industries. Then, using manufacturing and assembly processes, they will convert raw materials into parts or finished goods. For example, they may convert oils into plastics and then the plastics into toys. The construction industries are concerned with building roads and other transport networks. They also produce buildings for use as schools, hospitals, factories, shops, offices and homes.

Tertiary sector activities provide the services that support the distribution of raw materials, parts and finished goods between organisations. There are commercial services and personal services. Commercial (or indirect) services support the activities carried out in the primary and secondary sectors of production to help the product reach the consumer. Personal (or direct) services provide a service *directly* to a consumer. Commercial services include money to pay for the production and distribution of goods and services; communications to help arrange production and distribution; advertising to tell consumers about the products; transport and warehouses to store the products and insurance to protect against loss and damage. Personal services include health and beauty care; education; legal and financial advice and live entertainment.

The diagram in Figure 1.2 demonstrates how the three sectors are involved in the production process for printed material – like this student book.

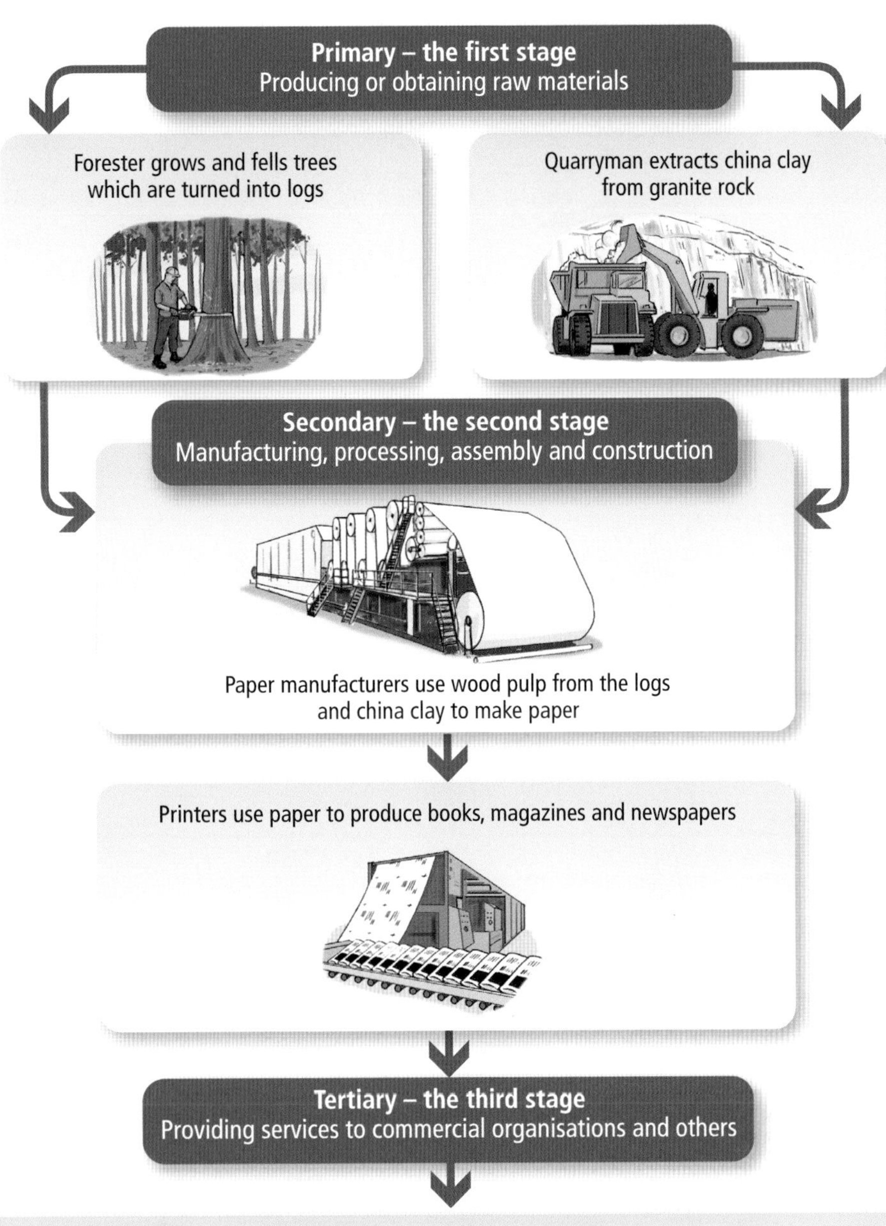

■ **Figure 1.2** *The three stages of production for printed material*

As you can see from the stages of production diagram there are a large number of separate organisations involved in the chain of production. Some organisations, such as Shell Oil Plc, actually play a part in all three sectors. Shell operates in the primary sector extracting oil, which is then passed on to the secondary sector refineries. They process the oil so it is suitable to be sold to consumers through the tertiary sector petrol stations.

Theory into practice

Produce a chain of production for the following goods. Make sure you clearly identify the industries involved in the chain from the primary, secondary and tertiary sectors until the product/service reaches its final consumer.

- A chocolate bar.
- A loaf of bread.

Theory into practice

Using the words Primary, Secondary and Tertiary identify which stage of production each of the following examples belongs to. For example, Hairdressers = Tertiary. Remember that some of the examples could be involved in more than one stage of production.

■ Hairdressers = Tertiary	■ Bank
■ Stone quarry	■ Oil refinery
■ Tulip grower	■ Carpet shop
■ Vineyard	■ Museum
■ Sheep farmer	■ Bakery
■ Car manufacturer	■ University
■ Hotel	■ Clothing shop
■ Petrol station	■ Supermarket
■ Insurance company	■ Paint manufacturer
■ Salmon fish farmer	■ Diamond mine

The percentage of primary, secondary and tertiary industries in every country changes constantly.

In the UK today, there has been a huge fall in primary and secondary industries and a rise in tertiary services. In 2004, 77.8 per cent of the UK's workforce was employed in tertiary industries. This figure would have been much lower 30 years earlier when the UK was a world leader in manufacturing. By contrast, China has seen a lot of growth in secondary industries and is regarded as one of the strongest economies of the early 21st century, with manufacturing being one of the country's greatest strengths today.

Internationally, there is a general overall growth in tertiary industries. There are many reasons for this:

- Services supplied by tertiary sector activities grow and fall in response to consumer demand and consumer wealth.
- Recent developments in the widespread use of information technology have made faster communication easier for many more people.
- Specialisation has allowed goods to be produced more cheaply, leading to lower prices and increased demand.
- People have more money and demand more luxury items such as mobile telephones, which may have to be obtained from other countries. They also demand more personal services such as private health care, eating out and foreign holidays etc.

Theory into practice

Look at the table below, which describes the industry sectors of a country, then answer the questions.

Industry	1000s employed in 1985	1000s employed in 2005
Agriculture, forestry & fishing	380	262
Energy and water supply	733	182
Manufacturing	7060	3705
Construction	1272	1195
Services	13888	20435
TOTAL	23333	25779

1. Identify one example of a primary, secondary and tertiary industry from the table above.
2. Calculate the total number of workers working in the primary, secondary and tertiary industries in 1985 and 2005.
3. What percentage of the total workforce was employed by services in 1985 and 2005 (rounded to the nearest whole per cent)?
4. Suggest one reason why more people were employed by services than any other sector.

1.2 Specialisation and division of labour

Think about the tourism industry in your country. What kinds of organisations are there within this industry? Make a list of at least ten of these organisations.

Specialisation

Within each of the three sectors of production we have discussed we can identify a wide range of activities and industries. There are a huge number of industries. The following list is just a small selection of some of the industries around the world:

- **Food and beverages (drinks)** – This includes all the processing activities involving food and beverages for final consumption, but it also includes intermediate products for other sectors – such as the tertiary tourist industry that will require food and beverages to give to its clients.
- **Electronics** – This includes all the manufacturing of electronic components and domestic and industrial electronic goods such as TVs, stereos, microwaves and production equipment.
- **Transport** – This includes all the organisations that provide transport services such as passenger transport by road, rail, air or sea, or distribution of goods or materials.
- **Motor vehicle** – This includes all car manufacturers, motorcycle manufacturers, heavy goods and passenger vehicle manufacturers.
- Some other major industries include: pulp and paper, heat and power, chemical, pharmaceuticals (medicines), steel, oil, tourism.

Specialisation – when individuals, organisations or whole economies concentrate on making a limited range of products or providing a specific service.

As you can see from the activity above, within each industry we have organisations that choose to specialise in one particular area. Whether an industry is in the primary, secondary or tertiary sector we can split it into the various types of work done. We call this **specialisation**.

Companies who specialise in a particular area employ workers to perform particular duties. These workers build up very specific skills through long experience and focused training, and become very efficient and effective workers. The different tasks are divided between workers depending on the skills and experience they have.

Specialisation has taken place because of increasing levels of competition. By concentrating on a limited range of products or services organisations can become highly efficient and produce huge quantities at very low prices. For example, in the food and beverages (drinks) industry we have producers such as Cadbury Schweppes, who specialise in making confectionery (sweets) and drinks, and Campbell, who specialise in making soups, fruit and vegetable drinks, and even biscuits.

Division of labour

Within an accountancy firm you can see evidence of division of labour. There will be staff who specialise in giving administrative help to everyone within the firm, corporate and personal tax consultants, auditors (book keepers), small business consultants and corporate business consultants. Within traditional manufacturing businesses there are accountants, marketing people, sales people, computer technicians, warehousing workers, production managers and administrators, to name just a few.

Division of labour – the selection and placing of workers within an organisation according to their experience and skills. They can carry out their duties quickly, accurately and efficiently, making sure that the organisation provides high-quality products or services.

Advantages of specialisation and division of labour

- An organisation and its workers can specialise in what they do best and become better and faster.
- Goods and services are produced at lower costs and in less time, but this is only helpful when there are a high number of consumers for the products or services.
- Equipment and machinery can be developed to allow workers to gain even more efficiency.
- Training for jobs is quicker because duties are easier to learn and workers don't need to move from one task to another.

Disadvantages of specialisation and division of labour

- Workers can become bored and stop being motivated if their tasks become repetitive, and this can lead to less efficiency.
- Goods produced by a range of manufacturers can become standardised. This means that they are similar in appearance and purpose so it can be difficult to tell the difference between competitors' goods.
- Smaller producers are not able to compete with the big producers.

Theory into practice

Tabard Clothing Ltd has been in the textiles (material and clothes) industry for over 70 years – making specialist clothing for sports enthusiasts, industrial protective clothing and bespoke (specially designed and ordered) uniforms. In recent years, sales of sportswear and industrial protective clothing have fallen due to increased levels of competition in these specialist areas.

1. What is specialisation?
2. Is there a case for specialisation in Tabard Clothing Ltd?
3. Explain the advantages and disadvantages of specialisation to Tabard Clothing Ltd.

Specialisation can take many forms. These include specialisation by:

- **Country** – A supply of services, goods, raw materials etc. that has in the past come from a particular country because of the naturally occurring resources or traditional craftsmanship that exist there. For example, diamonds from Africa, lamb from New Zealand, carpets from Turkey and watches from Switzerland.
- **Region** – The supply of services, goods, raw materials etc. will come from a particular region of a country. For example, in most countries there are regions associated with tourism, usually found on coastlands or in regions of great natural beauty. Another example would be the north-eastern region of Thailand, which is one of the country's largest silk production areas.
- **Town** – A town or city within a country can become linked with a particular industry. For example, Bang Tapang Noi in north-east Thailand is one of the main centres of silk production where, traditionally, female family members make silk by hand (in order to increase their families' small incomes as rice farmers).
- **Firms** – A firm or organisation may split itself up into specialised units. For example, Cadbury Schweppes Plc now has a number of divisions to deal with its many drinks and sweets that are consumed internationally.
- **Factories** – An organisation may focus each of its factories on a particular product type. For example, Heinz, the global US food manufacturer, has factories that specialise in manufacturing ketchups and sauces, and also factories specialising in manufacturing frozen meals, soups and children's meals.
- **Individual** – An individual can specialise in providing one type of service or product. For example, this could be an accountant who specialises in providing financial and tax consultancy services to private individuals.

1.3 Commerce, trade and aids to trade

Commerce

In the introduction to this unit we looked at what was involved in getting a carton of fresh orange juice to the breakfast table. We don't often think about the huge number of organisations and people who are involved in producing goods and making sure they reach us in perfect condition.

To produce a carton of orange juice the first thing needed is the fresh oranges. These are probably grown on specialised farms with a large number of specialist employees who make sure that the fruit is insect-free and picked at just the right time so that the juice is nice and sweet.

The oranges then need to be delivered to the factory to be processed and to have their juice extracted. This will involve a range of **commercial activities** such as transport to get the fruit from the farm to the factory, and insurance in case the fruit is lost or damaged while it is being transported.

Commerce or ***commercial activity*** is the means by which raw materials and finished goods are distributed to those people or organisations who have a need for them and the money to pay for them. Commerce includes trade and the various 'aids to trade'.

The owners of the factory will need to arrange payment for the fruit, which may involve taking a loan from their bank or organising an electronic transfer of money from the organisation's bank account to the farmer's bank account. Already we have seen a wide range of commercial activities that are involved in bringing a carton of orange juice to your table and we haven't even put the juice in the cartons yet!

Commerce is all about the wide range of activities or jobs that have to take place when transporting raw materials from primary industries to manufacturers in the secondary industry, and when transporting the finished goods manufactured by secondary industries to consumers. The orange juice example shows how complex commerce is.

Without commercial activities the movement of raw materials and goods or services between organisations, consumers and sectors would not be efficient. For example, large food retailers all rely on fast and efficient harvesting, processing and distribution of fresh foods to their stores to ensure they keep the food choice and quality their customers want.

There is a wide variety of commercial services supporting the movement of raw materials, semi-finished products and finished goods between businesses where buying and selling (known as **trade**) is always taking place. The commercial services which support trade are referred to as **aids to trade**. These are shown in the chart overleaf (Figure 1.3). We will look at trade (home and international) and each aid to trade in more detail throughout this book.

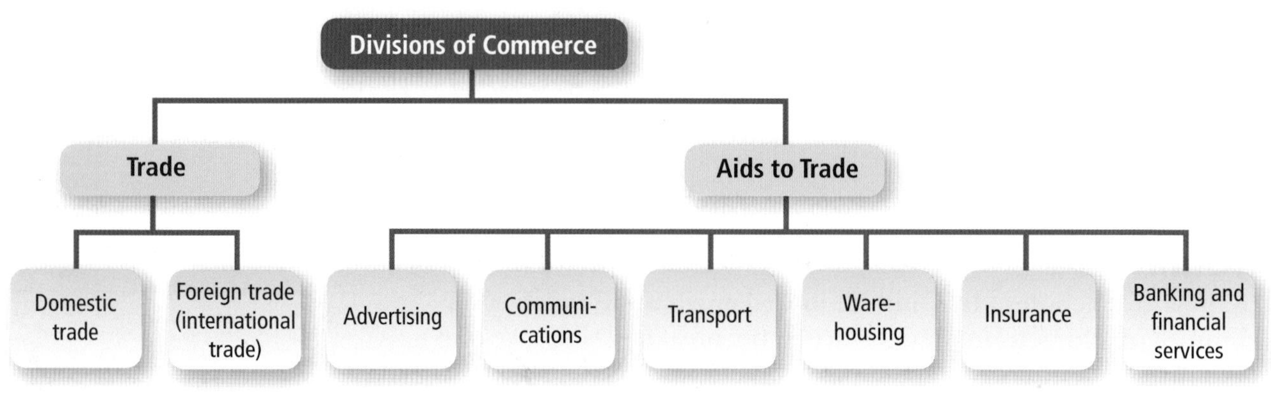

■ **Figure 1.3** *The divisions of commerce*

Trade

Trade – the process of buying and selling to make a profit.

We can use our example of a carton of orange juice to show that trade can take place in many different ways. A manufacturer can choose to sell its cartons of orange juice to home customers (customers in their own country) or to overseas customers (customers in other countries). This is referred to as **home trade** and **international trade**.

Home trade

Home trade – the whole range of activities involved in buying, selling and distributing goods within a specific country.

Home trade is important to a country's economy. Manufacturers and traders who choose to buy from home suppliers are supporting their own country's industries and economy. However, they will only choose to buy from home suppliers, rather than from increasingly strong overseas competition, if the terms and prices are good when compared with the overseas alternatives.

If the juice manufacturer chooses to sell its orange juice in its own country then it will need to decide whether it will sell its cartons of orange juice to wholesalers in very large quantities or directly to retailers in smaller quantities. This is usually called **wholesale** or **retail trade**:

- **Wholesaling** – Traditionally, manufacturers produce goods and sell them in very large quantities to wholesalers who distribute the goods to smaller wholesalers or retailers. This is an essential service that enables smaller retailers to obtain goods from a number of different manufacturers when they need them. The wholesaler is able to 'bulk buy' products (buy very large numbers) and sell them to retailers at a small profit margin. The retailers are then able to sell to the consumers with an additional profit margin added to the cost price. (You will find out more about wholesaling in Unit 5.) However, this process is changing and will be explored in more detail later in this book.
- **Retailing** – This is an extremely important part of the trading process. The location of shops and other retail outlets, how they price and promote the goods on their shelves, and what they choose to stock and sell to their consumers will either support or not support traders in goods and materials. (You will find out more about retailing in Unit 2.)

Can you think of any products or services in your own country that customers are encouraged to buy just because they have been made or supplied by home manufacturers or suppliers? For example, customers buying lamb in New Zealand are told that New Zealand lamb is the best in the world!

International trade

If a manufacturer chooses to sell their goods to customers in other countries, this will involve the services of **exporters**. If the manufacturer has to actually buy its oranges from another country then this will involve the services of **importers**. These are the areas of international trade. No single country in the world is able to produce all the materials and goods needed and wanted by its home businesses and consumers. For example, people in the UK may want tropical fruits that cannot be grown in the UK. Therefore, traders will **import** such materials and products. For countries to be economically stable they must then sell materials and products to other countries and this is called **export**. (You will find out more about importing and exporting in Unit 7.)

International trade (also known as foreign trade) – the range of activities concerned with the importing and exporting of materials, goods and products between countries.

International trade is very important because it allows consumers to obtain a much greater range of materials and products that are often not available in their own country.

Trade occurs between manufacturers and wholesalers or retailers who will decide how much of a certain product will be bought and at what unit cost (price of each item). The cost to the wholesaler or retailer will depend, for example, on how long they have been trading with the manufacturer and how much they wish to buy, as it is likely that the manufacturer will offer discounts (reduced prices) for large or bulk purchases. Trading occurs at every stage of the chain of production as goods or materials move from one organisation to another.

Aids to trade

The commercial services that support trade are referred to as *aids to trade* or 'indirect services' as they exist to help trade to take place. They are introduced below and will be looked at in more detail later in this student book.

- **Banking and finance** – Banks and other financial organisations make it possible for traders to obtain finance (maybe in the form of loans, mortgages or overdrafts) so that they can purchase raw materials, equipment, land and/or buildings that are necessary if they are to produce goods or provide services. Without necessary finance it is impossible for trading between organisations to take place. Finance is therefore essential for any company. Money can be borrowed for many different purposes and for different lengths of time. We will examine the many different types of finance available to organisations and the purposes they are generally used for in Units 3 and 15. We also need to realise that banks do not only provide sources of finance. They provide organisations with a range of other services including bank accounts to keep the company's money secure, administration of money being paid into and out of these accounts, and financial advice and other financial services such as insurances. We will investigate the services of banks in more detail in Unit 13.

- **Communications** – Good communications are extremely important for trading. Traders need to be in constant contact with each other to provide information, agree terms of trade, arrange delivery details and deal with after-sales issues. Today there is a much wider variety of efficient communication methods available to traders than in the past. (You will find out more about communications in Unit 9.)
- **Advertising** – The number of products and services sold by traders is strongly linked to how well they have been advertised and promoted to their consumers. Some organisations will design their own advertising campaigns by employing specialist marketing staff. However, many businesses do not have the necessary specialists and will use professional advertising agencies. Advertising has to create the desire for products or services. This desire or demand encourages materials and products through the production chain until products and services are readily available to consumers. (You will find out more about advertising in Unit 8.)
- **Transport** – This is a complicated part of the trading process. Transport and distribution services are about getting the right materials and products to the right place at the right time using the best forms of transport, whether by land, air or sea. Late delivery of materials or goods could lead to lost production time or lost sales. (You will find out more about distribution and transport in Unit 10.)
- **Warehousing** – Materials and goods delivered to the consumer or organisations that need them have to be stored until they can be used or developed. Some products, ice-cream for example, are wanted at particular times of year and may need to be stockpiled until they are in demand. (You will find out more about warehousing in Unit 11.)
- **Insurance** – There is a great deal of movement of material and goods in the production chain, so there is always a risk that they may be damaged, destroyed or stolen. Most businesses will insure their materials or goods against such a loss by using insurance brokers. This means that if the goods are damaged, stolen or destroyed, the business will receive compensation. There are few businesses that would send goods or materials by air or sea without insuring them first. (You will find out more about insurance in Unit 12.)

Theory into practice

LesJones Ltd makes good-quality acoustic and electric guitars which it sells directly to musical instrument retailers and music schools in its own country and overseas.

1. Identify six aids to trade or direct services that support the transfer of guitars from LesJones Ltd to retailers and schools.
2. Explain how each of these six aids to trade support the trading activity.

1.4 The relationship between industry, commerce and direct services

When we discussed the chain of production earlier in the unit it became clear that organisations and their consumers are highly **dependent** upon each other. Organisations rely on their consumers to pay for the products they manufacture in order to make their income and profits. Consumers rely on organisations to supply them with the products they require. Organisations and their consumers are 'mutually dependent' because they rely on each other. This is called **interdependence**.

For example, farmers increasingly depend on food retailers, such as Spar, or food manufacturers, such as Heinz, for orders of their produce (crops or animal). Heinz is dependent both on the farmers – who supply the food that goes into their meals and canned goods – and producers/ organisations that make steel and paper, so that they can produce the packaging for their goods. Meanwhile, the steel and paper industries are dependent on iron-extracting organisations that produce the raw materials for the production of steel sheeting and on the forestry workers/ organisations that cut down trees which are then processed into paper.

There is also interdependence between the organisations in the chain of production and those commercial organisations that exist to support it, such as banking and insurance institutions, distribution businesses and advertising agencies. Figure 1.4 on the following page, shows the interdependence that exists between organisations and commercial service providers in the car manufacturing industry.

Industries and commercial organisations also rely on a range of **direct services.** These support the activities that are carried out within and between the industrial sectors, and also support the delivery of services and goods directly to consumers. As you can see from Figure 1.4, transport is an important service to the manufacturers of cars and their suppliers, and between the manufacturers and the shops they sell their cars to in large quantities. However, transport is also extremely important to the dealerships that rely on it to distribute their goods to consumers.

Interdependence in the car manufacturing industry

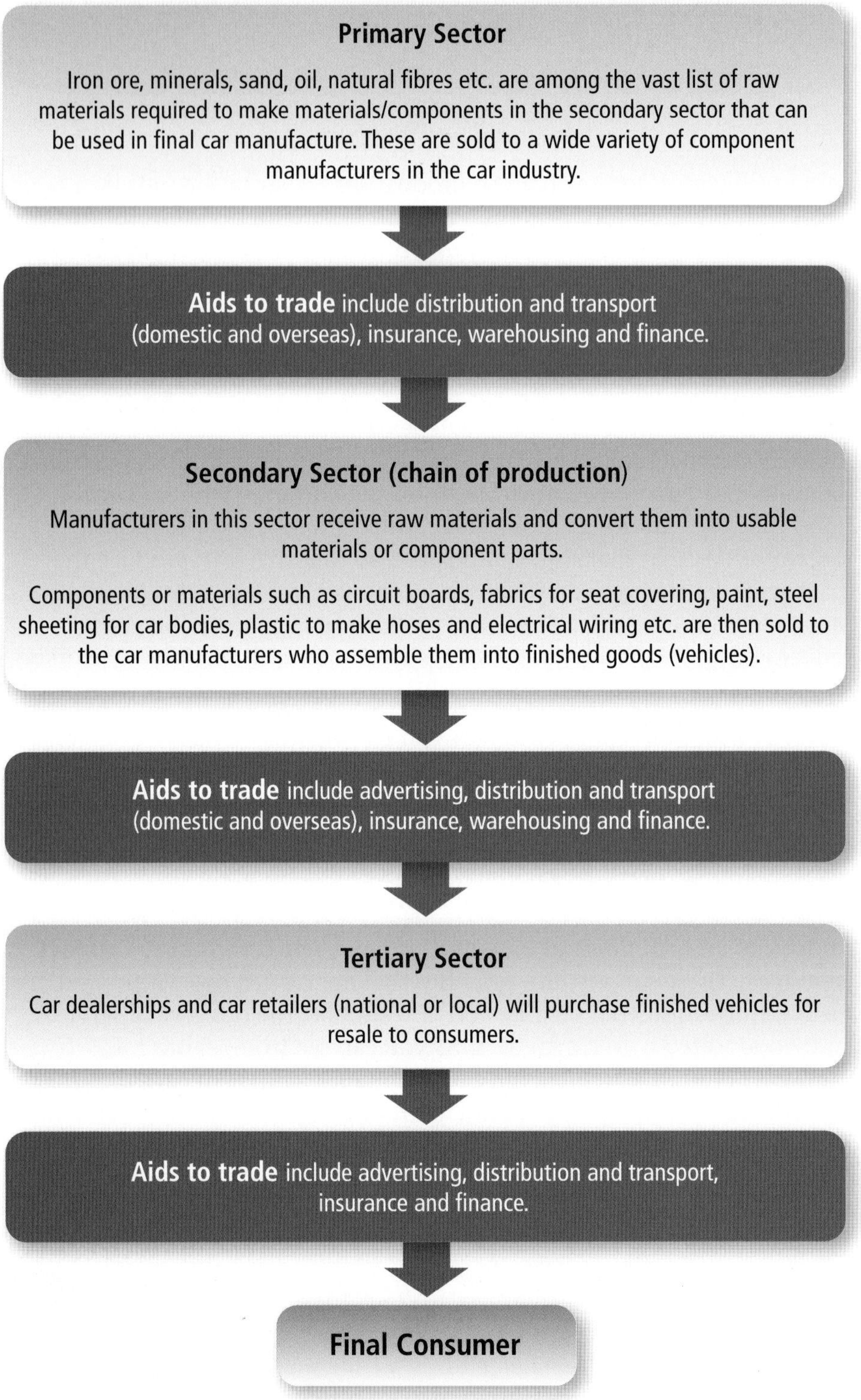

Primary Sector

Iron ore, minerals, sand, oil, natural fibres etc. are among the vast list of raw materials required to make materials/components in the secondary sector that can be used in final car manufacture. These are sold to a wide variety of component manufacturers in the car industry.

Aids to trade include distribution and transport (domestic and overseas), insurance, warehousing and finance.

Secondary Sector (chain of production)

Manufacturers in this sector receive raw materials and convert them into usable materials or component parts.

Components or materials such as circuit boards, fabrics for seat covering, paint, steel sheeting for car bodies, plastic to make hoses and electrical wiring etc. are then sold to the car manufacturers who assemble them into finished goods (vehicles).

Aids to trade include advertising, distribution and transport (domestic and overseas), insurance, warehousing and finance.

Tertiary Sector

Car dealerships and car retailers (national or local) will purchase finished vehicles for resale to consumers.

Aids to trade include advertising, distribution and transport, insurance and finance.

Final Consumer

■ **Figure 1.4** *The relationship between industry and commerce in car manufacturing*

Theory into practice

Earlier in this chapter we were looking at the chain of production for guitars made by LesJones Ltd. The chain of production demonstrated a high level of interdependence in the musical instruments industry.

1. What is meant by the word 'interdependence'? Use the guitar example to help you explain.
2. Describe an example where there is a high level of interdependence between industries in different sectors in the country in which you live.
3. Name two possible commercial services you think LesJones Ltd would rely upon on a regular basis. Briefly explain the role of each service in your own words.
4. Which direct services would be of value in the following situations experienced by LesJones Ltd?
   - An employee has stolen two guitars from the shop.
   - A competitor of LesJones Ltd has just started making an exact copy of one of their best-selling guitars.
   - One of their most experienced craftsmen is about to retire.

Summary of main points: Unit 1

- Production takes place when resources such as labourers, equipment and energy are used to convert raw materials into components or finished goods.
- The chain of production describes the stages involved in the production process from the primary sector, through the secondary sector and finally to the tertiary sector.
- Primary sector industries extract raw materials such as coal, or grow raw materials such as wheat, which are then used by manufacturing companies in the secondary sector.
- Secondary sector industries purchase raw materials that have been extracted or grown by primary sector industries. Using manufacturing processes the raw materials can be converted into components or finished goods to be used or sold by tertiary sector organisations.
- Tertiary sector industries are service based and usually support the distribution of raw materials, components and finished goods between trading organisations.
- Trade is the process of buying and selling between organisations with the aim of making a profit. Trade can take place in the home country (with traders in the same country) or internationally (with traders in other countries; this is sometimes called foreign trade).
- Home traders consist of wholesalers and retailers.
- International traders consist of importers and exporters.
- Aids to trade are the commercial services that support trade and enable the activities of trading to take place. They include banking and finance, communications, advertising, transport, warehousing and insurance.

Test your knowledge

Practice multiple choice exam questions

Read multiple choice questions carefully to make sure you understand what is actually being asked. If you do not know the answer straight away, try working out which of the four options you know are wrong to reduce the number of options you have to choose from.

1) Basic human needs are provided for by?
   a) Commerce
   b) Division of labour
   c) Production
   d) Trade

2) Examine the chain of production shown below:

   Primary sector producer → X → Wholesaler → Retailer → Consumer

   Which of the following is 'X' in the chain of production?
   a) Customer
   b) Broker
   c) Importer
   d) Manufacturer

3) The word 'trade' refers to:
   a) The movement of goods and services.
   b) The exchange of goods and services for other goods and services.
   c) The buying and selling of goods and services to make a profit.
   d) The relationship between an organisation and its consumers.

4) Which of the following is in the secondary sector?
   a) Coal mining
   b) Dairy farming
   c) Healthcare
   d) Car manufacturing

5) Which of the following is a definition of the word 'specialisation'?
   a) When businesses select and place staff within their organisation according to their experience and skills.
   b) A collection of businesses which provide similar products or services.
   c) When businesses, individuals and whole economies concentrate on making a limited number of products and services.
   d) A process which takes place when a business uses resources and converts them into goods or services.

Test your knowledge *continued*

Practice stimulus response and structured exam questions

1) The following table shows the number of people employed productively in a country. Use the table to answer the questions below.

Farming	750,000
Fishing	150,000
Manufacturing	800,000
Construction	300,000
Commercial services	1,200,000
Direct services	800,000
Total employed	4,000,000

a. Identify one example of a primary industry. (*1 mark*)

b. (i) Calculate how many people are employed in the secondary sector of production. (*2 marks*)
   (ii) Calculate the percentage of the total workforce employed in commercial services. (*2 marks*)
   (iii) Suggest one reason why more people are employed in commercial activities than in any other sector. (*2 marks*)

c. Giving an example of each, explain what is meant by:
   (i) Commercial activities (*3 marks*)
   (ii) Direct services. (*3 marks*)

d. Are some of the sectors of production shown interdependent? Explain your answer. (*3 marks*)

e. One of the main crops grown in the country is wheat, which is used for bread-making. Explain how value is added at each stage of production until the bread reaches the final consumer. (*4 marks*)

(CIE Commerce Specimen Paper 2, 2005)

- Question 1a asks you to **'identify'** and only gives one mark. Keep answers to these types of question short. Do not be tempted to waste time by providing a more detailed answer.
- Question 1c asks you to give **'examples'**. The examiner encourages you to provide good examples that make use of businesses (local, national or international) known to you.

2) 'Human wants are satisfied by commercial activities.'

a. Giving examples, explain the terms:
   (i) Human wants (*3 marks*)
   (ii) Commercial activities. (*3 marks*)

b. Show how commercial activities assist the satisfaction of human wants. (*14 marks*)

(CIE Commerce Paper 1, May/June 2000)

Always make a note of the command words that start most questions. For example, question 2b asks you to **'show'** and is allocated 14 marks. A developed and detailed answer is required here that gives examples of commercial activities and shows how each helps to satisfy particular human wants. These questions allow you to demonstrate the extent of your commercial knowledge.

Test your knowledge *continued*

3) Production involves industry, commerce and direct services.
   a. Explain why production takes place. (*4 marks*)
   b. Define the terms 'industry' and 'commerce'. Give one example of each. (*8 marks*)
   c. Explain what is meant by 'direct services' and show how a private individual might make use of these services. (*8 marks*)

(CIE Commerce Paper 1, October/November 2003)

Question 3b asks you to give **'definitions'** for given terms. Using appropriate commercial language you are required to give a concise (short and clear) explanation of what is meant by the term.

4) 'Aids to trade assist both primary and secondary industries.'
   a. (i) Using examples, distinguish between primary and secondary industry. (*4 marks*)
      (ii) Explain how two aids to trade may assist both primary and secondary industry. (*10 marks*)
   b. Explain the advantages of 'specialisation' for a manufacturer of shoes. (*6 marks*)

(CIE Commerce Paper 1, May/June 2003)

Always take note of the marks given to different parts of questions.
This indicates how much time you should spend on developing your answer. For example, more time should be spent on question 4a (ii) than on part (i).

5) In the table below are details of the three stages of furniture production.

A – Lumberjack felling trees	B – Furniture-making business	C – Furniture shop	D –

   a. Identify the three stages of production shown in A, B and C above. (*3 marks*)
   b. (i) Who is the person you would expect to find at the end of the chain of production in D? (*1 mark*)
      (ii) Explain why this person is important. (*4 marks*)
   c. Explain how transport may assist the production of furniture. (*6 marks*)
   d. Choose two other aids to trade and show how they might assist the selling of furniture. (*6 marks*)

(CIE Commerce Paper 1, October/November 2002)

2 Retail trade

What do I need to study?

- Describe and explain the role of the retailer in the 'chain of distribution'.
- Identify the different types of retailers.
- Describe and explain the various selling techniques and trends in retailing.
- Explain the implications of e-commerce on retailing.
- Describe the different methods of home shopping.
- Explain large-scale retailing and identify its advantages and disadvantages.
- Explain how small-scale retailers can survive in a changing commercial environment.

Introduction

Retailer – an organisation that specialises in bringing services and goods in small quantities to the final consumer.

Retailing is one of the four branches of trade you will study in this student book; the others are wholesaling, importing and exporting. Each branch is concerned with the buying and selling of goods in different ways. Retail trade aims to make sure that consumers are supplied with the goods they need. **Retailers** also provide a range of other complementary services. These may include giving advice about products or providing a delivery service for goods purchased by consumers.

Chain of distribution – the route taken by finished goods from where they are produced to where they are finally consumed. There are many kinds of chains of distribution. The route taken depends on the type of goods being distributed.

Have you ever stopped to think about how the items you desire or need actually get to your favourite retailer or shop so that you can purchase them? Look at the labels on your clothes or your favourite game at home. Do they say made in Hong Kong, China, Taiwan or Great Britain? Your clothes and games may have travelled half way across the world to be hung up in a shop or put on a shelf for you to try on or pick up and buy.

The reality is that when you go into a shop or retailer to buy a text book like this one, or when you order a DVD from an Internet retailer, there are a lot of organisations involved in making the item easily available to you. This process is called the **chain of distribution**.

Throughout this unit, we will investigate the many chains of distribution in commerce.

2.1 The role of the retailer in the chain of distribution

Chains of distribution

Most commercial activity is focused on getting goods and services from the people who manufacture or provide them, to consumers who need and desire them. As we have already seen, goods travel through a chain of distribution.

Figure 2.1 summarises four of the most common routes that goods take from the manufacturer to the consumer.

You can see from this diagram that retailers play a very important role in this distribution process. The ways in which goods pass from the manufacturer to the final consumer are quite varied. Some goods pass directly from the manufacturer to the consumer, other goods are passed through a range of intermediaries (businesses in the middle) including wholesalers, small-, medium- and large-scale retailers and even mail order or Internet companies.

Distribution chain 1 is the most commonly recognised and used way of distribution. Manufacturers produce massive quantities of particular products and sell them in large quantities to wholesale chains or independent wholesalers. The wholesalers then distribute or sell smaller quantities of those products to small or medium-sized retailers. The wholesaler is providing a valuable service to manufacturers, who have limited storage space, and to retailers, who want to purchase a wide variety of goods to meet demand from their customers. However, it is

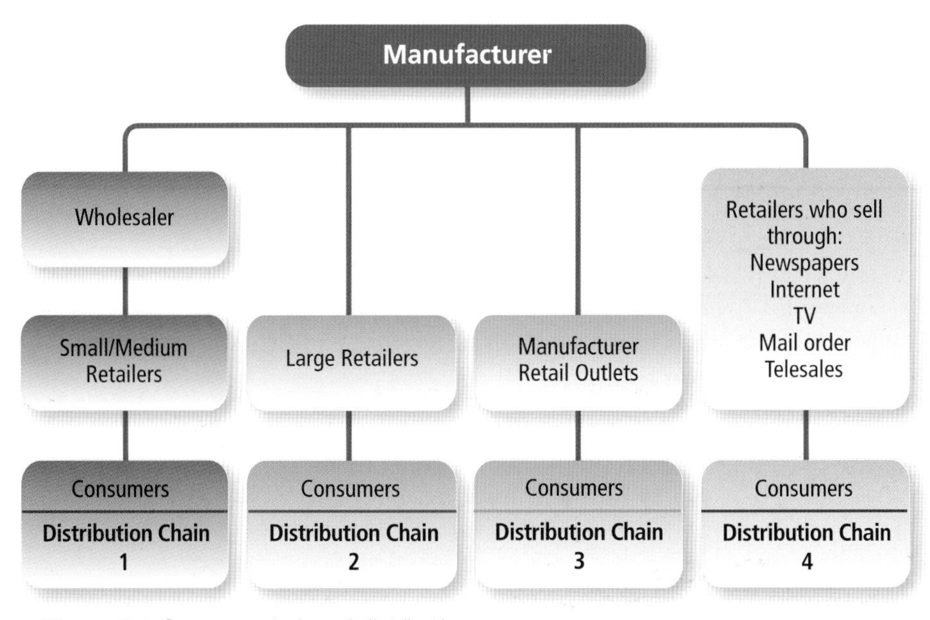

■ **Figure 2.1** *Common chains of distribution*

important to look at distribution chain 3 and see that some manufacturers are now realising that there is an opportunity to make more profit by opening their own retail outlets. This means that they can sell products directly to consumers at a higher price than they would get from wholesalers, who would expect very large discounts for ordering goods in large quantities.

Retailers

This section focuses on the organisations that exist to provide consumers with the services and goods they demand – the retailers.

Manufacturers and wholesalers carry out a specific function within the distribution chain, which is producing and distributing goods in very large quantities. Retailers, however, provide many different functions that benefit consumers. They are focused on responding to consumer needs and expectations.

The functions of retailers are listed below:

- **Providing outlets to sell manufacturers' goods** – Retailers act as 'middlemen' (the people in the middle) between manufacturers and consumers. (The term 'middlemen' can also be used to describe wholesalers who purchase large quantities of goods from the manufacturer and sell them directly to retailers and other traders.)
- **Breaking of bulk** – This is the term used for buying goods in large quantities from wholesalers or manufacturers to sell to customers individually or in smaller quantities. This is a very important service provided by large-scale retailers that enables consumers to purchase goods in small quantities. For example, they can buy one can of beans instead of a case or box of 24.
- **Offering a choice of goods** – Retailers usually stock goods from many manufacturers so that consumers have a choice. For example, a supermarket may offer the customer a choice between more than 20 varieties of shampoo.
- **Supplying goods when needed** – Retailers stock goods which are demanded by their customers and will try to make sure that they are always in stock (available).
- **Providing information and advice** – Retailers know a lot about the products they sell because it helps them to make more sales. For example, electrical appliance retailers will be able to advise customers on the best items to satisfy their needs and to fit their budget from the vast selection they offer.
- **Providing after-sales service** – Retailers can provide services after the product has been purchased, such as repairs or spares. For example, car dealerships will have a long relationship with their customers, offering servicing of the vehicles to help keep them working properly.

- **Offering credit facilities and finance** – Retailers of high-value goods, such as furniture or electrical items, might offer customers credit facilities or loans. This makes it possible for the customer to 'buy' the item they want at once, even if they cannot afford to pay for it straightaway.
- **Providing delivery services** – Retailers of large goods such as kitchen appliances (a washing machine, for example) will sometimes offer a delivery service as part of the purchase. Customers will consider delivery costs when choosing where they will buy high-value, large goods.

Theory into practice

Imagine you are purchasing each of the goods listed below from a specialist retailer. Using the information you have read about the functions of retailers, identify which function(s) would be most important for each item. For example, you may decide that after-sales service is of particular importance when purchasing a sports car in case you experience any mechanical difficulties. You may find it helpful to discuss each item with a friend or parent who has purchased these goods. Make sure to explain the reasons for each function that you choose.

- Sports car
- Washing machine
- Computer
- Television.

Think it over...

'Retailers will only purchase goods which are demanded by their customers and which satisfy their needs and expectations.'

Discuss in pairs the importance of this statement to wholesalers and manufacturers. Talk to the rest of your group about what you think.

2.2 Types of retailer

■ *A small, counter-service independent retailer*

There are many different types of retailer – from small counter-service shops to large department stores. Look at Tables 2.1–2.6 to find out what the main types of retailer are and the advantages and disadvantages of each type to the consumers who use them.

Independent retailers/Unit retailers – These are usually small retail outlets or unit retailers that are run by the people who own them. Examples include newsagents, fruit and vegetable shops or small groceries. They generally offer a personal 'counter service' where customers are served individually. Goods are usually not displayed on shelves for customers to select themselves, although some do offer self-service.

Advantages	Disadvantages
Personal and friendly service	Goods are generally more expensive because the retailer cannot buy in bulk (large quantities)
Convenient local location	There is a more limited range of products available
Long opening hours	Only one shopkeeper can mean that it takes longer to be served at the counter
May take and deliver orders	May only take cash payments

■ **Table 2.1** *Advantages and disadvantages of independent/unit retailers*

Self-service retailers – These are shops where goods can be selected by customers themselves. They are slightly larger than independent retailers and usually have more than one checkout. Examples include local 'convenience' stores.

Advantages	Disadvantages
A larger variety of cheaper goods can be offered than by independent retailers	Space is still limited so a full range of products is often not on offer
Personal and friendly service	Prices are not as cheap as large supermarket chains
Convenient local location	
Long opening hours	
A greater variety of payment types are accepted	

■ **Table 2.2** *Advantages and disadvantages of self-service retailers*

Supermarkets – These retail outlets are larger than self-service stores. They operate on a self-service basis and offer a wide variety of groceries (food) and non-food items. Supermarkets have a lot of space that is usually divided into sections where you can find particular product types. Examples of supermarkets include Tesco and the French chain, Carrefour.

Advantages	Disadvantages
They can buy in bulk (large) quantities at competitive prices. This means they can offer reduced prices to the customer	Service can be less personal, although supermarkets take their customer service and staff training seriously to stop this being a problem
Spacious (large) shopping environment encourages shoppers to return	Can be very busy at weekends
Car parks	There is an increased need for security
All methods of payment are accepted	

■ **Table 2.3** *Advantages and disadvantages of supermarkets*

Superstores/Hypermarkets – These are basically even larger supermarkets that sell many thousands of product lines. Examples include Tesco and Walmart superstores which provide a 'one-stop' shop where busy people can buy their weekly food shopping, pick up a pair of new jeans and fill their cars with fuel on the way home. Superstores are generally located away from town centres where land is less expensive and they can provide excellent parking and other facilities.

Advantages	Disadvantages
Often very low prices	Their location makes them difficult to get to if you don't own a car
A very wide choice and range of product types offers the customer a 'one-stop-shop' experience – in other words, they can get everything they need in one place	The cost of petrol to travel there may make these stores uneconomical if you only need a few items
Locations are generally very pleasant and easy to reach through established transport networks	They are very large shops and are criticised for not providing a personal service
Some offer late opening or even 24-hour opening	
Excellent additional facilities, such as restaurants	

■ **Table 2.4** *Advantages and disadvantages of superstores/hypermarkets*

Department stores – These are single retail outlets divided into different specialist departments, such as electrical goods, men's clothing or jewellery. Some department stores offer extra facilities, including restaurants or cafes. Famous examples include Selfridges and Harrods in London and Macy's in New York.

Advantages	Disadvantages
Comfortable and enjoyable shopping experience with an excellent choice of products	Found mainly in large towns and city centres so some customers may find them difficult to get to because of poor transport systems or lack of car parking facilities.
High level of service from well-trained assistants	Very large and impersonal
Store cards and credit facilities available	Prices can be very high to cover the high costs of city locations
Delivery service for large items	

■ **Table 2.5** *Advantages and disadvantages of department stores*

Multiple chain retailers – These are groups of retail outlets or branches that specialise in selling a particular type of produce. Examples include the electrical retail chain, Currys, The Disney Store, or the sportswear specialist, Foot Locker.

Advantages	Disadvantages
All stores offer a similar experience	Sometimes large and impersonal stores
Prices can be very competitive because of their ability to buy products in bulk from manufacturers at very low prices	Often located in retail parks on the edge of town making them difficult to get to if you do not have your own car
A large variety of items related to a specific need, e.g. toyshops	
The chain stores are familiar to customers through branding and advertising	

■ **Table 2.6** *Advantages and disadvantages of multiple chain retailers*

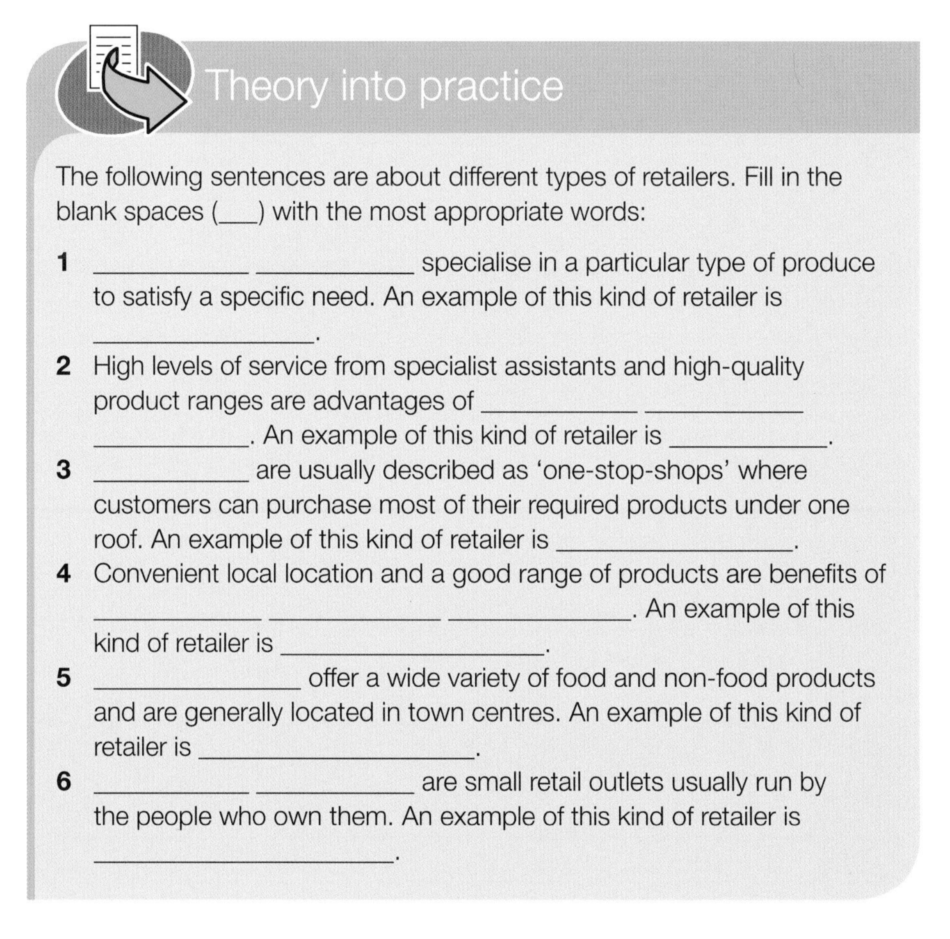

Theory into practice

The following sentences are about different types of retailers. Fill in the blank spaces (___) with the most appropriate words:

1 ____________ ____________ specialise in a particular type of produce to satisfy a specific need. An example of this kind of retailer is ________________.

2 High levels of service from specialist assistants and high-quality product ranges are advantages of ____________ ____________ ____________. An example of this kind of retailer is ____________.

3 ____________ are usually described as 'one-stop-shops' where customers can purchase most of their required products under one roof. An example of this kind of retailer is __________________.

4 Convenient local location and a good range of products are benefits of ____________ ____________ ____________. An example of this kind of retailer is ____________________.

5 ________________ offer a wide variety of food and non-food products and are generally located in town centres. An example of this kind of retailer is ____________________.

6 ____________ ____________ are small retail outlets usually run by the people who own them. An example of this kind of retailer is ______________________.

If you look back at Figure 2.1 on page 23, which shows the different channels (ways) of distribution that exist in trade, you can see that distribution chains 1 and 2 are the most useful to retailers. However, where distribution chain 1 used to be the most commonly used channel we are now finding that distribution chain 2 is increasingly used. Retailers are growing in size and we only have to look around our own towns to notice that smaller independent shops are being replaced by large retail chains and department stores such as Marks & Spencer. Retail chains have become so big that they now have enormous purchasing power and can negotiate lower prices with manufacturers. They have set up their own distribution and warehousing facilities to store the products they sell in large quantities. This is something that smaller retailers could never do. Large retail chains can do the same activities that wholesalers do, such as buying products in bulk, storing the stock and then redistributing goods in smaller quantities to their own retail outlets or branches. We will investigate this trend in more detail in the next section.

2.3 Selling techniques, trends in retailing and the implications of e-commerce

Selling techniques

As we saw in Unit 1, adding value to products is one of the most important activities performed by manufacturers. But there are other ways in which manufacturers and retailers will try to attract consumers.

Branding

Consider one of the most well-known drinks in the world, Coca-Cola. It is made mostly of water, flavourings, sugar and the manufacturer's famous 'secret ingredient'. Some value is added to the ingredients by the manufacturing process, but the real value of the product has been added by the years that Coca-Cola has spent building up their world-famous **brand**. Coca-Cola is an instantly recognisable name which millions of people associate with quality and fashion. We are more 'brand aware' today than we have ever been, so retailers use brand awareness and the promotional activities of manufacturers to sell more products through their outlets.

Some multiple retailers and supermarkets, like Tesco, have used their brand image to sell own-branded product lines (items displaying the logo of the retailer). If customers trust the retailer and associate the store with quality and value for money, they are more likely to buy products that display their logo.

Packaging

This refers to the way goods or services are presented to customers. Packaging has many functions; it makes the product look attractive, and protects it during transport and when it is put on shelves. Packaging is strongly linked to the creation of a successful brand image. Supermarkets sell many own-branded goods. Some are packaged simply and plainly and presented as 'value-for-money' budget items. Some are packaged in highly decorated and complicated packaging and are presented as 'luxury' items. Packaging means that customers can instantly recognise the product and brand. This is done by using colour, shape and design, and by making sure that logos or brand names can be easily seen. For example, the famous golden arches of the McDonald's 'M' logo are bright and instantly recognisable. If packaging is not eye-catching and attractive then customers will not notice or desire the product.

Brand – is the identity of a specific product or service created by a business to make their products or services instantly recognisable to potential and existing consumers. The main purpose of a brand is to ensure that consumers will always seek the brand-owner's products or services in preference to those of its competitors. Branding is created with words or advertising slogans such as Nike's 'Just Do It' and eye-catching, easily remembered logos and images.

Think about the last trip you made to your local grocery store. There was probably a wide variety of products available to you. List at least four products you can remember seeing. For each item find a picture from the Internet or draw what the item looks like. Explain why each product was so memorable and attractive to you and your friends. What do you think it is about the packaging that was designed to appeal to you?

Self-service

Impulse buying – when customers buy goods that they did not intend to buy because the items are carefully displayed, and encourage consumers to see them as an item that is very good value – an opportunity not to be missed.

Most customers want to be able to walk into retail outlets like supermarkets, look at the range of products on the shelves and choose what they want from a huge range of different items. This is one of the reasons that most retailers have become self-service. If customers are given time to view all the products on offer, they usually end up buying extra products that they did not need or plan to buy. This is referred to as **impulse buying**.

Retailers use a variety of methods to get customers to buy more and spend more on their purchases. For example:

- Expensive products are placed on shelves at eye level so that they are seen first by the customers.
- Cheaper products are usually located on the bottom shelf.
- Products that are being promoted as 'buy-one-get-one-free' or '50 per cent extra free' are usually placed at the end of rows (on what supermarkets call 'gondola ends'). This is where the products will get the most attention and is also where customers will do a lot of their impulse buying.

After-sales service

This is the range of services offered to consumers to ensure customer satisfaction so that they return to the retailer again. After-sale services may include:

- delivery services (paid or free of charge)
- installation services (for example, installing a washing machine by connecting it to your water supply)
- repairs, maintenance and servicing of goods
- advice, training in a product's use, and telephone helplines that you can call if you have a problem with the product
- customer service desks or customer service telephone lines.

Depending on the nature of the retailer, these after-sales services will vary. For example, electronic appliance retailers may offer all these services, but clothes retailers may only offer customers fashion advice and customer service desks (in case the goods have to be returned for any reason). There is no need for fashion retail outlets to offer 'installation' of the clothing purchased! After-sales services are essential in order to meet the needs of customers and to ensure they use the retailer again.

Trends in retailing

Growth of large-scale retailers

There are an increasing number of multiple retailers, superstores, hypermarkets and out-of-town shopping 'villages'. They have the power to negotiate low prices because of the large orders they place. This is known as **economies of scale**: that is, the bigger the store, the bigger their order from the manufacturer; so they can negotiate a lower price with the manufacturer and sell the item to the customer at a lower price while still making a profit. Customers are attracted to retailers which offer them value for money, and because most families now own cars they can more easily get to out-of-town retailers.

Economies of scale – the decreases in the cost of production or purchase price per unit (item) made possible as a result of producing or purchasing goods in very large quantities.

Some retailers offer consumers in-store loyalty cards to encourage them to return. These loyalty or customer reward systems offer, for example, points which can be exchanged for goods or discounts on items bought in the store to encourage customers to shop there again.

While all this is good for the consumer, there are also problems. Many people are against the changing retail trade and the growth of superstores and multiple retailers. They say that this trend is leading to the decline of town centres as some shops are forced to close – these are usually independent retailers who are too small to compete with the prices and range of products and services offered by the superstores. The opening of a superstore in one area can mean that local traders lose a lot of money and customers. People also protest against the development of more superstores and retail villages because they are often developed on greenbelt land (land that has not been built on), and therefore contribute to the destruction and pollution of the countryside.

Theory into practice

Your uncle runs a very successful independent shoe shop, called Hudson's Shoes, in the local town. You sometimes help him out on a Saturday which is his busiest day of the week. In the local newspaper this week there was an advertisement for a major new clothing retailer who has opened a store in the retail park on the outskirts (edge) of the town. They have their own exclusive range of shoes in-store.

What are the implications of this (what will this mean) for your uncle's business? Make sure you explain each of your points in detail.

Computer technology

Computer technology has completely changed the retail sector. It enables retailers to check levels of stock and reorder goods so they have just the right amount. This means that goods that are in demand are on the shelves for people to buy. It also means that produce with a short shelf life (that cannot be on the shelves for very long because they will not stay fresh, like fruit or vegetables) is not wasted by going past its 'sell by' date before it can be sold.

To help retailers get their stock levels right, they also have access to management information that they could not have had in the past. They know exactly what is being purchased and how much of it, so they can more accurately predict when they might need higher stock levels of certain products. This means that they can satisfy high points of demand such as that experienced at weekends in supermarkets. Supermarkets receive deliveries of fresh produce on a daily basis but they will receive less fruit and vegetables on a Monday and more on a Friday.

Computers are helping retailers to become far more efficient. A few of the technological advances helping retailers to ensure they have the right products in their stores at the right price and at the right time are described below.

Electronic point-of-sale (EPOS) till systems, bar codes and scanners

These highly advanced, computerised till systems use scanners (laser reading equipment) to read the bar codes on individual products. These bar codes contain price and product information about the item and are printed on all products for sale. The computerised till feeds the details in the bar codes to the central computer system which uses this information to reduce the number of a particular product on the stock system. This means that the computer – and therefore the retailer – knows exactly when replacement stock needs to be ordered. In the past, this information had to be found out by staff counting stock on a daily basis.

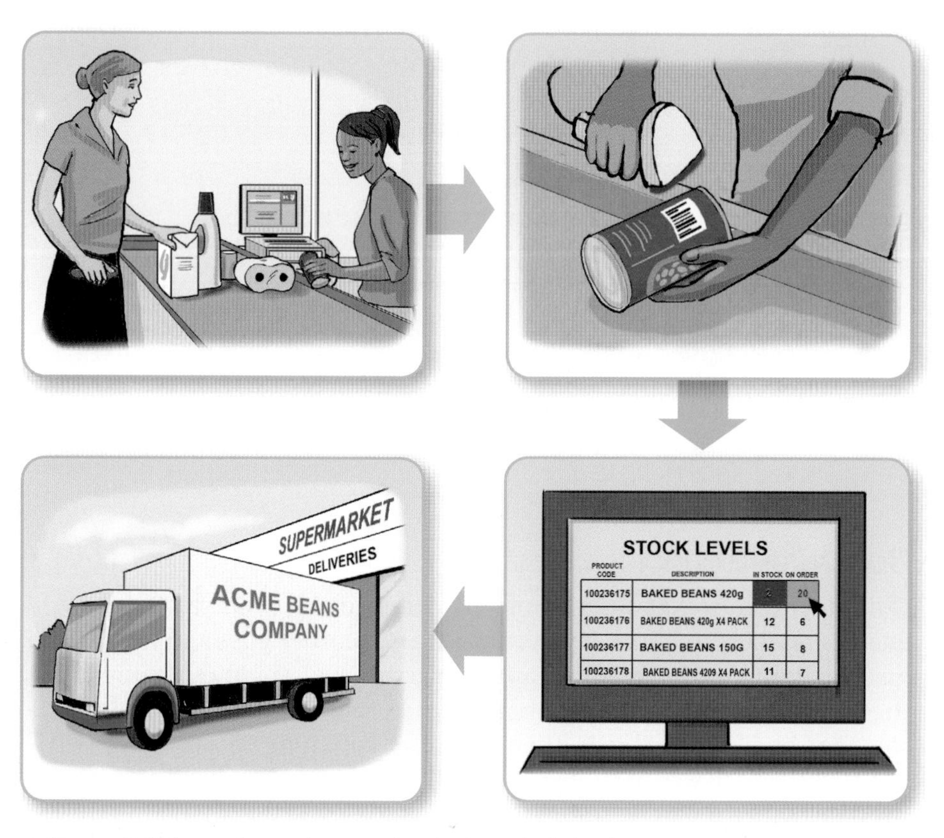

■ **Figure 2.2** *Computer systems make stock control simple*

The main EPOS systems are:

- **Electronic data interchange (EDI)** – This is used by most medium- to large-scale retailers. Computers monitor (watch) stock levels of all products and communicate directly with the computerised systems of their suppliers to make orders automatically and receive their invoices electronically. Humans put instructions into the computer, stating what level the stock should fall to before an order needs to be made. From that point on everything is done automatically. This has enabled supermarkets to employ fewer staff and to reduce errors in ordering stock.
- **Electronic funds transfer at the point of sale (EFTPOS)** – These systems make purchasing products even easier. Customers are able to pay for an item using their bank debit cards and the system automatically transfers money from the purchaser's account to the account of the supermarket. This means that customers do not need to carry large quantities of cash.

Overall, the impact of computer technology has led to more efficient retail operations, less waste and fewer disappointed customers. Using computer technology, multiple retailers can now get products from another one of their stores if they don't have what a customer wants in stock. For every benefit, however, there is a downside. As computers are relied on more, even to do routine (everyday) tasks, there is less need for staff on the shop floor. This has led to many job losses in some retail businesses.

Computer technology has had a huge impact on retailing in recent years.

1. List three advantages to retailers of computer technology.
2. How might consumers benefit from computer technology?
3. Describe a possible disadvantage to computer technology in stores.

The implications of e-commerce

E-commerce (electronic commerce or EC) means buying and selling goods and services on the 'Internet' or the 'World Wide Web'. E-commerce has probably had a larger impact on retailing than any other development. Online retail selling is now commonly referred to as **e-tailing**.

The USA has seen astonishing growth of e-commerce. It is estimated that in 2008 the value of online sales will be more than double what it was in 2003. It is also estimated that as much as 10 per cent of all sales made in the USA in 2008 could be from e-tailers.

e-tailing – This refers to retail selling that takes place online. This is the process whereby customers use the Internet to purchase goods rather than travelling to the stores themselves.

Established retailers who have responded to their consumers' desire to purchase goods on the Internet from the comfort of their own homes have seen huge sales growth, e.g. Tesco and Nordstrom. Those who are not using the Internet to their advantage are potentially losing business. Some retailers (especially new businesses) choose to carry out business only over the Internet because of its low cost to them.

Benefits of e-tailing

E-tailing has benefits both for consumers and the e-tailers themselves. These are shown below:

Benefits of e-tailing for the consumer

- They can identify different suppliers of particular goods and select the one that offers cheap prices and quick/free delivery. There are websites such as www.dealtime.com that will compare prices of particular products for you across thousands of possible suppliers.
- Purchasing can take place 24 hours a day and 7 days a week.
- Some e-tailers allow customers to track the progress of their orders online, e.g. Amazon.
- It is less time-consuming for consumers as they do not have the expense and inconvenience of going to the shops to find and purchase a product.
- The excellent levels of product advice and information available online help consumers with their decision to purchase.

Benefits for the e-tailer

- All transactions are electronic, which greatly reduces the need for paperwork.
- Orders can be processed and sent out quickly, e.g. some e-tailers can have products to you by the next working day.
- The Internet allows retailers to access an almost unlimited audience. Traditional retail outlets usually only attract local customers.
- Small e-tailers have very low running costs (the amount of money it costs them to operate) and can therefore compete with larger retailers when it comes to price.
- They can receive orders 24 hours a day and 7 days a week, not just during shop opening hours.
- Prices and product information can be easily and quickly changed.
- Fewer staff are required to run an e-tailing operation so employment costs are lower.

2.4 Home shopping

There are more purchasing options open to customers than ever before. We can go into a shop, see items on a TV shopping channel and order them over the phone, respond to a newspaper advertisement or even request catalogues and get items delivered directly to our homes. Over recent years, the Internet has also been responsible for a change in how goods are distributed from manufacturer to the final consumer. As shown in Fig 2.1, the most recent addition to the common chains of distribution is distribution chain 4 which shows how easily consumers can purchase goods at home without needing to visit a retail outlet.

In this section of the unit we will look at the most common methods of shopping from home.

Internet shopping

This is probably the largest home-shopping method at the moment and it is growing in popularity every day. We discussed the value of Internet shopping to retailers and consumers in the previous section.

Mail order

This is where manufacturers, retailers or wholesalers sell goods to the public by the following methods:

- Sending catalogues to consumers – consumers can select and order products either by post, via a telephone ordering line or on the Internet using a personal customer account.
- Advertising products in magazines and newspapers – often these advertisements include an order form that can be completed and returned free to the supplier.
- Employing agents who work from home – these agents sell products from catalogues to friends, family members and neighbours and receive either a percentage of the goods sold or discount off their own purchases.

Mail order is a popular means of retailing. Most mail order companies offer consumers easy-to-obtain credit terms so that they can receive products and pay for them over an agreed period of time. It is a very convenient method of shopping because the consumer does not need to leave home and the products are received on approval – which means they can be sent back if they are not satisfactory. Remember that mail order is only an effective method of retailing if the retailer's catalogues and advertising attract consumers.

Telesales

This is a sales tool that was developed in the USA and involves businesses contacting possible new customers in their home by phone. This method has been criticised for intruding on people's home life, and this has damaged the reputation of the businesses that use it. It is often used by financial services trying to sell products such as credit cards or by companies selling expensive home improvements such as new kitchens or double glazing. It is an inexpensive method of selling but it is not suitable for all products and services.

TV shopping

This is a quite recent sales innovation that has been made possible by satellite and digital television. TV shopping benefits consumers because it allows them to see a thorough demonstration of the product on the television. They can also telephone the company to ask questions before purchasing. The on-screen sales people are very persuasive, but the real challenge for the business is making sure their target customers (the customers most likely to buy the product) are watching!

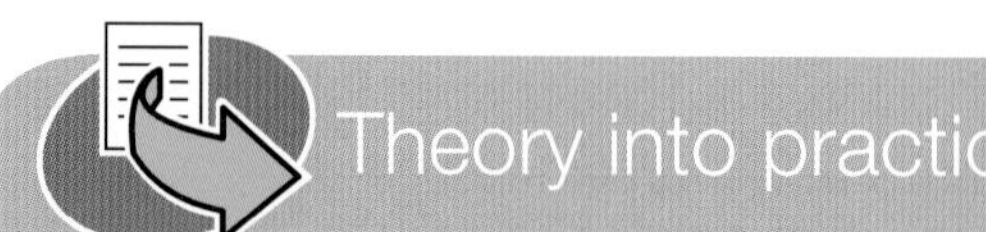

Theory into practice

Each year there is a large increase in the amount of goods and services being purchased on the Internet or through a variety of other home-shopping methods. Conduct a survey of your family and friends on the benefits of home shopping compared with visiting retailers. You can present your findings as part of a class discussion.

2.5 Large-scale retailing

This unit has shown how the retail trade is evolving (changing) and increasing – with more department store retailers, hypermarkets and superstores opening every week. Some of the advantages and disadvantages of these changes are summarised below:

Advantages of large-scale retailing

- **Economies of scale** – The larger the retailers become, the larger their orders for products become. If retailers are buying more they are better able to negotiate lower prices for what they purchase. In addition, bigger supermarkets can stock a greater range of products without having to hire more staff. These cost savings can then be passed on to consumers in the form of reduced prices.
- **Convenience** – Consumers benefit from a convenient, one-stop-shopping experience as they can find almost all their shopping requirements in one shop or out-of-town retail village. Because the large-scale retailers are usually located on the outskirts (edge) of town, they have the space to provide free car parking and therefore easy access to shops.

Disadvantages of large-scale retailing

- **Wholesalers** – Traditionally, most manufacturers distributed their products through wholesalers, but because retailers have grown so large they have been able to develop their own warehouses and distribution networks. Most supermarkets and multiple retailers will negotiate directly with manufacturers and buy products in bulk. These products are delivered to the retailer's own warehousing facilities where they are divided and distributed to retail outlets across the country. Large-scale retailers have no real need for wholesalers any more.
- **Other retailers** – Economies of scale mean that large-scale retailers are able to offer products so cheaply that small, local, independent retailers cannot compete. This has caused a big decline in the number of small independent retailers.
- **Consumers** – The consumer shopping experience in large-scale retail outlets is impersonal. Smaller independent retail outlets can offer a more personal and friendly shopping experience. Also, because small independent retailers are struggling to compete with large-scale retailers and many are closing down, consumers now have much less choice over where they buy their shopping.

Survival of small-scale retailers

Despite the growth of large-scale retailers there will always be some small retailers that will survive. In section 2.2 of this unit we investigated small-scale independent retailers, such as corner shops and grocers, in some detail. Although it is harder for these retailers to compete with larger retailers they do have some competitive advantage. They are usually located near to their customers' houses, they are more familiar with their customers' preferences so are able to stock the goods that their customers' want, and they are often open for long hours on a daily basis.

Theory into practice

A supermarket chain is about to build a very large, modern hypermarket near to your home and school. A large proportion of the local community are in favour of it but there are groups of the community who feel that yet another large-scale retailer is not needed in the area. Your school newspaper has asked you to produce an article explaining the possible advantages and disadvantages of this new hypermarket to your local community.

Summary of main points from Unit 2

- The 'chain of distribution' is the route taken by finished goods from where they are produced to where they are finally consumed. The route taken depends a lot on the type of goods being distributed.
- A retailer is an organisation that specialises in bringing goods and services in small quantities to the final consumer. There are many types of retailer including independent retailers, self-service retailers, supermarkets, superstores, department stores and multiple retailers. Each offers a range of advantages and disadvantages to customers.
- Branding is a much-used selling technique that uses words, advertising slogans and eye-catching and memorable logos and pictures. A brand is the identity of a specific product or service created by a business to make their products/services instantly recognisable to new and old consumers, e.g. Nike and Coke.
- Packaging is another selling technique which, if it is designed to be eye-catching and attractive, will create customer interest and desire.
- There are an increasing number of multiple retailers, superstores, hypermarkets and out-of-town shopping villages which have led to the decline of some local town shopping centres and independent retailers in many countries.
- Computer technology has completely changed the retail sector. It enables retailers to check trends in purchasing (which goods are being bought) and stock levels and order goods automatically, quickly and efficiently so that there is never a time when a highly demanded good is out of stock.
- E-commerce is the buying and selling of goods on the Internet and through the World Wide Web. E-commerce has probably had a bigger effect on retailing than any other development or trend. E-tail brings a number of benefits to consumers and e-tailers (organisations that have decided to have an online shop).
- Customers have many more purchasing options than ever before. These options can be grouped under the heading of 'home shopping' methods and they include Internet shopping, mail order, telesales and TV shopping.

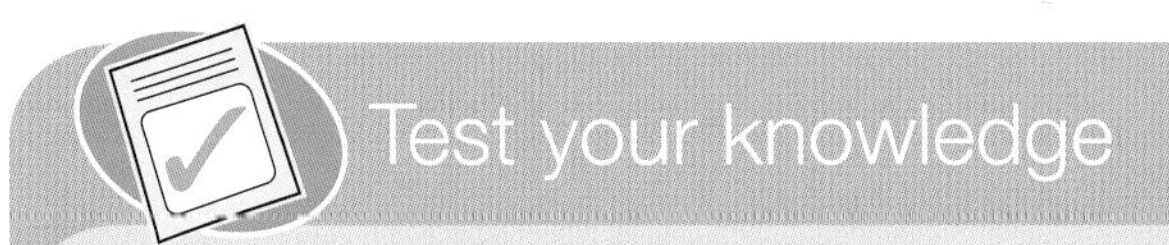

Test your knowledge

Practice multiple choice exam questions

1) Which of the following is **not** an advantage of e-tailing to consumers?
   a) Access to a wider variety of goods.
   b) Ability to buy goods 24 hours a day, 7 days a week.
   c) Delivery time for goods to reach consumer.
   d) Ability to track orders online.

2) A small-scale retailer is considering making his retail outlet self-service rather than counter-service. Which of the following could be a disadvantage of self-service to a retailer?
   a) Fewer sales assistants may need to be employed.
   b) A wider range of goods may need to be offered.
   c) Costs of keeping the store secure may increase.
   d) Customers may purchase more due to impulse buying.

3) Many retailers choose to use an EPOS (electronic point of sale) system. What is the main benefit of this system?
   a) Customers can use the system to find out the price of goods.
   b) The retailer can check stock levels and predict when more stock may be needed.
   c) A more personalised service can be offered to customers.
   d) Customers can use the system to apply for credit to pay for their goods.

4) Retailers provide a range of additional services to their customers. One of the most important is 'breaking of bulk'. Which of the following options describes what is meant by 'breaking of bulk'?
   a) To provide a wide range of goods.
   b) To enable customers to buy small quantities of goods they need or desire.
   c) To act as a middleman.
   d) To supply goods when and where they are desired.

5) Which of the following options is **not** considered to be a strength of large-scale retailers?
   a) Providing a personalised service.
   b) Good road access and parking facilities.
   c) Lower costs due to economies of scale.
   d) Access to a wide range of products under one roof.

Practice stimulus response and structured exam questions

1) A new hypermarket has opened in a shopping centre on the outskirts of a city.
   a) State and explain one difference and one similarity between a hypermarket and a shopping centre (shopping plaza). (*4 marks*)
   b) What are the benefits to the customer of shopping in a hypermarket? (*4 marks*)
   c) Why is a good system of roads essential to the location of a shopping centre? (*6 marks*)

(CIE Commerce May/June 2000)

Test your knowledge *continued*

2) Samuel Moyo is a trader running a general hardware shop in a small town.
   a) State three services Samuel might provide for his customers. (*3 marks*)
   b) Explain why some customers prefer to shop at national chains of large-scale retailers rather than use small, independent shops close to their homes. (*5 marks*)

(CIE Commerce Specimen Paper 2 2005)

Question 2a asks you to **'state'** and only gives one mark per service stated. Keep answers to these types of question short. Do not be tempted to waste time by providing a more detailed answer.

3) Mr Ndlovu owns a chain of self-service shops. The shops sell food, drinks, newspapers and stationery.
   a) Explain three advantages of owning a chain rather than owning one shop. (*6 marks*)
   b) What factors have led to the growth of the self-service system of retailing? (*6 marks*)
   c) Mr Ndlovu is thinking of installing vending machines to sell drinks outside his shops. Discuss the arguments for and against installing these machines. (*8 marks*)

(CIE Commerce Paper 1 Oct/Nov 2003)

Question 3c asks you to **'discuss'**. Questions that ask for this usually require you to see both sides of an argument. In this case you need to discuss in detail the advantages and disadvantages of what is being proposed.

4) Many department stores, supermarkets, multiple chains and unit retailers are located in city shopping centres.
   a) State two characteristics of:
      i. department stores (*2 marks*)
      ii. unit retailers. (*2 marks*)
   b) Explain why retailers are often located in shopping centres. (*6 marks*)
   c) Why do many multiple chain stores buy direct from manufacturers? (*4 marks*)
   d) Why do many consumers prefer to buy food from supermarkets rather than unit retailers? (*6 marks*)

(CIE Commerce Paper 1 May/June 2003)

Questions 4c and 4d ask you **'why'** something occurs. Using your commercial understanding you are required to suggest reasons from the perspective (point of view) of the business or customer depending on the question. Providing illustrations or examples may help you to explain your reasoning.

5) Ming Na's family have owned a supermarket for many years.
   a) State two characteristics of a supermarket. (*2 marks*)
   b) Explain why supermarket shopping has grown in importance in recent years. (*8 marks*)
   c) Explain why, given the growth in supermarket shopping, there are still many small shops selling food. (*10 marks*)

(Author Sept 2006)

3 Customer credit

What do I need to study?

- Explain what is meant by the concept (idea) of credit.
- Why is there an increased use of credit?
- What are the advantages and disadvantages of credit to buyers and sellers?
- Identify the different types of credit available and describe their features.
- What are the advantages and disadvantages of using the different types of credit?
- Suggest different methods of credit in certain circumstances and explain the reasons for their suitability.

Introduction

Credit – a means of borrowing money from a person or company and returning it at a later date, usually with additional interest charged on the original loan.

Credit is a widely used way of encouraging customers to buy more items, or items of a higher value, even if they do not have the money in the bank to purchase them at that time. However, offering customer credit can actually help an organisation improve its turnover (and possibly its profits) at the same time as enabling the customer to more quickly enjoy an expensive item like a new car. In this unit we will investigate the increased use of credit and the consequences of this to traders and customers.

3.1 The use of credit

The concept of credit and its increased usage

Credit is a general term used for any type of financial loan that is extended to private customers, usually on an 'unsecured' basis (that is, it is not 'secured' against the customer's home, for example) and is repaid on a weekly or monthly basis over an agreed period of time. It is a convenient way for customers to 'buy today and pay tomorrow', purchasing high-value products or services instantly and paying for them at a later date.

There are very few days when customers are not seeing TV advertisements or junk mail (advertising leaflets that have not been asked for by the customer) offering thousands of dollars' worth of credit for a variety of purposes. In fact, the amount of customer credit taken in western and developed countries is growing at a worrying rate. Here are some interesting facts about customer credit in the USA.

- In October 2003 the USA's Federal Reserve reported that Americans owed $1.98 trillion compared to $1.4 trillion five years earlier in 1998, an increase of 41 per cent.
- In 2003 the average American household owed approximately $18,654.
- Over 40 per cent of households in the USA spend more than they earn on a yearly basis.
- On average, a typical American family owes $8,000 on credit cards.
- The number of private individuals declaring themselves bankrupt (not having enough money and possessions to sell to cover their debts) doubled between 1994 and 2003.

So, why has there been such a large increase in the amount of customer credit or, to look at it another way, customer debt?

- There is an accepted idea that we can have what we want today and pay for it later (but at an increased cost).
- Interest rates on credit cards and other sources of credit are attractively low, particularly for new customers, but the rates rise quickly after being introduced.
- There is an increased amount of advertising to customers about the availability of credit and special credit offers.
- The increase in Internet purchasing has led to an increase in credit card transactions which have become the easiest and preferred method of payment online.
- Increasing costs of living such as housing and rental costs are forcing people to rely on their credit cards more often.

What cannot be denied is that there is a relationship between the increasing amount of customers obtaining credit and the number of individuals declaring themselves bankrupt (they have no money to pay their debts).

Advantages and disadvantages of credit to buyers and sellers

Credit has its advantages and disadvantages to both buyers (or customers) and sellers (retailers who offer goods or services on credit).

Advantages to buyers of using credit

- Instant purchase of items with the option to pay for them in smaller amounts over a long period of time.
- Convenient credit sources like credit cards for Internet or overseas transactions.
- Some credit cards offer protection from fraud and identity theft (stealing and using someone's credit card number and personal information).

Disadvantages to buyers of using credit

- Customers who use credit but fail to pay it back by the agreed date may have to pay expensive fees and high rates of interest.
- All credit sources are more expensive than paying with cash.
- If customers take out a lot of credit they may find themselves unable to afford the normal costs of living because of the high repayment costs. A lot of customers therefore choose to 'consolidate' their debt. This means taking out a long-term loan to settle *all* their current credit. They will then have only one loan to repay over a long period of time, slightly reducing their total monthly repayments.
- If you miss or fail to meet an agreed repayment, you may find it difficult to get credit at a later date. This is sometimes called being 'blacklisted'.
- Accumulated debt stops private individuals from investing in pension funds or high-rate saving accounts, which means they are unable to save for their futures.

Theory into practice

Your friend has just gone to university and is looking for a part-time job, but he is also considering applying for a credit card so he can buy some furniture for his room. Write a letter to your friend giving him advice about the advantages and disadvantages of using credit cards.

Advantages to sellers of offering credit

- There is a fast flow of money into the organisation.
- It is easy and convenient for customers to purchase on credit and this may cause them to buy on impulse or to buy more goods than they intended.
- Certain credit methods offer automatic currency conversion for sales with overseas customers. This is particularly useful for Internet retail.
- Customers now expect to be able to use credit cards or credit facilities and if a retailer does not offer these they may lose sales. Visa is an association owned by 21,000 members of financial institutions. They developed one of the most well-known international payment systems and say that if a retailer accepts credit cards, they can increase their sales by 30–100 per cent.
- Where credit such as hire purchase or finance agreements (paying for something in instalments – see the next part of this unit) are offered to customers, the retailer will receive a commission (a percentage of the price) from the credit company.

Disadvantages to sellers of offering credit

- The level of credit card fraud is increasing, with criminals making illegal transactions using false cards or a card stolen from another customer.
- Offering credit can be expensive. If a retailer accepts credit cards they have to pay the credit company a fee to use their payment systems and a percentage of each sale made using credit.

Theory into practice

Shahana Ali has just set up her first retail outlet, selling greetings cards and inexpensive gifts to customers in a small town centre. She has been operating for six months and has been sent information on the benefits of installing a payment system such as Visa from her bank. List three possible benefits that might be included in the information.

3.2 Types of credit

Hire purchase

Customers use hire purchase (or HP) to buy expensive items and pay for them over a long period of time. However, this means that the item remains the property of the hiring company until the last payment is made. The total cost of the repayments is usually much more than the original cost of the item, sometimes making this a very expensive source of credit. The main advantage of hire purchase is that the agreements are usually very flexible and enable customers to obtain goods that they would not normally be able to afford. The agreement usually asks for a series of small payments and then a final large payment, which the customer will save for while they have the use of an item.

For example, a customer buys a car worth $20,000 on hire purchase. He pays $350 a month for 36 months and then, at the end of that period, he can decide whether to pay the final payment of $10,000 if he wants to keep the car, or simply return the car to the hiring company.

He will have paid $2600 above what the car was originally worth if he pays the final instalment of $10,000.

Advantages of using hire purchase

- It spreads the cost of expensive items over a long period of time.
- Repayments are decided at the beginning of the agreement and will not go up or down.
- Other credit options may mean more expensive monthly payments so hire purchase allows people to have items they might not normally be able to afford.
- If all the hire purchase payments are made, the customer owns the item.
- If the item becomes out of date or worth less than its original price, the customer may choose not to make the final payment and to return the item to the hirer.

Disadvantages of using hire purchase

- If payments are not made, the hiring organisation may repossess (take back) the item and all the earlier payments will be lost.
- During the hire purchase period the item may become out of date or worthless.
- Hire purchase agreements may encourage customers to live beyond their means by buying things that they would not otherwise be able to afford on their income.
- It is more expensive than paying cash.
- Hire purchase items are usually priced very highly.

Theory into practice

The family next door rely on their car to get the children to school 5 miles away, to collect their shopping and to get to their places of work. Yesterday, their old car broke down and the mechanic said it could not be repaired. The $3000 they have saved would only be enough to buy an old and possibly unreliable car. Alternatively, they could use hire purchase to buy a new car worth $15,000, for which they will need to pay $150 a month for five years and then a final repayment of $9000 to secure ownership of the car. They have come to you for some financial advice. List the advantages and disadvantages of buying a cheap car with their savings compared with purchasing a new car on hire purchase.

Extended credit (deferred payments)

This source of credit is very similar to hire purchase where agreed payments are made over a period of time. However, with extended credit the buyer may not have to start making payments immediately after receiving the goods. Another difference is that the item becomes the property of the purchaser straight away and not on the final payment. Deferred payments are often used for goods which have a poor resale value; e.g clothes.

Customers who apply for extended credit also purchase high-value goods like furniture or electrical items but do not have to make any payments immediately. However, in most cases, interest is charged over this introductory 'free' period *and* over the rest of the loan period. This interest is added to the amount loaned, making the repayment cost much higher than the original loan. Customers will use this type of credit in order to have expensive items that they need or want now and will start paying for them later when they can afford to do so.

Retailers of expensive items such as furniture or cars often offer extended credit terms to their customers. This allows their customers to purchase an item, pay nothing for a year and then pay back the value of the item over the following three years.

Advantages of using extended credit

- The items purchased will not be repossessed if payments are missed or delayed.
- The items belong to the purchaser right away.

Disadvantages of using extended credit

- If repayments are not made the purchaser may be taken to court to demand payment of the outstanding amount (the amount left to pay) on the agreement.
- Purchasers cannot end their agreement and return the item.
- Interest rates are usually very high and expensive to the purchaser.

Credit cards

Credit card companies (including banks and other financial institutions) give their customers an account and a credit card. The customer can use this card at a variety of retailers, to purchase items on credit which they can take home immediately and pay for at a later date. Each card holder can spend up to a limit agreed with the lender. Every time the customer uses the card they have to sign a form or, more commonly now, type in a personal identification number (PIN) which is usually four digits long. This keying in (typing) of a PIN number at the checkout is more commonly known as 'Chip and PIN'. The credit card has a small computer chip in it which prevents thieves from copying the card and using it illegally to purchase goods and services without the card holder's knowledge. In the United Kingdom all retailers must use the chip and PIN system to limit and prevent fraud. After its introduction to the UK in 2005, there was a reduction of nearly £60m in counterfeit (copying a credit card) and fraud on lost and stolen cards compared to figures in 2004.

The card holder receives monthly statements from the credit card company showing how much is owed and what was purchased that month using the credit card. The card holder has to make at least a minimum payment, which is usually about 2–5 per cent of the total balance (amount owed) on the account. However, if they do not pay the full amount on their card, interest is charged on the balance left on the card, increasing the amount of money that is owed. Figure 3.1 shows the different stages in a credit card transaction.

Advantages of using credit cards

- It is easy to purchase high-value items without having to spend time completing confusing forms and documents.
- It is safer to carry a credit card instead of large amounts of cash.
- If the balance at the end of the month is paid off then no interest is charged.
- Credit companies may give their card holders 'rewards' or money back to encourage them to use their cards more often.

Many people use credit and store cards instead of cash when they shop

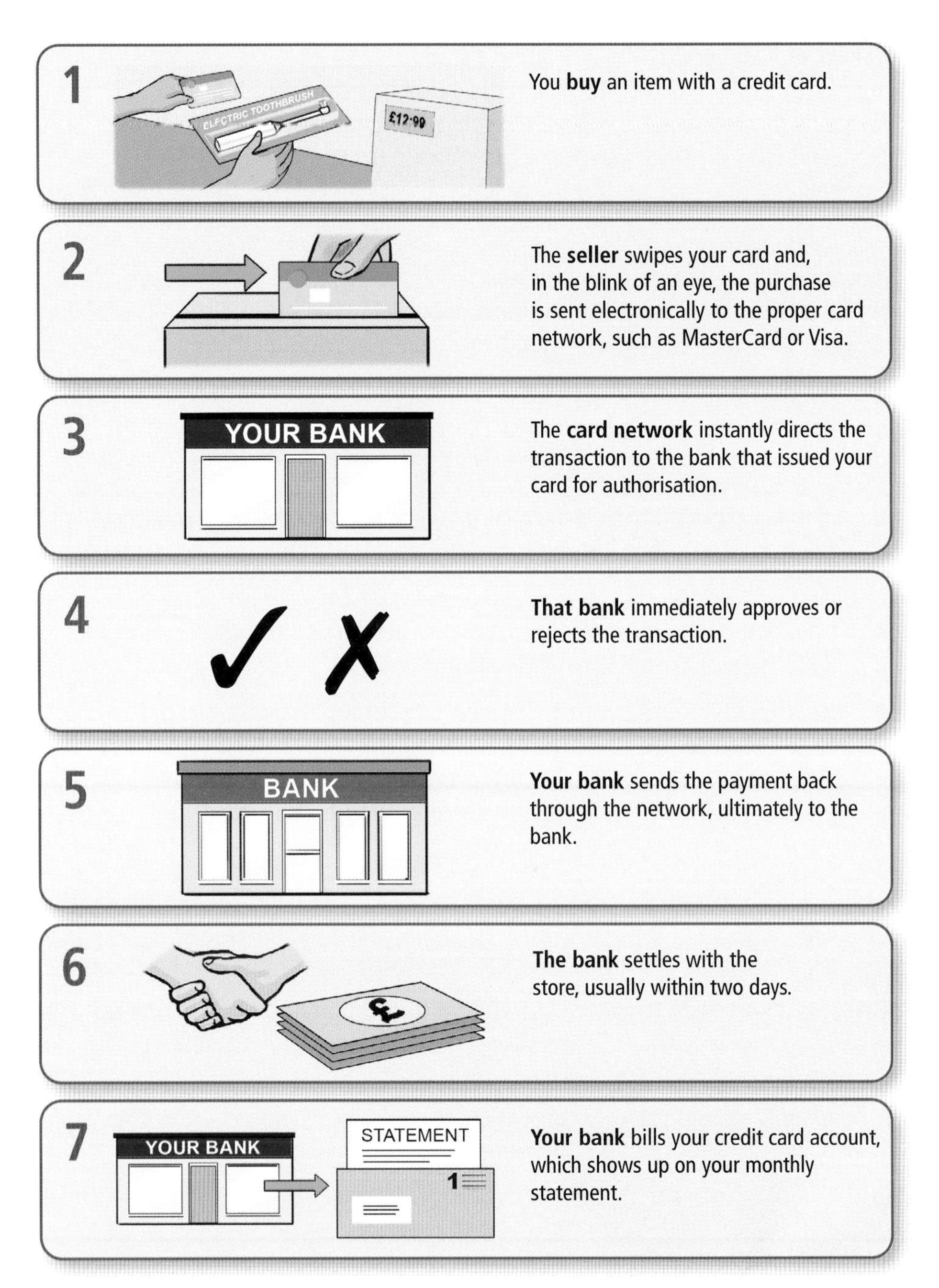

■ **Figure 3.1** *How credit cards work*

Disadvantages of using credit cards

- Credit cards charge a high rate of interest compared with other credit methods like bank loans.
- The fact that it is easy to use credit cards encourages card holders to spend more, which can result both in high repayments and interest being charged.

Store cards

Store cards are very similar to credit cards but card holders can only use them in the stores which give them. Stores promote their cards to customers when they are paying for goods (in the store or on the Internet), and usually offer an incentive such as a large discount on that day's purchases if the card is applied for there and then.

APR/Annual Percentage Rate – the interest rate charged on loans or credit cards. This figure takes in not only the interest payable over the term of the loan or period of credit but also any other charges or fees. It is regarded as the best way to compare the cost of credit from one financial institute to another.

Advantages of using store cards

- As long as you pay off your card balance at the end of the month you can have free credit and avoid interest charges.
- The card may entitle you to special store discounts not available to others.

Disadvantages of using store cards

- **Annual percentage rates** of interest, known as APRs, are usually extremely high and can be more than double the rate of standard credit cards.
- Stores regularly try to encourage card holders to purchase more by sending exclusive information about sales by e-mail or post.
- The rewards and discounts offered encourage the card holder to spend more at the store that gave the card rather than looking for cheaper alternatives. They may even spend so much that they are unable to afford the minimum repayment on their card.

Theory into practice

You have decided to go to your favourite clothes shop to buy some new clothes. You can only afford to spend $100 (which has taken you 12 weeks to save). When you arrive at the store the customer service assistant starts to tell you about their new store card. If you take up a store card you could spend up to $400 that day *and* receive a 10 per cent discount on your first transaction (which would save you $40). In addition to this, for every $100 you spend, you will get $1 back. Will you accept the card? Explain the reasons for your answer.

Suitability of methods of credit in certain circumstances

As you have seen, it is possible to get a variety of different types of credit, but these types of credit are often better suited for use for different things. Table 3.1 shows a variety of different types of credit, as well as a discussion of when they are suitable for use and why.

Type of credit	Suitable for	Reasons for choice
Hire purchase	High-value items like cars and expensive electrical items required for immediate use.	Allows customers to use the items immediately in return for relatively small monthly payments with the option to make a large final payment to secure ownership of the items.
Extended credit (deferred payments) sometimes referred to as 'buy now and pay later'	Goods with a poor resale value, e.g clothing.	Allows customers to buy items that they cannot afford to start paying for immediately. These credit terms allow customers to buy items for immediate use, and to make repayments at a later date. These payments are spread over a very long period of time, so that the repayments are affordable to the customer.
Credit cards	Inexpensive, everyday purchases like food shopping, clothing and fuel for vehicles. Expensive items and services like the cost of hotels or flights, or purchases when on holiday.	Allow customers to access a sum of money (usually a maximum of $2000 to $3000 per credit card) to pay for small to medium purchases that they may not be able to afford immediately using their bank accounts. Customers can repay the loan over a long period of time but with the cost of interest added every month. Credit cards are quick to get and customers do not need to get approval for every item they purchase on credit.
Store cards	Purchases from the store that issued the card. They are often available in department stores and clothes retailers. Store card holders may purchase low- to medium-value items which may be luxuries such as new clothes or decorative items for a house.	Customers use store cards because they have a long-term purchasing relationship with the store that is issuing the card. They may be attracted by discounts and special offers as a reward for holding a store card and making purchases in that retail outlet. Customers need to be aware that the rewards may not be worth the very high costs associated with store cards in terms of the APRs charged compared to other credit types.

■ **Table 3.1** *Suitability of methods of credit*

Theory into practice

Suggest, with appropriate reasons, the most suitable method or methods of credit to use for the purchase of the following items:

- A new kitchen ($12,500)
- Uniform for children starting back at school after the holidays ($230)
- A television ($1300)
- The weekly food shop ($75)
- A bicycle ($599)
- Living room furniture ($4599)

Summary of main points from Unit 3

- Credit is a means of borrowing money from a person or company with the aim of paying it back at a later date, usually also paying the added interest charged on the original amount that was loaned for the purchase of something specific.
- In recent years the amount of customer credit taken in western and developed countries has hugely increased. So too has the number of people declaring themselves bankrupt!
- Hire purchase (HP) is one credit method usually used to purchase expensive items like cars or furniture. They can be paid for over a long period of time. The item will not belong to the consumer until their final HP payment is made.
- Extended credit is similar to HP but the date that repayments are made can be delayed for a significant amount of time. They are used again for high-value items such as cars or furniture.
- Credit cards provide card holders with the flexibility and freedom to purchase goods and services up to an agreed credit limit, when they want to, even if they do not have any money in their bank account. The amount loaned can be paid off over a long period of time by paying off small amounts each month. Interest rates are usually very high because this credit method is very convenient.
- Store cards are similar to credit cards but can only be used to purchase items from the named store. Again, store cards usually have very high rates of interest if the balance on them is not paid off quickly.

Test your knowledge

Practice multiple choice exam questions

1) Accepting credit cards in a shop can be costly to the retailer as a small percentage of each transaction is paid to the credit card company. Why do shops accept credit cards?
   a) To increase profit made by the retailer.
   b) To reduce the amount of cash handled within the shop.
   c) To increase the amount of turnover made by the retailer.
   d) To reduce the overheads of running the shop.
2) Which of the following options is an advantage to a purchaser of hire purchase?
   a) Payments of regular amounts can be made by instalments straight out of a bank account.
   b) On paying a deposit the goods become the property of the purchaser.
   c) Some retailers may provide a discount if hire purchase is used.
   d) A wide variety of products can be purchased.
3) Which of the following is an advantage of extended credit or deferred payments to a purchaser?
   a) Any kind of goods can be purchased.
   b) Discount will be given when the sale is made.
   c) Payments can be made by regular instalments.
   d) The purchaser becomes the owner of the goods on paying the deposit.

Test your knowledge *continued*

4) Which of the following is a disadvantage to credit card holders?
   a) It is easy to purchase items without complicated paperwork.
   b) Cards are more secure than carrying cash.
   c) Allows you to spend more than you earn.
   d) When balances are cleared monthly credit is free.

5) Which of the following is a disadvantage to retailers offering credit?
   a) Convenience to customers
   b) Increased average sale orders
   c) Fees payable on each credit card transaction
   d) Impulse sales

Practice stimulus response and structured exam questions

1) Josephine and Boniface own a shop. They accept debit cards but not credit cards as payment for goods.
   a) Explain why they accept debit cards and not credit cards. (*4 marks*)
   b) Explain one possible disadvantage to their business of not accepting credit cards. (*3 marks*)

(CIE Commerce Paper Oct/Nov 2002)

Question 1 asks you to **'explain'**. Questions that ask for explanations often have more marks awarded for them. Your answers need to be more developed depending on the marks awarded.

2) State a method of payment you would use for each transaction below. In each case choose a different method and give two reasons for your choice.
   a) Payment for batteries from a street trader. (*3 marks*)
   b) Purchase of a jacket costing $200 from a department store. (*3 marks*)

(CIE Commerce Specimen Paper 2 2005)

3) Explain why retailers will usually accept the following payments for debts.
   a) Cash (*3 marks*)
   b) Credit cards (*4 marks*)

(CIE Commerce Paper 1 Oct/Nov 2003)

4) A new hypermarket has opened in a shopping centre on the outskirts of a city.
   a) State two advantages and disadvantages to customers of using credit cards to purchase goods in the hypermarket. (*4 marks*)
   b) State one advantage and one disadvantage to the hypermarket of accepting credit cards. (*2 marks*)

(CIE Commerce May/June 2000)

5) A family member is considering purchasing a new car. He can afford a $10,000 loan over five years for a small family car that will cost him $200 a month. Alternatively he could buy a sports car worth $18,000 on hire purchase for the same monthly repayment.
   a) State three advantages of hire purchase. (*3 marks*)
   b) State three disadvantages of hire purchase. (*3 marks*)
   c) Explain the difference between hire purchase and extended credit. (*2 marks*)

(Author Sept 2006)

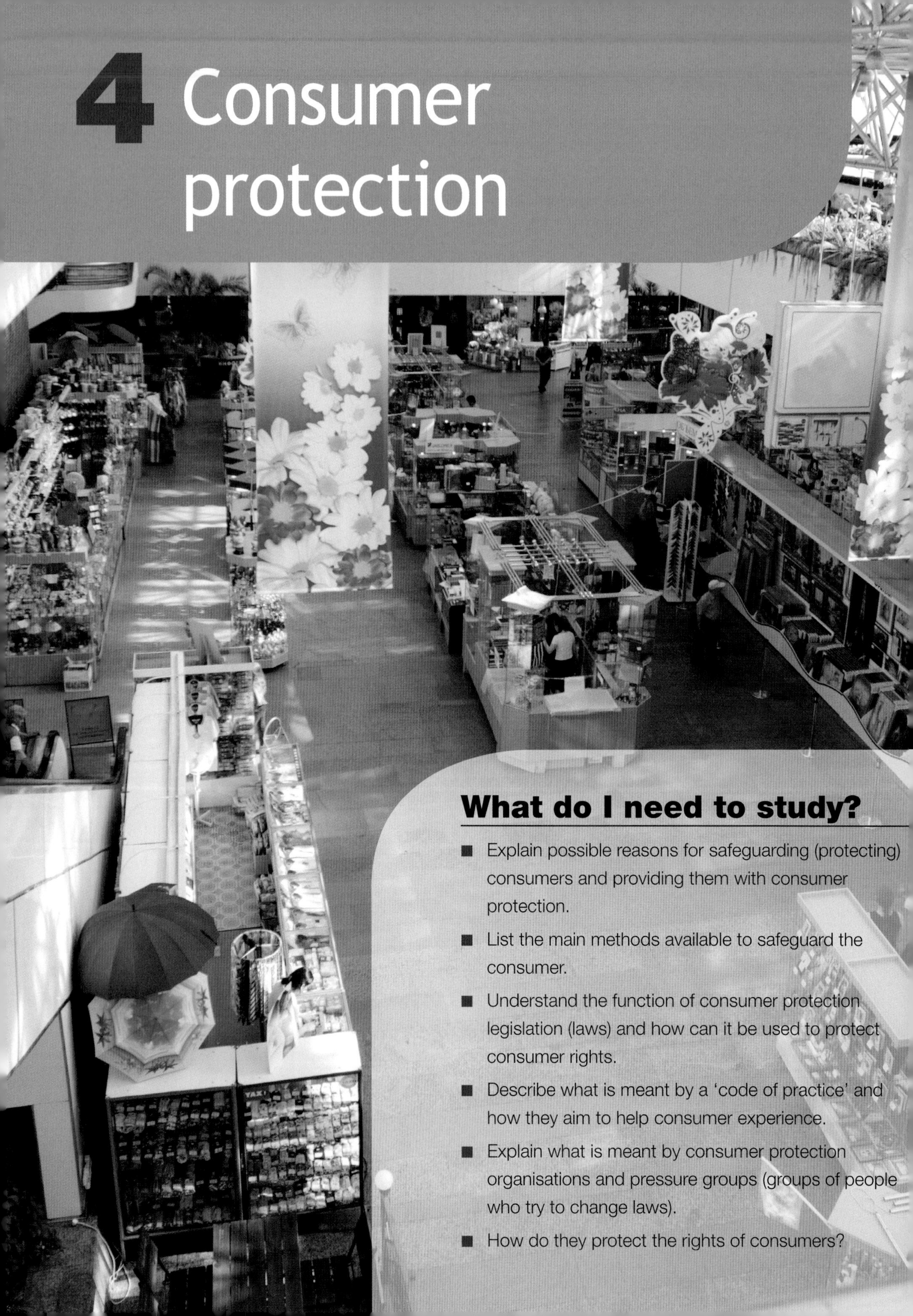

4 Consumer protection

What do I need to study?

- Explain possible reasons for safeguarding (protecting) consumers and providing them with consumer protection.
- List the main methods available to safeguard the consumer.
- Understand the function of consumer protection legislation (laws) and how can it be used to protect consumer rights.
- Describe what is meant by a 'code of practice' and how they aim to help consumer experience.
- Explain what is meant by consumer protection organisations and pressure groups (groups of people who try to change laws).
- How do they protect the rights of consumers?

Introduction

In this unit we will look at the methods used to protect consumers from dishonest traders who think it is alright to take advantage of consumers or even put the health of consumers at risk in order to make a profit. Consumers are protected by a complex range of consumer protection legislation. In addition to this, there are codes of practice which have been developed by organisations in certain industries to safeguard consumers' health and make sure they are provided with the goods and services they paid for. We will also investigate the organisations set up by governments to represent consumers and protect and improve consumer rights in the future.

It can be hard to understand how consumer protection might apply to you. Ask yourself, what stops a chocolate manufacturer from promising in their advertising that you will become more intelligent if you eat their latest chocolate bar? What stops major sports shoe manufacturers from agreeing with each other never to charge less than $80 for their sports shoes? What stops food manufacturers from using cheap but dangerous ingredients in their products, making them potentially harmful to consumers' health? The answer is consumer protection.

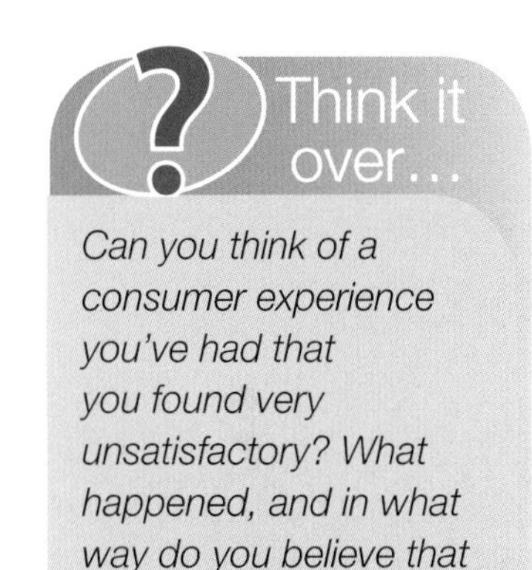

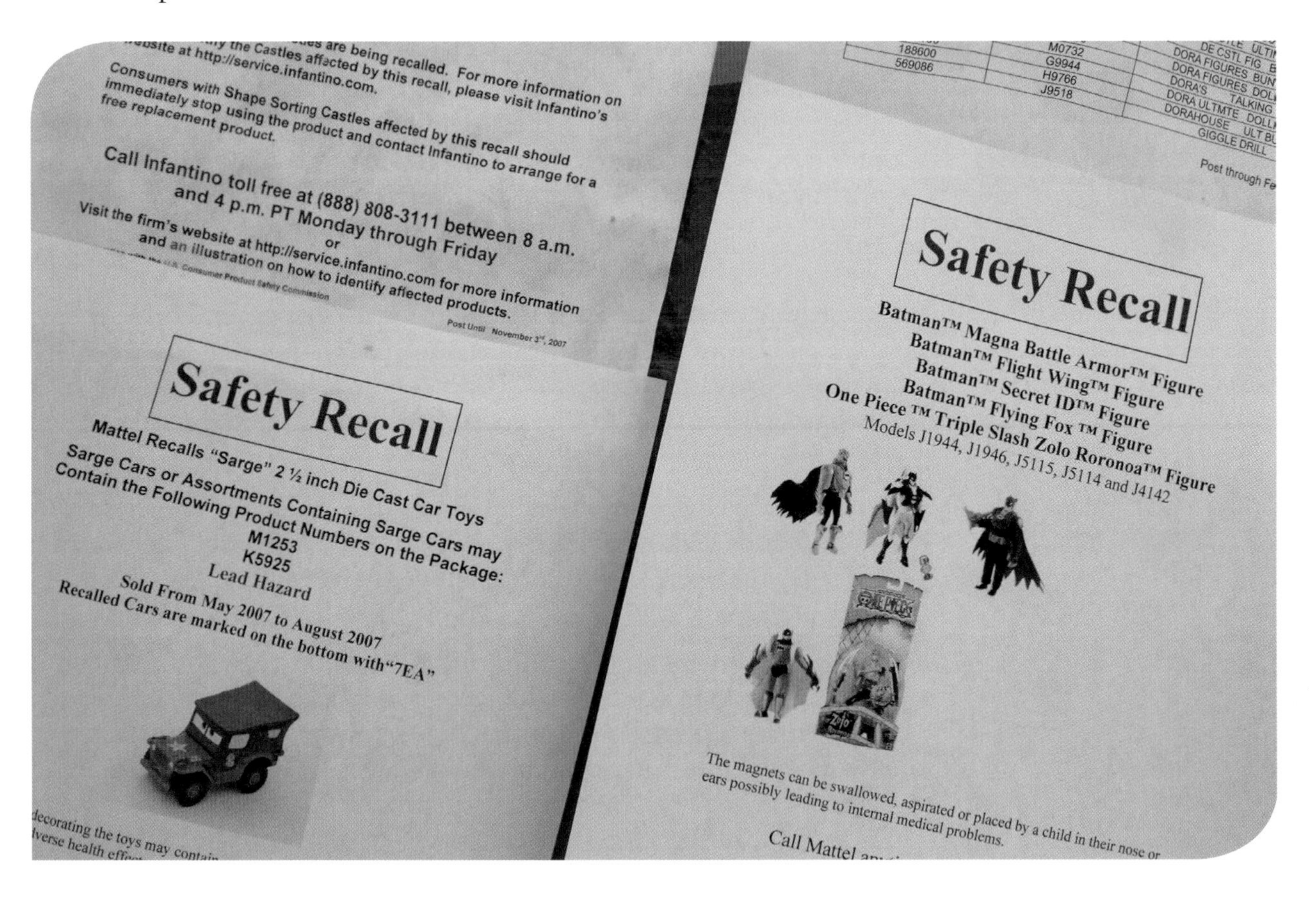

4.1 Safeguarding the consumer

Why do consumers need protection?

The main objective of most commercial organisations is to survive and, in increasingly competitive markets, to sell products or services to customers at the highest profit levels they can achieve. In order to make higher profits, organisations can be tempted to try to cut material costs by using cheaper, poor-quality suppliers. Without consumer protection, legislation and codes of practice, organisations may not spend a lot of money designing products that are safe for consumers to use. The quality of finished goods may not be properly inspected for safety and suitability before sending to retailers. This could mean that there is an increased risk of unsafe goods reaching consumers and causing harm, injury or even death. This means that there is a real need for consumer protection.

Some organisations, if left alone, will try to influence the market and exploit their customers, doing anything they can to increase sales and reduce costs. Some examples of how traders may take advantage of their customers are as follows:

- **Higher prices:** organisations may form cartels. This means that a group of leading suppliers of a product or service will agree to set prices at a level that is higher than it would naturally be if competition was allowed between them. Consumers are disadvantaged by having to pay higher prices for goods and products they need, e.g. petrol, because there are no other alternative suppliers offering lower prices in the market.
- **False expectations:** traders may encourage consumers to buy products or services by giving misleading information in their advertising or labelling. This may include overexaggerated claims of price reductions – giving consumers the impression that they are getting a 'bargain' when they are not – or inaccurate descriptions of products and services so that consumers have false expectations of what they are purchasing.
- **Poor value for money:** organisations may supply underweight products, packaging up less than is shown on the product label, so that they make more profit per gram of product sold.
- **Safety:** organisations may fail to consider the safety of their consumers when manufacturing goods or providing services. They may choose to make unsafe goods that are cheap to manufacture by using inferior, inexpensive or even dangerous materials which help them to keep costs per manufactured item as low as possible. A Chinese manufacturing company, International Playthings, recalled a product for safety reasons when a problem was discovered. They felt

it was their responsibility to inform consumers who had bought their toy mobile phone that parts that could break off and present a possible choking risk to a small child.

Theory into practice

In groups, discuss the possible ways in which consumers may be exploited by the following traders.

- Building firm
- Clothing retailer
- Toy manufacturer

Explain why consumers might need to be protected in each case. Try to give examples where possible.

Appropriate forms of consumer protection are necessary to safeguard the health and rights of the consumer. In the next section of this unit, we will consider the different methods there are of safeguarding consumers.

4.2 Methods of safeguarding the consumer

Protection for consumers can be provided in the following ways:

- consumer law
- codes of practice
- consumer protection organisations
- other consumer organisations and pressure groups.

Consumer law

Most countries have laws to protect the rights of their consumers, from food shoppers to car owners to hotel guests. In this section we will investigate the main consumer protection laws or Acts that exist in a variety of different countries, showing how they aim to protect consumers.

Consumer Protection Acts

Most countries have developed their own legislation to protect their consumers against faulty, unsafe and poor-quality products and services. We will look at the consumer protection laws in a number of different countries (the UK, the Maldives and India). You will notice that the legal requirements vary between countries but they all aim to protect consumers.

UK – Consumer Protection Act 1987

This Act was developed to reduce the chance that consumers might have their safety put at risk by poorly designed or manufactured goods in the UK. There are now strict regulations that apply to the manufacture of goods. For example, toys for very young children must not have any small loose parts that could be swallowed by a child; and soft furnishings, such as sofas, must be made of fire-retardant fabric (fabric that will not easily catch fire). This Act is important because it forces manufacturers to make and supply safe products. If they fail to comply with regulations and a product causes harm to a consumer, the organisation responsible may have to pay compensation money or even go to prison.

Maldives – Consumer Protection Act 1996

This Act was created in 1996 to protect consumer rights. It contains very specific guidelines which all organisations must follow. The Act helps to ensure that consumers are protected from organisations that might lie about the quality of their goods. It states that consumers should be given all the information they require before deciding to purchase their goods, such as accurate price, any faults that might exist or, in the case of food, a list of ingredients and an accurate date that it should be eaten by (expiry date). If a consumer buys an item that is faulty or damaged, then the Act states that they have the right to return that item and receive a full refund. Failure to follow these regulations will result in the organisation involved having to pay a fine.

India – Consumer Protection Act 1986

The Consumer Protection Act of India 1986 also aims to protect the interests of consumers. It encouraged the setting up of consumer councils to handle consumer complaints and protect their basic rights. The Act and the councils work to ensure that Indian consumers are accurately informed about the quality and price of the goods they wish to purchase, and that they are given access to a variety of goods and services at competitive prices. The councils also work to educate the consumer so that they are aware of their rights and are able to seek compensation when they feel that they have been badly treated by traders. These requirements are very similar to Pakistan's Islamabad Consumer Protection Act of 1995.

Codes of practice

Governments such as those in India and the UK encourage organisations and industries to take responsibility for consumer protection and customer satisfaction. This could involve setting up specialist trade associations which develop their own voluntary **code of practice**. If consumers know that traders within an association keep to the standards of their code of practice they can be confident that the traders care about the quality and safety of the products and services they provide.

Code of practice – a set of guidelines adopted by traders within common industries to ensure the quality and safety of products and services supplied to consumers.

Examples of codes of practice include the Advertising Standards Authority (ASA) in the UK and the Advertising Standards Council of India (ASCI). The ASA and the ASCI aim to make sure all advertising meets the standards that have been set in their country's code of practice. For example, a soft drinks company in the UK used poster advertising in and around public swimming areas showing children drinking their products under the water. Because children are vulnerable members of society and it is unsafe to drink up to an hour before swimming, let alone to drink in the pool, the ASA in the UK upheld complaints that the advertising could lead to children being physically harmed. Figure 4.1 shows an extract from India's advertising code of practice. You can see how the codes within a certain country can be influenced by cultural practices.

As with consumer legislation, advertising codes of practice around the world are quite similar. Table 4.1 shows a summary of some of the advertising regulations for different products in China and India.

	China	India
Alcoholic drinks	Official permits must be obtained to advertise drinks with over 39% alcohol. Most alcohol adverts are actually banned in China despite this.	Advertising alcoholic products is not allowed in India except on satellite television.
Cigarettes	Advertising cigarettes is banned in Beijing but in other regions of China it may be approved.	Advertising cigarettes in India is not allowed on media such as TV, satellite TV and radio.
Medicines	A 'Medicine Advertising Permit' must be obtained before advertising medicines.	There are strict rules on the advertising of medicine in India.

■ **Table 4.1** *Advertising regulations in China and India*

India's advertising code of practice

1. Advertising should not offend the morality, decency and religious beliefs of those exposed to the adverts.

2. No advertisement will be permitted that:
   (i) discriminates against any race, caste, colour, creed, gender or nationality
   (ii) is against any provision of the Constitution of India
   (iii) incites people to commit crime, cause disorder or violence
   (iv) presents criminal activities as desirable
   (v) exploits the national emblem of India, or any part of the Constitution of India or the person or personality of a national leader
   (vi) portrays women in a manner that emphasises passive, submissive qualities and encourages them to play a subordinate, secondary role in the family and society.

3. The goods or service advertised shall not suffer from any defect or deficiency as mentioned in the Consumer Protection Act 1986.

4. No advertisement shall contain information which may lead the public to consider that any of its ingredients has some special or miraculous or supernatural property or quality, which is difficult or impossible to prove.

5. No advertisement which endangers the safety of children or creates in them any interest in unhealthy practices or shows them begging or in an undignified or indecent manner shall be aired.

6. Indecent, vulgar, suggestive, repulsive or offensive themes or treatment shall be avoided in all advertisements.

■ **Figure 4.1** *India's advertising code of practice*

Quality assurance – a general term used to mean all the activities carried out by an organisation to ensure products and services that reach customers are of the highest quality all of the time. Traders will attempt to always identify improvements to the development, design, marketing, manufacturing and selling of products or services. This will allow them to benefit from the advantages of becoming known as a high-quality and innovative manufacturer.

Thankfully, most organisations today are run honestly and ethically and do not try to deceive or mislead their consumers. Traders realise that if they fail to satisfy their customers they will not benefit from their repeat purchases or word-of-mouth recommendations, two of the most important forms of advertising an organisation can have. In fact, most organisations have very comprehensive systems of **quality assurance** to try to ensure their goods work properly. If, for some reason, faulty products reach consumers they will do everything in their power to correct the fault, replace the product or refund the consumer.

Think it over...

In small groups decide on a product, service or industry in your country that particularly interests you and find out the following:

- *Does the industry have a trade association? If so, what is its name and what are its main aims?*
- *For the product, service or industry, find out if there is a recognised code of practice. Try to find out what the main concerns of the code of practice are and briefly explain their importance to consumers.*
- *What advice does the trade association give to consumers who feel unhappy about their consumer experiences?*

Theory into practice

Mr Chopra has worked as a carpenter for 25 years but he was recently made redundant. He used his savings to set up a small firm manufacturing traditional painted wooden toys for tourists visiting his town. Giving relevant examples, explain how the Consumer Protection Act 1996 of India may apply to him.

Consumer protection organisations

It would be almost impossible for governments and their consumer councils to deal with every consumer complaint or example of exploitation. Therefore, there is a range of consumer protection organisations who work together to ensure consumer safety by applying the relevant consumer protection laws.

If a consumer has purchased a product or service and is unhappy with it or it has caused harm to them, they are likely to go back to the trader or retailer and complain. The trader or retailer may:

- replace the product with a new or a similar item, or provide the service again
- give a full refund
- do nothing.

If the trader or retailer does nothing then the consumer can go to the following types of government-funded consumer organisations:

- **Local trading standards organisations**
  These organisations deal with complaints about faulty products or poor standards of service. They will support the consumer by enforcing consumer protection legislation so that consumers receive appropriate compensation and traders operate more ethically in the future.

- **Local environmental health organisations**
  These organisations deal with complaints that concern the standard of food and how clean the places are where food is prepared or sold, e.g. restaurants or food manufacturing plants. They will investigate complaints from consumers about poor standards of cleanliness and, in very serious cases, situations where consumers have experienced food poisoning. These organisations have the power to stop food traders from operating if they do not meet the standards.

- **Local consumer advice centres**
  These centres provide people with a wide variety of sources of information and advice about consumer choice and consumer rights. They will help the consumer to decide whether they have a valid (true) complaint and show them how to pursue their claims.

Other consumer organisations and pressure groups

The groups we have investigated so far support the consumer, but there are many other organisations that go further and try to influence *future* consumer experiences. They may try to put pressure on organisations or traders to operate in a more ethical way or demand that the government changes or develops consumer protection legislation to give consumers better protection.

- **Consumer associations and pressure groups**
  These pressure organisations test products and then report on the performance and standards of manufacture. They will compare these results with those of other similar products and this information can be made available to consumers so that they have good-quality, reliable and independent information to help make their buying decisions.

  A well-known consumer association in the UK publishes a magazine called *Which?* In its reports it gives readers a summary of the suppliers and manufacturers of certain services and products so that the reader can make the best consumer choice for their needs.

  In the image on page 66 you can see someone using special climbing equipment to keep them safe. It is very important that equipment like this is carefully tested. Climbers rely on this equipment to hold their weight high up a mountain. Would you use equipment that hadn't been tested?

- **International and National Consumer Councils**
  These organisations aim to communicate consumers' views to governments, large organisations and industries, particularly where people are unable to deal with their own consumer complaints. The councils are usually made up of a range of influential people from a wide variety of backgrounds and countries. Governments will often consult the consumer councils to get a consumer view before they make any new policies, regulations or legislative changes. Here are some examples of these councils:

■ *Specialist equipment needs to be thoroughly tested before use*

i. The *Network for Consumer Protection in Pakistan* – their main objectives are to protect and promote the interests of all Pakistani consumers. They provide people with education about their consumer rights by giving them independent information about everyday goods and services. As well as representing the interests of consumers, they aim to influence new government policies relating to consumer protection.

ii. The *Consumer Protection Council of India* – a voluntary organisation that promotes and develops public consumer awareness while trying to prevent the exploitation of consumers.

iii. The *Consumers International Organisation* – aims to support and represent the rights of consumers on a global basis, addressing the challenges of consumer protection internationally. Representatives from 113 countries make up Consumers International. They work together to defend the rights of all consumers by supporting smaller national consumer groups and using international pressure to change policies and laws in different countries.

- **Standards institutions**
  Most countries have standards institutions that set minimum standards for the design and manufacture of goods to guarantee their quality, performance and safety. In America there is the American National Standards Institute and in the UK there is the British Standards Institute. The European Commission's rules on product manufacture and service provision create standards in Europe and internationally there is the International Standards Organisation.

  Most of these organisations aim to establish voluntary standards of manufacture or service provision and will test products for quality and safety. Products that meet standards in the UK are labelled with a 'Kitemark' and the standard reference number. This indicates to the consumer that the product has been fully tested and that it satisfies certain basic standards of quality and safety. It is a very valuable mark to manufacturers because many consumers would look for it when purchasing goods or services.

The British Standards Kitemark

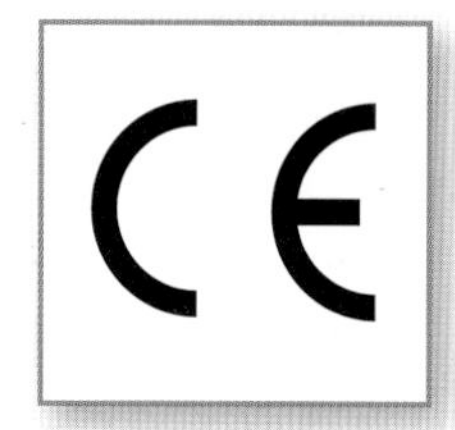

The European CE mark

■ **Figure 4.2** *Examples of safety standards markings*

Figure 4.2 shows examples of marks that manufacturers can use on their products once they have achieved the necessary level of safety, quality and consumer protection as laid down by specific legislation for each type or category of product. The British Standards Kitemark is displayed on products that meet their standards. In Europe, products will display the CE mark to demonstrate that they comply with the relevant European laws or directives.

Theory into practice

Find five common items you use on a daily basis, either at home or at school. Check them to see if they show any particular markings like the ones above. Find out what all the different markings on your products mean.

Theory into practice

Mai Saitou is very upset. The wooden doll she bought for her granddaughter came apart soon after the child had started playing with it, exposing a very dangerous, sharp nail. The trader refuses to do anything for Mai, saying that the toy had not been reasonably cared for and shouldn't have been given to such a young child. Write a list of the different organisations that Mai could approach for help.

Summary of main points from Unit 4

- Consumers are protected from dishonest traders by a complex range of consumer protection legislation, the most important of which are the Consumer Protection Acts. Each country has their own version of these acts.
- Legislation prevents traders from charging falsely high prices, misleading consumers by falsely advertising or labelling products, providing services and goods that are poor value for money and selling goods and services that could put the safety of consumers at risk.
- Consumers can also be protected when industries form and follow their own 'codes of practice' which are voluntary guidelines on how to produce goods and services to ensure the safety of consumers.
- Consumer protection organisations that are sometimes run by government agencies also work to represent the victims of dishonest traders and provide advice on their consumer rights. These organisations help consumers to seek compensation for the actions of dishonest traders and prevent other consumers from becoming victims.
- Pressure groups aim to expose unethical organisations and their unfair practices. They try to force these organisations to change the way they conduct their business activities and prevent consumers from being unfairly affected by their actions in the future.

Test your knowledge

Practice multiple choice exam questions

In exams, make sure you express yourself clearly and always check that you have answered the question that is being asked.

1) British Standards is a standards association in Great Britain. Which of the following describes its main function?
   a) To ensure advertising of products and services is accurate and not misleading.
   b) To represent consumers who have a complaint against a manufacturer.
   c) To ensure the design and construction of products meet certain requirements for safety.
   d) To ensure that within an industry there are no incidents of price fixing such as that associated with cartels.

2) What is the best way a consumer can protect themselves from unfair trading practices?
   a) Check products for safety stamps and labels.
   b) Use well-known mail order organisations.
   c) Join a consumer group or organisation.
   d) Try the goods before buying.

3) The increased variety of goods produced and the dangers of misleading advertising have led to the growth of:
   a) Advertising agencies
   b) Consumer protection
   c) Informative advertising
   d) Insurance companies

Test your knowledge *continued*

4) Which of the following four methods is not a common method for safeguarding consumers?
   a) Consumer law
   b) Customer care functions
   c) Consumer protection legislation
   d) Codes of practice

5) How does a standards association protect consumers?
   a) It advises consumers to buy wisely.
   b) It controls prices of basic commodities.
   c) It passes laws against unfair trading practices.
   d) It tests products for quality.

Practice stimulus response and structured exam questions

1) a) Why do consumers need protection? (*3 marks*)
   b) Describe and explain three ways in which traders may exploit their customers. (*9 marks*)

2) Most countries have consumer laws to protect the rights of their consumers. The most well known are Consumer Protection Acts. Describe five ways in which a Consumer Protection Act tries to protect consumers. (*10 marks*)

3) a) What is a 'code of practice'? (*2 marks*)
   b) What contribution do trade associations make to consumer protection? Give a relevant example. (*8 marks*)

4) a) What is meant by the term 'quality assurance'? (*2 marks*)
   b) How does an organisation that has quality assurance procedures ensure its consumers are protected and safe? Provide an example in your answer. (*8 marks*)

5) In most countries there is a range of consumer protection organisations that work together to ensure consumers' safety and protection by applying the relevant consumer protection laws. Give a brief explanation of what the following organisations can do for consumers.
   a) Trading Standards (*2 marks*)
   b) Environmental Health (*2 marks*)
   c) Consumer advice centres (*2 marks*)
   d) Consumer organisations and pressure groups (*2 marks*)

   Note that the examiner has asked for a 'brief' explanation in Question 5. You need to ensure that you point out the main function of the organisation and briefly explain what it does for consumers. Do not give more detail than requested in the question.

5 Wholesale trade

What do I need to study?

- Describe the role of the wholesaler in the chain of distribution.
- Identify the functions and services of the wholesaler.
- Understand the role of intermediaries (people in the middle) such as merchants and agents in the distribution of goods.
- Explain the trends in wholesaling: the forces making for the elimination and the survival of the independent wholesaler.

Introduction

Wholesaler – an organisation which specialises in buying goods in very large (or bulk) quantities from manufacturers and then selling them on to smaller retailers in much smaller quantities.

In this unit we are going to look at wholesale trade. Wholesale trade is one of the four main branches of trade; the others being retail, import and export trade. **Wholesalers** hold stocks of goods and materials bought directly from the manufacturers in large quantities, and then supply them to retailers. Wholesalers therefore provide an essential link between manufacturers and retailers.

Smaller local retailers, which we looked at in detail in Unit 2, are the most likely to use wholesalers. But why don't smaller shops buy their goods directly from the manufacturer? Surely it would be cheaper than paying the wholesaler's prices with their profit margins added on top of the goods price? The reality of the situation is that small independent retailers do not often buy direct from manufacturers because manufacturers are only interested in selling large orders. They are not prepared to pay the cost of delivering small quantities of their products to small independent retailers around the world. Instead, they concentrate on selling large quantities of their products to a small number of wholesalers. The wholesalers then distribute the goods to retailers on the manufacturers' behalf but for a small profit margin. They buy products in large quantities and sell them on in much smaller quantities to retailers.

5.1 The role of the wholesaler in the chain of distribution

There are many different chains of distribution, as we saw in Unit 2. The most common chain of distribution for many years is shown in the diagram below.

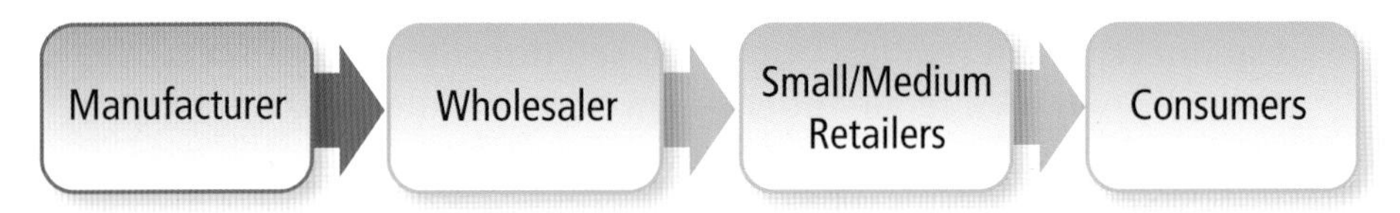

Figure 5.1 *The traditional chain of distribution*

As we have seen, manufacturers make the products and sell them to wholesalers in very large quantities. Wholesalers then divide the products into smaller quantities and sell them to small independent and medium-sized retailers. However, in the last 10 to 15 years, the way goods get to consumers has begun to change dramatically. Today, wholesalers are becoming less important than they were in the past. There is a trend developing where wholesalers are increasingly being removed from the distribution chain. There are many different reasons for this:

- **Increasing size of large retailers**
  Large retailers are generally growing in size and number and we are seeing a move towards 'large-scale retailing'. Many retailers are large enough to have their own warehousing and distribution facilities, which means that they don't need to rely as much on wholesalers and are able to buy goods directly from manufacturers in bulk quantities themselves. By not using a wholesaler, large retailers can negotiate reduced prices with the manufacturers. As these retailers become bigger we can see a decline in the demand for wholesalers' services.
- **Declining number of small independent retailers**
  The growth in the number of large-scale and multiple retailers opening outlets on the outskirts of towns and cities means that there are fewer customers in towns and city centres, which has led to very difficult trading conditions for the small independent retailers based there. As a result, many retailers are closing down. Wholesalers' customers tend to be those small independent retailers who are declining in numbers and we can only assume that if this decline in small retailers continues, wholesalers will have fewer customers to supply and might go out of business themselves!
- **Improved systems of transport and communication**
  Large-scale retailers have developed such good relationships with manufacturers that many have 'linked' computer systems. This

means that orders can be automatically placed when a retailer's computer system notices that a particular type of product is running low in stock so that the retailer rarely runs out of goods demanded by customers. Excellent road and rail networks mean that orders made can be delivered within hours or days of the order being placed. Wholesalers cannot offer this standard of convenience and efficiency in their service to retailers. This makes it difficult for them to compete with manufacturers who decide to supply retailers directly.

- **Manufacturers dealing directly with retailers and consumers**
  Some manufacturers are choosing not to deal with wholesalers and to deal directly with retailers or even to sell directly to consumers through their own retail outlets, mail order or Internet sales sites. This means that manufacturers have more control over the sales of their products and can sell to certain customers at increased prices.
- **Increased mass production and branding of products**
  Manufacturers, in an attempt to become more competitive, are using advertising and branding to create awareness and desire for their products. They have realised that they cannot rely on wholesalers to promote their products more than their competitors' products, but by establishing good trading relationships with large-scale retailers they can ensure their products appear on many more retailers' shelves.

  Retailers encourage manufacturers to use various sales promotion methods such as 'buy-one-get-one-free' and '50 per cent extra' to help them sell as many of their products as possible. The strong relationships that are forming between manufacturers and retailers are reducing the need for wholesalers' services.

Theory into practice

The number of retailers served by wholesalers is falling significantly. There are more and more large-scale retailers – supermarkets, hypermarkets and multiple chain retailers – who choose to be located on the outskirts of towns and cities. These days, retailers are more likely to deal directly with manufacturers than with wholesalers. Answer the questions below, giving reasons for your answers.

1. Who are the typical customers of a wholesaler?
2. How have large-scale retailers had an effect on the decline of wholesaling?
3. How have manufacturers had an effect on the decline of wholesaling?
4. Why do small independent retailers tend to pay more for goods from wholesalers than large retailers do from the manufacturers?

5.2 Functions and services of the wholesaler

Types of wholesaler

1. **General or traditional wholesalers** – This type of wholesaler can be regional (serving local retailers only) or national, with wholesale distribution outlets across the country. They usually stock a wide variety of goods including food and non-food items. These wholesalers send their sales representatives to retailers to take orders, which the wholesaler will then deliver. The retailer will benefit from **trade credit**, which allows them to receive goods now and pay for them later.

   It is probably the general or traditional wholesaler that has been most affected by large-scale retailers dealing directly with manufacturers and this has led to their decline in numbers.

2. **Specialist wholesalers/merchants** – These wholesalers deal with a particular trade. For example, there are specialist wholesalers or merchants for the building trade who supply materials and equipment specifically for building sites. Other examples include fish merchants and fruit and vegetable wholesalers who sell their products directly to specialist retailers like fishmongers and grocers.

3. **Cash and carry wholesalers** – As traditional wholesale outlets decline we are seeing more cash and carry wholesalers. These wholesalers are trying to make it as easy as possible for small independent retailers to compete with large retailers by offering goods at the lowest possible prices they can. Cash and carry wholesalers are able to do this because they do not send out sales people to collect orders or deliver stock to their customers. This means that the costs of running their wholesale organisation are kept as low as possible. Small retailers have to go to the cash and carry wholesaler themselves, pick their own items, put them on to a trolley and pay for them with cash as they leave. This means that cash and carry wholesalers do not offer trade credit to small retailers.

Trade credit – an arrangement to buy goods 'on account'. This means that retailers are able to receive goods without having to pay the wholesaler in cash straight away. The terms of the arrangement can vary but usually retailers can have goods for four weeks before they need to pay the wholesaler.

Theory into practice

There are wholesalers all around you, whether you realise it or not. Let's investigate the wholesalers that serve retailers in your local area.

1. Using the Internet, telephone directories or other trade directories, make a list of the different wholesalers in your area.
2. For each wholesaler on your list, decide whether you think they are general, specialist or cash and carry wholesalers.

Functions of wholesalers

Wholesalers provide many different services to manufacturers, retailers and consumers.

For manufacturers:

- Wholesalers provide a convenient outlet for manufacturers to sell their goods to in huge quantities. This is particularly important for manufacturers who do not have enough warehousing space of their own to store their finished products.
- Wholesalers pay promptly for the goods they receive. This means that the goods are quickly turned into cash for the manufacturer's organisation rather than sitting on their shelves until they can be sold.
- Wholesalers take on the risk that the goods may not be what consumers or retailers want. By selling directly to the wholesaler, the manufacturers don't have to worry about not being able to sell their goods to the consumer and therefore losing money.
- Deliveries to wholesalers are made in large or bulk quantities. This is very cost-effective and means that the distribution and delivery costs for the manufacturer are much lower than if they had had to deliver small quantities to lots of small retailers across the country. You can see in the diagram below that many extra deliveries are needed when a manufacturer chooses to sell directly to the retailers rather than through a wholesaler, and this would be much less cost-effective.

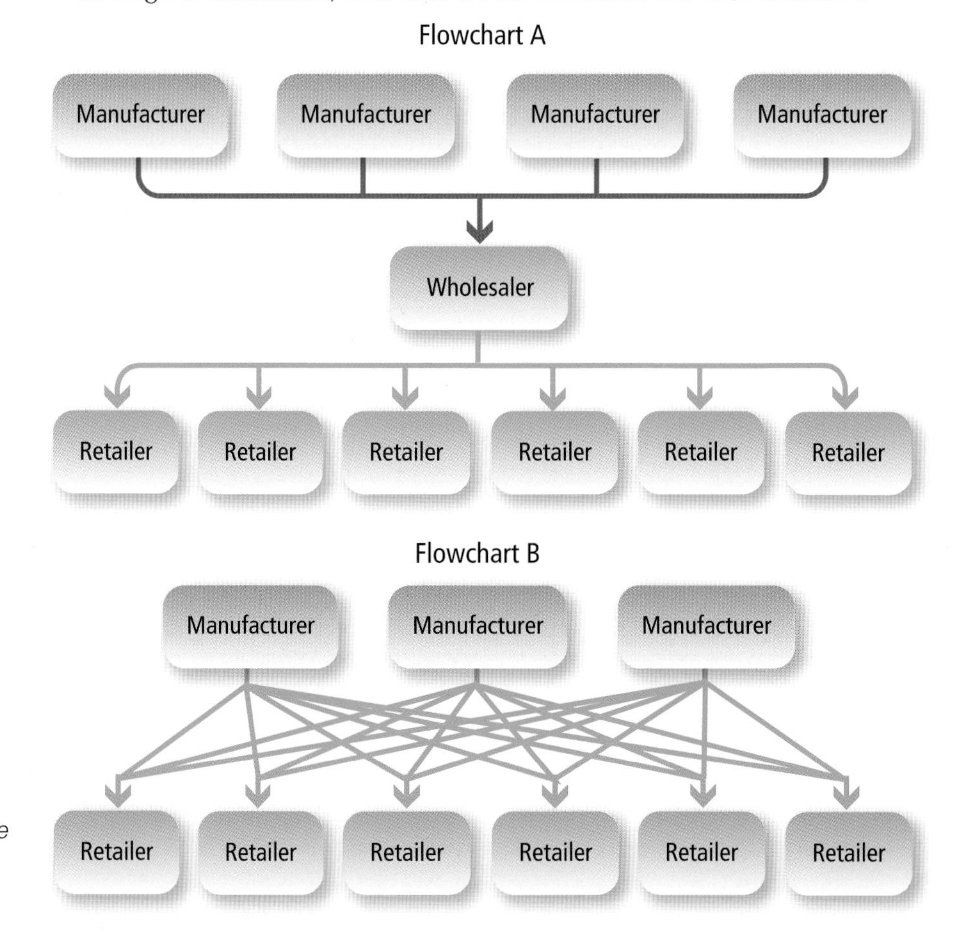

■ **Figure 5.2** *Fewer deliveries are needed if manufacturers use wholesalers to distribute their goods to retailers*

- Manufacturers rely on wholesalers to market their products to retailers using attractive displays and mail shots. Mail shots are eye-catching leaflets sent by post directly to retailers to tell them about existing and new product lines and any special offers that may be of interest to them.

For retailers and consumers:

- The wholesaler buys products in large quantities from manufacturers and sells them to retailers in smaller and more convenient amounts. This allows the retailers to stock products according to the needs and demands of their customers. This function of the wholesaler is called 'breaking bulk'.
- Wholesalers store large amounts of many different varieties and types of product. This means that retailers and consumers can be confident that they will get the products they need easily and quickly.
- Wholesalers allow retailers to stock very small quantities of new product lines so that they can test them in their own shops to see if their customers like them or not. If the customers don't want to buy the new product lines, then the retailer doesn't have to worry about having a large quantity of goods they can't sell on their shelves. It is the wholesaler, not the retailer, who purchases large quantities of these new products from manufacturers and takes the risk of being left with lots of stock that they cannot sell.
- As we have seen at the start of section 5.2 under the heading, 'General or traditional wholesalers', some wholesalers offer trade credit to their regular retailer customers. This means that they can sell the product in their stores for up to four weeks before they have to pay the wholesaler. This helps small retailers to stay in business because they do not need to take out expensive loans to stock their shops.
- Some wholesalers may offer delivery services to retailers who have trade accounts with them.
- Wholesalers provide retailers with information on the newest products available so that they can plan ahead and stock products which may be demanded by customers in the future.

'Distribution of goods through wholesalers is more cost-effective, economical and environmentally friendly.'

How relevant do you think this statement is to wholesalers, manufacturers, consumers of products, and the general public?

5.3 Intermediaries

The 'middlemen'

There are a variety of traders who provide links between organisations within the chain of distribution:

- **Merchants** – These are professional traders who deal in goods that they do not make themselves. They buy goods directly from a manufacturer and are then responsible for selling and promoting those goods to their buyers. They make the sale and arrange for transport of the goods directly from the manufacturer to the buyer. Lots of merchants do not actually see or handle the goods themselves.
- **Brokers** – These are agents who work on behalf of manufacturers or suppliers of primary sector materials like oil. The broker finds buyers for their products or materials. Brokers have long-standing links within certain industries and they receive a commission based on how much of a product or material they sell. Like merchants, brokers do not have any contact with the product. They are responsible for setting up a relationship between the supplier and the buyer.
- **Factors** – These are another type of agent but they *do* handle the product and have it with them when they go out to seek buyers. They are rewarded financially by receiving a commission based on the value of the goods they have sold. Factors only deal in goods and not services.
- **Forwarding agents** – These are agents who specialise in receiving and distributing goods for export to overseas customers. They allow companies to have much easier access to overseas markets by offering them a range of different warehousing and transport services. It would be very difficult for organisations to arrange for the warehousing and distribution of their goods in other countries because they would be unlikely to have the connections that the forwarding agent has.

Theory into practice

Ling has been operating a small furniture-making firm called Ling's Furniture for nearly 20 years. He supplies to wholesalers who sell the furniture on to small retailers at home and abroad. Recently he considered supplying furniture directly to small retailers, leaving out the wholesaler's stage altogether and getting a better price for each piece of furniture he sold. Write a brief summary of the services that the following intermediaries could offer to Ling's Furniture:

- Merchants
- Forwarding agents

Summary of main points from Unit 5

- A wholesaler is an organisation which specialises in buying goods in very large quantities from manufacturers and then sells them on to small retailers at a slightly higher unit cost than the price they paid the manufacturers.
- Wholesalers operate as intermediaries or middlemen within the chain of distribution, providing a link between manufacturers and retailers who want to stock certain products.
- Wholesalers are becoming increasingly removed from the distribution chain due to the growth of retailers, who are becoming so large that they can purchase directly from manufacturers in large quantities and store the goods in their own warehouses. In addition, wholesalers are declining because there are fewer small independent retailers who use their services, and also manufacturers are choosing to remove the wholesaler stage of the distribution chain because they want to deal directly with retailers and consumers instead.
- There are many types of wholesaler. Each has their own specific specialism:
  - General or traditional wholesalers
  - Specialist wholesalers
  - Cash and carry wholesalers.

Test your knowledge

Practice multiple choice exam questions

1) Wholesalers have many functions. Which of the four options below describes the main function of a wholesaler?
   a) To act as after-sales providers to consumers.
   b) To promote manufacturers' goods and materials.
   c) To put limits on what is demanded from retailers.
   d) To link manufacturers and retailers.

2) Which of the following options describes the main function of brokers?
   a) To label goods with their company name.
   b) To provide a guarantee that goods imported from overseas will be sold.
   c) To provide storage and warehousing facilities.
   d) To establish trading relationships between buyers and sellers.

The letters below represent the traditional channel of distribution. Use this flowchart to answer questions 3, 4 and 5.

A → B → C → D

3) What is represented by the letter 'A'?
   a) Retailer
   b) Consumer
   c) Wholesaler
   d) Manufacturer

Test your knowledge *continued*

4) What is represented by the letter 'C'?
   a) Manufacturer
   b) Consumer
   c) Wholesaler
   d) Retailer

5) What is represented by the letter 'D'?
   a) Wholesaler
   b) Manufacturer
   c) Retailer
   d) Consumer

Practice stimulus response and structured exam questions

1) Mrs Boah owns a cash and carry wholesaling company. What are the benefits of this kind of warehouse for:
   a) Mrs Boah? (*3 marks*)
   b) The retailers she supplies? (*3 marks*)

(Author 2006)

2) Samuel Moyo is a sole trader running a general hardware shop in a small town.
   a) Samuel buys many of his television supplies from a wholesaler rather than direct from a manufacturer. Give three reasons why he does this. (*6 marks*)

(CIE Commerce Specimen Paper 2 2005)

3) Answer the following questions on the wholesale trade:
   a) Name four services a wholesaler might provide for a retailer but not for a manufacturer. (*4 marks*)
   b) Explain why retailers charge higher prices than wholesalers. (*4 marks*)
   c) Explain the trends that have contributed to the decline of the wholesaler. (*6 marks*)
   d) In what circumstances is a wholesaler still likely to be used by retailers? (*6 marks*)

(CIE Commerce Paper 1 May/Jun 2004)

Question 3a asks you to **'name'** four services and only gives one mark for each one named. Keep answers to these types of question short. Do not be tempted to waste time by providing a more detailed answer.

4) Explain the purposes of a wholesaler in the chain of distribution. (*10 marks)*

(CIE Commerce Paper 1 Oct/Nov 2004)

5) A furniture manufacturer has been selling to wholesalers and retailers and is considering selling directly to consumers.
   a) Explain two methods the manufacturer might use to sell the furniture directly to consumers. (*4 marks)*
   b) Explain the benefits this manufacturer might obtain from selling directly to consumers. (*6 marks)*
   c) State and explain two problems the manufacturer is likely to meet when selling directly to consumers. (*4 marks)*

(CIE Commerce Paper May/Jun 2002)

6 Documents of trade

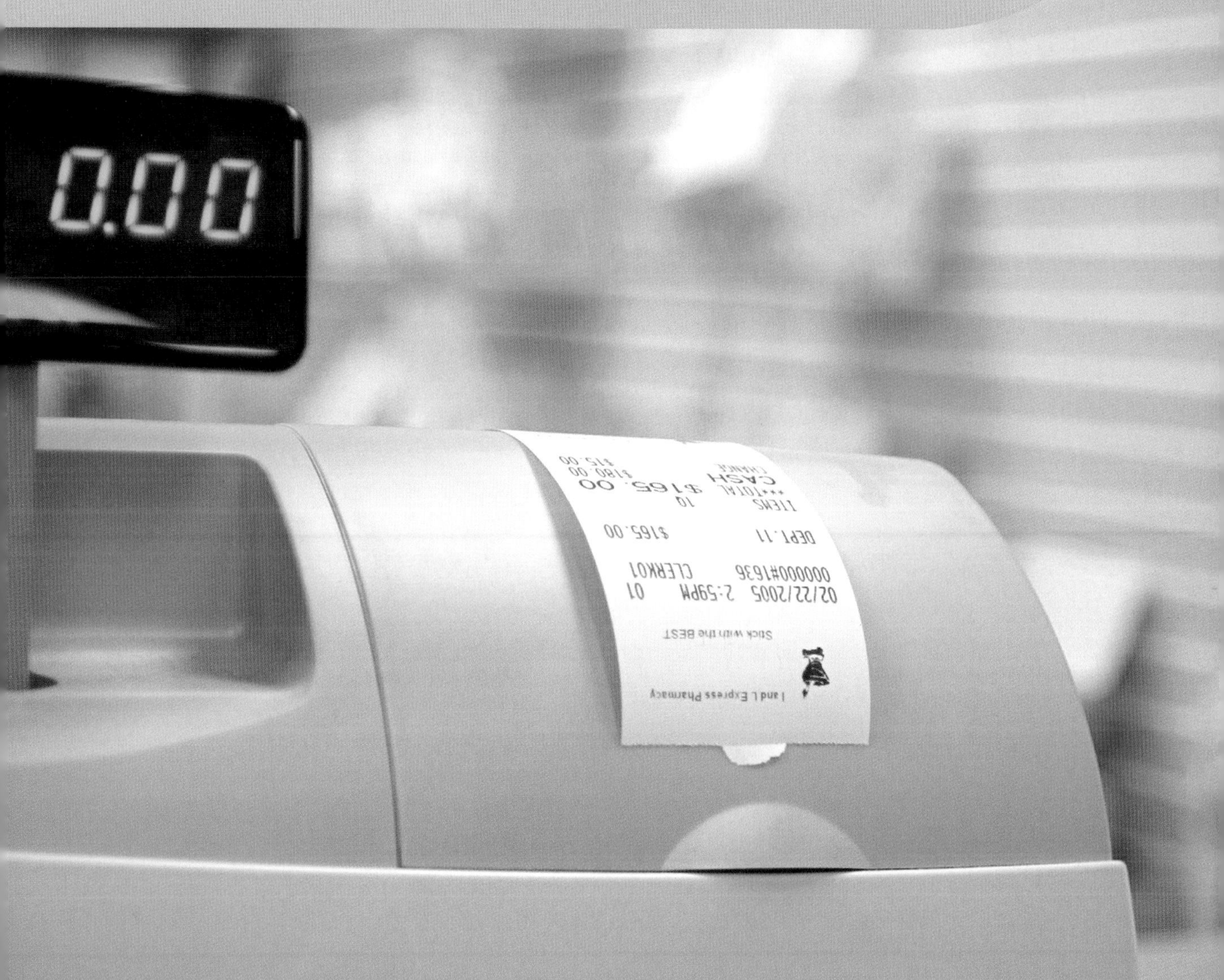

What do I need to study?

- List the main documents used in home trade.
- Explain the purpose of these home trade documents.
- List the key information contained in these documents.
- Define what is meant by terms of payment.
- What are the reasons for cash and trade discounts, and mark up?

Introduction

All the commercial activities we have read about so far in this book can be referred to as **trade**. What we mean by the word 'trade' is the purchase of goods and materials in exchange for money or other goods and materials. Trade is generally divided into two main branches: home trade (or domestic trade) and international trade (or foreign trade). We have seen in Units 1, 2 and 5 that goods and materials can pass between several different organisations before reaching the final consumer. We refer to the buying and selling of goods and materials between organisations as **commercial transactions**.

Commercial transactions – agreements made between sellers and their buyers which may involve the transfer of goods and services in exchange for money.

Organisations can conduct thousands of commercial transactions in a year, a month, a week or even in a day. This means that they need a way of recording where goods are going, where they have come from, how much was charged for them and whether or not they have been paid for. Documents of trade provide records of the details of commercial transactions.

6.1 Documents of home trade

Organisations have developed a number of documents where they can record transactions to make the process of exchanging products or information simple, quick and efficient. In this unit, we will look at the purposes of each of the documents that organisations use and the type of information that is being passed between buyers and sellers. The documents we will be investigating are:

- Enquiry
- Quotation
- Catalogue
- Price list
- Order
- Advice note
- Delivery note
- Invoice
- Credit note
- Statement of account
- Receipt

Enquiry

This document is sent from the buyer who wants to purchase goods (for example, a new car), material supplies (for example, wheat, sugar and fruit required by breakfast cereal manufacturers) or services (for example, the repair or maintenance of electrical goods in your home) to their potential suppliers (sellers).

When a buyer wants to purchase particular goods or services, they will send an 'enquiry' to a range of sellers who specialise in these goods or services. An enquiry can be sent by e-mail or post, or the information can be requested by telephone or by a salesperson who is visiting the supplier. However the buyer chooses to contact the seller, they will be 'enquiring' about the following things:

- Can they supply a list of the desired features of the goods/services required?
- What price will they charge?
- Can they deliver by the date required?

Buyers can find suitable suppliers for the goods or services they wish to purchase by looking at the suppliers' catalogues, price lists or business directories.

Quotation

This document is sent by the seller to the buyer in response to an enquiry.

Sellers who have received enquiries will prepare and send back quotations for the goods or services. The quotation contains all the information requested by the company wanting to make a purchase. The company can then compare all the quotations they have received from the different sellers and decide which one best satisfies their needs.

A quotation will be very detailed, giving the following information:

- Prices of goods/services charged
- Delivery conditions
- Special conditions requested by the customer. For example, they may have asked for a material that is not normally used in the making of a particular product
- Any discounts that may be offered.

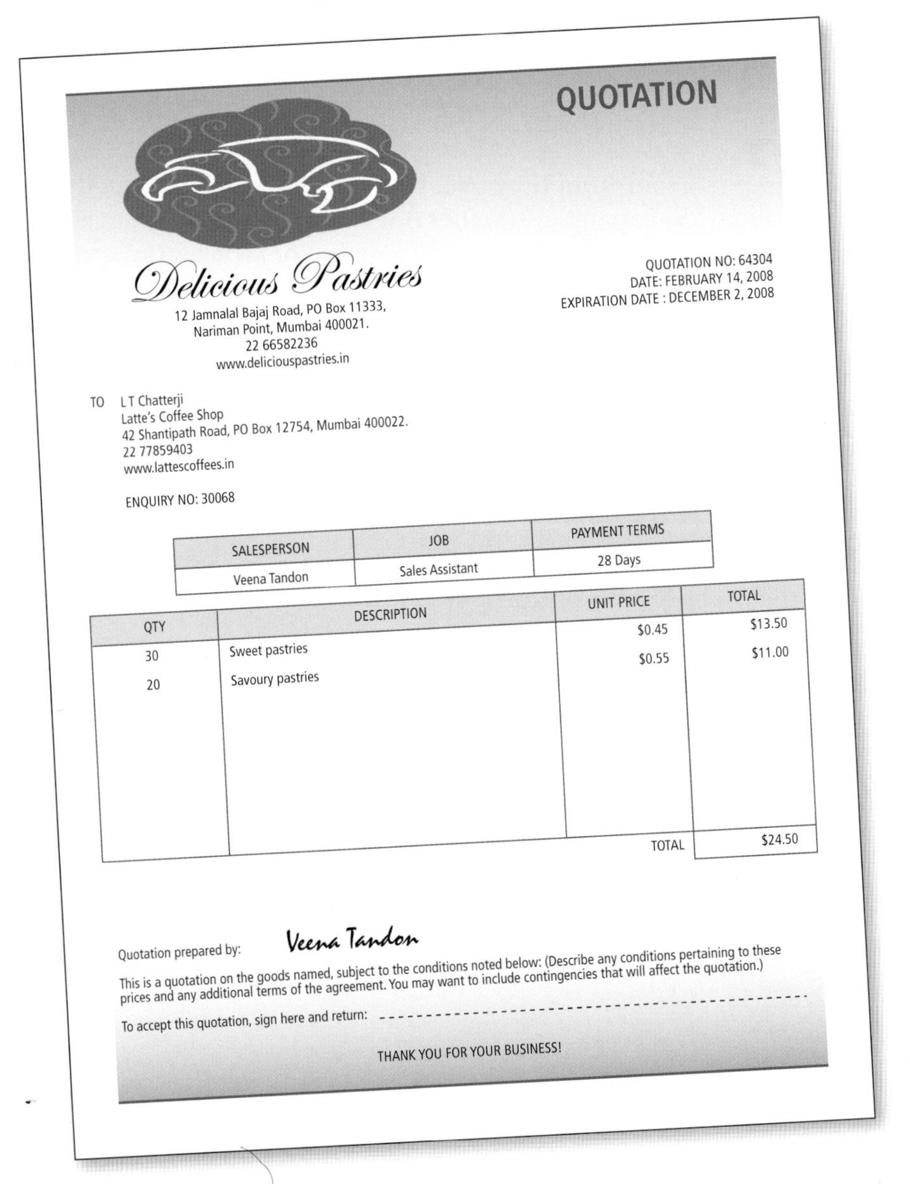

QUOTATION

Delicious Pastries
12 Jamnalal Bajaj Road, PO Box 11333,
Nariman Point, Mumbai 400021.
22 66582236
www.deliciouspastries.in

QUOTATION NO: 64304
DATE: FEBRUARY 14, 2008
EXPIRATION DATE : DECEMBER 2, 2008

TO L T Chatterji
Latte's Coffee Shop
42 Shantipath Road, PO Box 12754, Mumbai 400022.
22 77859403
www.lattescoffees.in

ENQUIRY NO: 30068

SALESPERSON	JOB	PAYMENT TERMS
Veena Tandon	Sales Assistant	28 Days

QTY	DESCRIPTION	UNIT PRICE	TOTAL
30	Sweet pastries	$0.45	$13.50
20	Savoury pastries	$0.55	$11.00
		TOTAL	$24.50

Quotation prepared by: Veena Tandon

This is a quotation on the goods named, subject to the conditions noted below: (Describe any conditions pertaining to these prices and any additional terms of the agreement. You may want to include contingencies that will affect the quotation.)

To accept this quotation, sign here and return: ______

THANK YOU FOR YOUR BUSINESS!

■ **Figure 6.1** *An example of a quotation*

Catalogues and price lists

These are sent by the seller to potential buyers.

Sometimes enquiries received from buyers are very general and do not ask for a particular quantity or type of goods and services. When this happens, the seller may choose to send a catalogue instead of a quotation to the buyer. The catalogue lists all the goods or services provided by the supplier as well as specific information about each product or service. Catalogues may include the prices of the goods, but this is not always the case. Catalogues are expensive to produce and distribute and the price of goods changes frequently. For this reason, sellers may choose to supply a price list instead of, or in addition to, their catalogue. Price lists are a simple, printed list of all the products which are offered by the seller and their prices. Price lists are much cheaper to produce and can be more easily updated every time the price of goods or services changed. If buyers require any extra information they can call the seller.

In the past, catalogues and price lists were usually sent by post, but now that more advanced computer technology is widely available many organisations choose to send them by e-mail or even on CD-ROMs sent in the post.

Order

This document is sent by the company wishing to make a purchase to their chosen supplier.

When a company has received all the quotations that it requested from suppliers it will select one supplier that offers the best **terms**.

> ***Terms*** – this word is used *here* to mean the agreements made between a seller and their customers. These agreements are likely to include any discounts offered by the seller, the prices charged, whether delivery will be free or not, payment terms (how long the customer has to pay for the goods) and product quality.

Orders form the basis of all commercial transactions and need to state clearly what the transaction consists of so that it is carried out accurately. An order will include most of the following information:

- Name and address of the buyer
- Name and address of the chosen supplier
- A request to supply the particular goods or services
- A unique order number and quotation number
- Descriptions of the goods with item codes where available
- The quantity of the goods required
- Prices
- Terms of delivery: where, how and by when the goods should be delivered
- Payment terms (e.g. when payment must be received)
- Date the order was made
- A signature of the buyer who is requesting the goods.

Contractual – A contract is a binding agreement between a buyer and seller. The seller promises to supply goods and the buyer promises to pay for them. These promises are the contractual commitments they agree with each other before goods are exchanged.

Orders are signed because they are important legal commercial documents. When the order is signed it becomes a **contractual** agreement between the buyer and seller of the goods or services that specifies payment terms, delivery dates, items ordered, quantities needed and all other obligations and conditions.

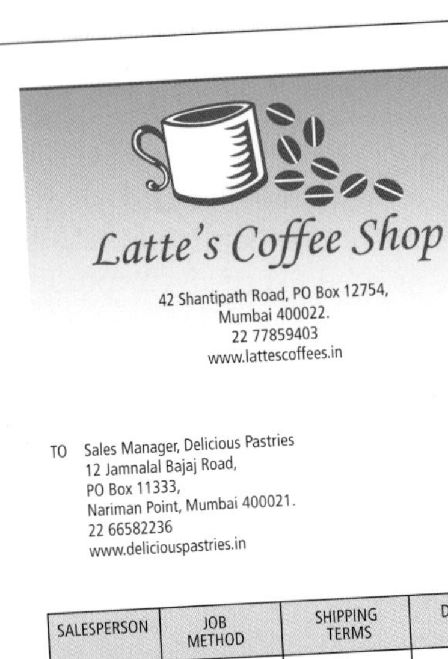

SALES ORDER

Latte's Coffee Shop

42 Shantipath Road, PO Box 12754,
Mumbai 400022.
22 77859403
www.lattescoffees.in

ORDER NUMBER: 65440
QUOTATION NUMBER: 64304
DATE: FEBRUARY 15, 2008

TO Sales Manager, Delicious Pastries
12 Jamnalal Bajaj Road,
PO Box 11333,
Nariman Point, Mumbai 400021.
22 66582236
www.deliciouspastries.in

SHIP TO Latte's Coffee Shop
L T Chatterji
42 Shantipath Road, PO Box 12754,
Mumbai 400022.
22 77859403
www.lattescoffees.in

Customer A/c No : L2345

SALESPERSON	JOB METHOD	SHIPPING TERMS	DELIVERY TERMS	DELIVERY DATE	PAYMENT TERMS	DUE DATE
Stuart Smith	Sales Assistant	Van	Free	22/2/08	Due within 28 days	20/3/08

Please supply the following:

QTY	ITEM #	DESCRIPTION	UNIT PRICE	DISCOUNT	LINE TOTAL
30	SW 1345	Sweet pastries	$0.45	Zero	$13.50
20	SA 1256	Savoury pastries	$0.55	Zero	$11.00
			TOTAL DISCOUNT	Zero	$0.00
				TOTAL	$24.50

■ **Figure 6.2** *An example of an order*

Theory into practice

Look carefully at the example of the sales order above and answer the following questions.

1. What is the name and address of the buying organisation?
2. Who is the buyer that placed the order?
3. What is the name and address of the supplying organisation?
4. What goods have been requested (type, quantity, price per item and item code)?
5. What is the order reference number?
6. What was the reference number of the original quotation?
7. How will the goods be delivered and how much will it cost the buyer?
8. What are the payment terms for this transaction? Explain clearly what you mean.
9. What is the date the order was placed?

Advice note

This is a document sent from the seller to the organisation wishing to purchase goods or services.

Sometimes goods that have been ordered take some time to be delivered. When this happens an advice note may be sent to the buyers to tell them that their order is being processed and will be delivered by a certain date. Advice notes usually include the following information:

- The date the goods are due to be sent out
- A description of the goods being despatched
- The quantity of goods being sent
- The relevant order number
- The type of delivery (for example, post, courier or delivery directly from the supplier using their own transport services).

Delivery note

This is a document from the seller that comes with the ordered goods when they are delivered.

The goods from the seller will arrive with a delivery note that includes the following information:

- The number of packages sent
- A description of the goods sent
- The quantity of goods sent
- An order number.

The buyer needs to check that they have received everything that is listed on the delivery note. They also need to check that they have received everything they have ordered by comparing the delivery note to the original order document. When they are satisfied, they will sign a duplicate (identical) copy of the delivery note and return it to the seller. This lets the seller know that the goods have been received and that the order has been completely delivered. The buyer should keep the duplicate delivery note on file.

Invoice

This document is sent from the seller to the buyer as a request for payment.

When the supplier has successfully delivered the goods, they will send the buyer an invoice. The invoice is a request for payment from the buyer in exchange for the goods or services that the supplier has provided. The supplier may ask for payment to be made immediately or, if credit terms have been agreed, at a later time. An invoice will include the following information:

- Date
- Name and address of the supplier

- Name and address of the buyer
- Address where the goods were received
- Description of the goods provided
- Quantity of goods sent
- Prices charged, including discounts
- Delivery costs
- Total cost.

The buyer should always check that the amount invoiced agrees with the quantity of goods that they received. They can do this by comparing the invoice to the duplicate delivery note that they kept when the goods were received. If the buyer spots any mistakes on the invoice then they can request a corrected invoice to be sent to them before making any payments.

Here is an example of an invoice that Delicious Pastries sent to Latte's Coffee Shop for goods that they have received.

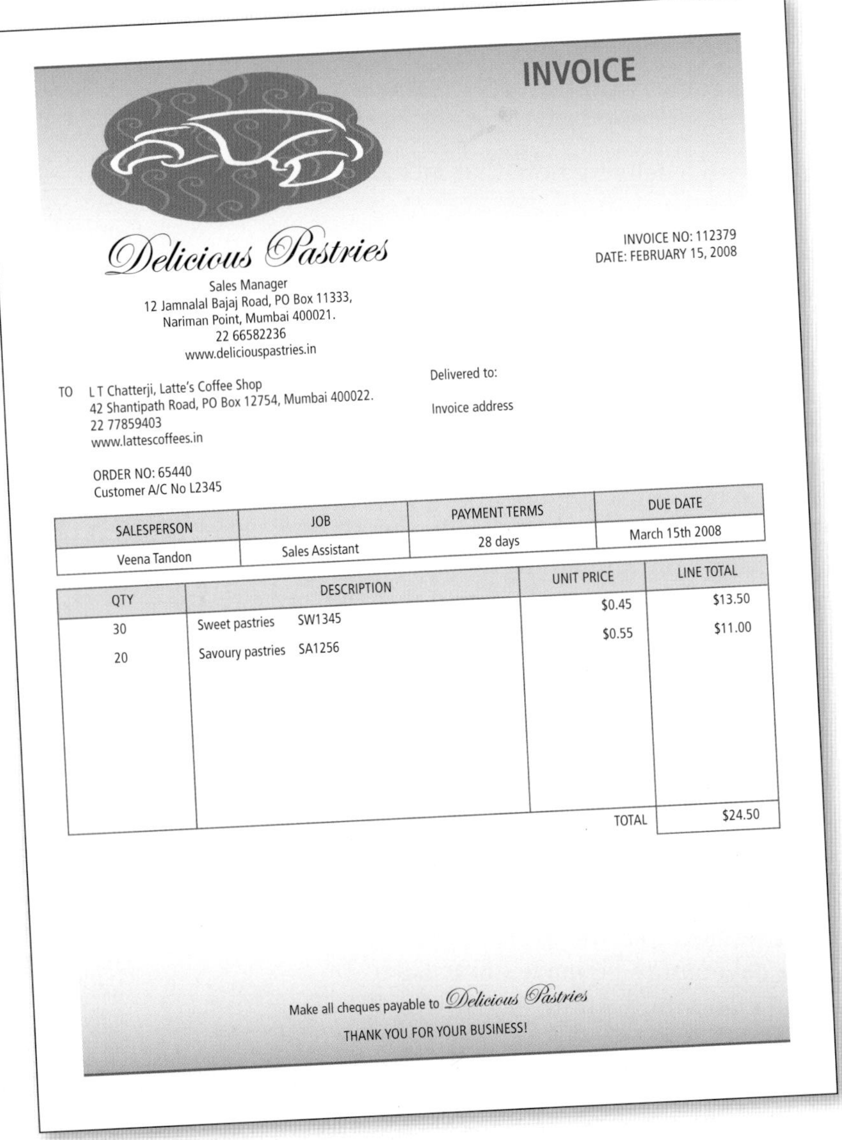

INVOICE

Delicious Pastries

Sales Manager
12 Jamnalal Bajaj Road, PO Box 11333,
Nariman Point, Mumbai 400021.
22 66582236
www.deliciouspastries.in

INVOICE NO: 112379
DATE: FEBRUARY 15, 2008

TO L T Chatterji, Latte's Coffee Shop
42 Shantipath Road, PO Box 12754, Mumbai 400022.
22 77859403
www.lattescoffees.in

Delivered to:

Invoice address

ORDER NO: 65440
Customer A/C No L2345

SALESPERSON	JOB	PAYMENT TERMS	DUE DATE
Veena Tandon	Sales Assistant	28 days	March 15th 2008

QTY	DESCRIPTION	UNIT PRICE	LINE TOTAL
30	Sweet pastries SW1345	$0.45	$13.50
20	Savoury pastries SA1256	$0.55	$11.00
		TOTAL	$24.50

Make all cheques payable to Delicious Pastries
THANK YOU FOR YOUR BUSINESS!

■ **Figure 6.3** *An example of an invoice*

Credit note

This document is sent from the seller to the buyer of particular goods or services. Sometimes mistakes are made during a transaction. For example:

- The seller may have put the correct amount on the invoice but then accidentally charged the buyer too much for the goods they purchased.
- The buyer may have been mistakenly charged on the invoice for goods that they *did not* receive.
- The buyer may have been mistakenly charged on the invoice for goods that they *did* receive but had to send back because they were damaged or faulty.

Credit notes are sent from the seller to the buyer. They are usually printed in red to distinguish them from normal invoices. This is because they are *not* a request for payment; they are letting the buyer know that it is the seller who owes money to the buyer. The amount on the credit note will be deducted (taken away) from the total amount owed by the buyer to the seller. The credit note provides evidence to the buyer that any errors on the original invoice have now been corrected.

There are also documents called 'debit notes'. These act in a similar way to credit notes, by correcting mistakes that may have been made. The difference between them is that debit notes are used to correct an error on a buyer's account that does not relate to a particular order or invoice. For example, if an accountant meant to type into the computer that the buyer paid $10 but accidentally keyed in $100, then a debit note will be raised for $90 to correct the error.

Figure 6.4 is a credit note sent to Latte's Coffee Shop by Delicious Pastries. Latte's Coffee Shop was charged for 20 savoury pastries that they did not receive because the person who prepared

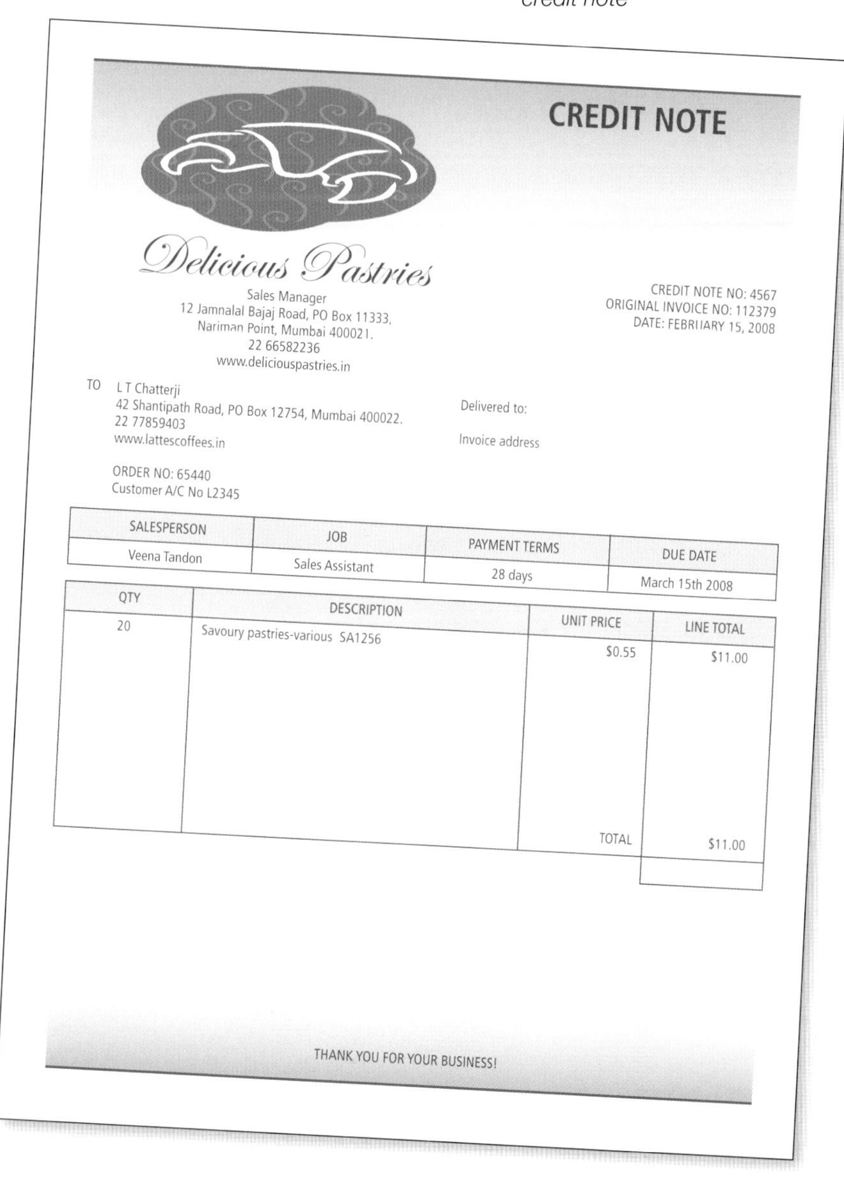

CREDIT NOTE

Delicious Pastries
Sales Manager
12 Jamnalal Bajaj Road, PO Box 11333,
Nariman Point, Mumbai 400021.
22 66582236
www.deliciouspastries.in

CREDIT NOTE NO: 4567
ORIGINAL INVOICE NO: 112379
DATE: FEBRUARY 15, 2008

TO L T Chatterji
42 Shantipath Road, PO Box 12754, Mumbai 400022.
22 77859403
www.lattescoffees.in

Delivered to:
Invoice address

ORDER NO: 65440
Customer A/C No L2345

SALESPERSON	JOB	PAYMENT TERMS	DUE DATE
Veena Tandon	Sales Assistant	28 days	March 15th 2008

QTY	DESCRIPTION	UNIT PRICE	LINE TOTAL
20	Savoury pastries-various SA1256	$0.55	$11.00
		TOTAL	$11.00

THANK YOU FOR YOUR BUSINESS!

■ **Figure 6.4** *An example of a credit note*

the order at Delicious Pastries forgot to put them on the delivery van. Delicious Pastries sent the credit note to correct the mistake that they had made.

Statement of account

This document is sent to the buyer and shows the total amount of money that they owe to the seller.

A buyer may have several transactions with the same seller over a period of time, a month for example. They will receive many invoices during that month and instead of paying each one individually, the buyer will pay all of them together at the end of the month. This is sometimes referred to as the buyer's account balance.

Every month, the buyer will receive a new statement of account from the seller listing all the transactions that have taken place during that month. The statement will include the following information:

- The amount owed at the start of the month; for example, money that is still owed by the buyer from the total shown on the previous month's statement.
- Invoices that have been sent during the month.
- Credit notes that have been sent during the month.
- Payments received from the buyer.
- The account balance owed at the end of the month.

A statement of account is a request for payment of the account balance that has not yet been paid. Figure 6.5 is an example of a statement of account sent by Delicious Pastries to Latte's Coffee Shop. It shows a list of invoices that have been sent and a credit note for some goods that were invoiced but which the buyer didn't receive.

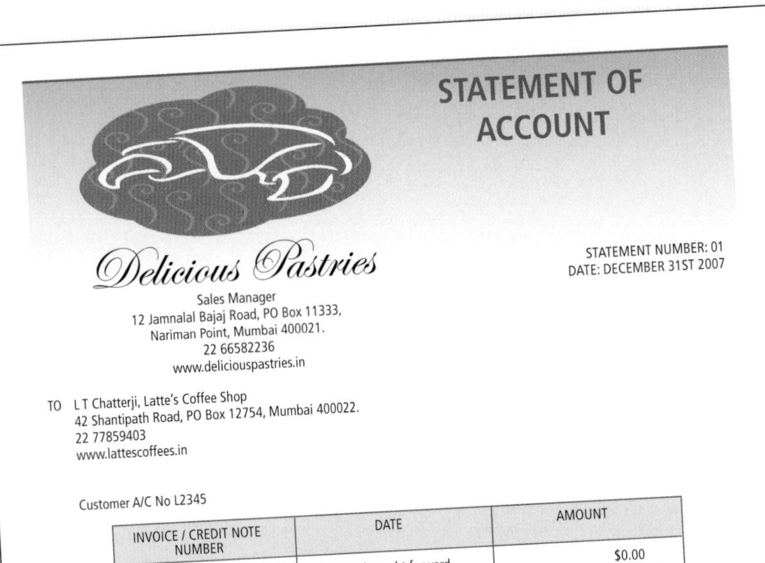

STATEMENT OF ACCOUNT

Delicious Pastries
Sales Manager
12 Jamnalal Bajaj Road, PO Box 11333,
Nariman Point, Mumbai 400021.
22 66582236
www.deliciouspastries.in

STATEMENT NUMBER: 01
DATE: DECEMBER 31ST 2007

TO L T Chatterji, Latte's Coffee Shop
42 Shantipath Road, PO Box 12754, Mumbai 400022.
22 77859403
www.lattescoffees.in

Customer A/C No L2345

INVOICE / CREDIT NOTE NUMBER	DATE	AMOUNT
	Balance brought forward	$0.00
112379	2/12/07	$24.50
4567	9/12/07	$11.00
134568	10/12/07	$24.50
136784	15/12/07	$24.50
143956	20/12/07	$35.50
	Amount Payable	$98.00

Make all cheques payable to Delicious Pastries
THANK YOU FOR YOUR BUSINESS!

■ **Figure 6.5** *A statement of account*

Theory into practice

Look carefully at the statement of account example above and answer the following questions.

1 What month does the statement relate to?
2 How much does Latte's Coffee Shop owe Delicious Pastries?
3 What was the value of the third invoice received in the month?
4 After this statement was sent the following additional transactions took place.
   * Invoice for $42.50 on 12/12/07 (no. 135672)
   * Invoice for $14.50 on 18/12/07 (no. 138976)
   * Credit note for $24.50 on 19/12/07 (no. 4938)

Can you work out what is now owed by the buyer (the new statement balance)? Remember that credit notes will be **deducted** (taken away) from the amount owed by the buyer to the seller.

Receipt

This document is given to the buyer after they have purchased a product or service. Before a receipt can be given, the buyer must arrange for payment to be made to the seller. Payments can be made in cash or via cheques, credit transfers, standing orders, direct debits, electronic transfers, debit cards or credit cards. We will look at these payment methods in detail in Unit 13. Once payment has been received, the seller will send a receipt to the buyer. The receipt is evidence that the customer has paid for the goods or services that they received. For this reason, receipts are often referred to as 'proofs of purchase'. The most common use of receipts is in retail.

Think about the last purchase you made in a retail outlet. Did you get a receipt with your change?

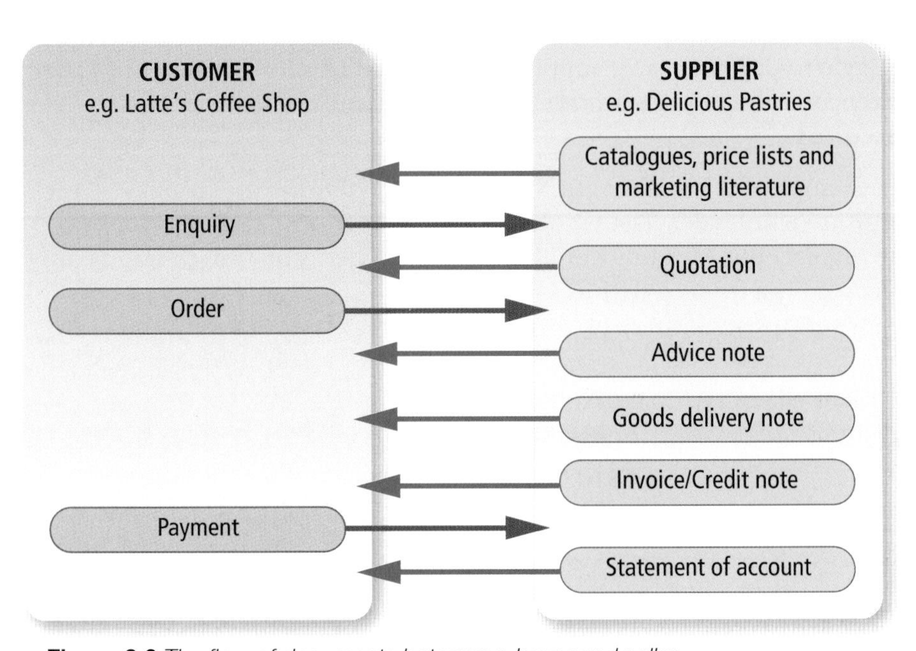

■ **Figure 6.6** *The flow of documents between a buyer and seller*

6.2 Terms of payment

The terms of a commercial transaction are agreed between the buyer and seller before any goods or services are exchanged, and before any money is paid. Payment terms refer to the amount of time buyers are given before they have to pay for the goods or services that they have received. The terms are usually included on the quotation that the seller sends to the buyer. Terms of payment are also often found on price lists and in catalogues.

Trade credit refers to the period of time before which a buyer has to pay for the goods or services they have received.

Most transactions are made on what is called **trade credit**. For most firms this credit is given for a time period of four weeks, but trade credit can be given for more or less time than this. Organisations need trade credit because it allows them time to sell some of the goods they have purchased before they need to pay the seller. The sales they have made will provide income and this money can then be used to pay their suppliers. There will, hopefully, be some money left over after the suppliers have been paid – profit for the firm.

Cash discounts

Cash discount – money that may be deducted from the total of an invoice if payment is made within a specified period of time; usually four weeks. The cash discount is calculated after any other discounts have already been deducted. Other discounts may include 'trade discount', a reduction on the price granted by a manufacturer or wholesaler to buyers in the same trade, and 'bulk discount' which is a reduction on the price charged to buyers when they have bought a large quantity of particular goods.

Money moves *through* a commercial organisation. It comes in when consumers pay the organisation for goods that they have received. It leaves when the organisation makes payments to suppliers of goods and services and when other bills, including employees' wages and the running costs of the organisation, need to be paid. So you can see that money is essential to all commercial organisations. Without a good flow of money, some organisations will fail to survive. Organisations offer their buyers incentives, in the form of large discounts, to encourage them to make prompt (quick) payments. They do this because they may struggle to pay their own suppliers if they can't collect money from their buyers on time. A discount for prompt payment is known as a **cash discount.**

For example, Mr Ling bought $10,000 worth of furniture from a furniture wholesaler. The wholesaler put a 5 per cent cash discount on the invoice. But Mr Ling would receive the 5 per cent cash discount only if he paid the invoice within four weeks.

The cash discount was calculated like this:

$$\textbf{Cash discount} = \text{invoice value (after trade discount)} \times \frac{\text{cash discount}}{100}$$

$$= \$10{,}000 \times \frac{5}{100}$$

$$= \underline{\$500}$$

Theory into practice

Your school has just purchased 30 desks for its new computer room. Each desk cost $99. The supplier has offered the school a 3 per cent cash discount if they pay for the desks by the end of the month.

1 What would the total value of the invoice be?
2 What cash discount would the school get by paying on time?
3 For what reasons would the supplier offer a 3 per cent cash discount to your school?

Trade discounts

Trade discount is different from cash discount. **Trade discount** is deducted from the amount invoiced for goods that have been supplied. The discount rate will vary depending on who the buyer is, how long they have been dealing with the company and the value of goods bought.

Here is an example of how trade discount works: Princess Toy Shop has been a trusted customer of a toy wholesaler for six years. They usually purchase about $1000 of goods a month. The wholesaler gives Princess Toy Shop 8 per cent trade discount and 5 per cent cash discount as an incentive to keep trading with them and to encourage them to pay within an agreed period of time (terms of payment).

The trade discount was calculated like this:

Trade discount $= \text{value of invoice} \times \frac{\text{trade discount}}{100}$
$= \$1000 \times \frac{8}{100}$
$= \$80$

Cash discount $= \text{invoice value (after trade discount)} \times \frac{\text{cash discount}}{100}$
$= (\$1000 - \$80) \times \frac{5}{100}$
$= \underline{\$46}$

The cost to Princess Toy Shop if they pay within 28 days (one month) will be:

price to pay = value of invoice – trade discount – cash discount
= $1000 – $80 – $46
= $874

Trade discount – money off purchases given by one organisation to another. These discounts are usually given by organisations in the same trade, for example, within the building trade. Trade discounts are also given to retailers by wholesalers to allow retailers to make a profit on each item bought and sold in their retail outlet.

Think it over...

A wholesaler offers one retail customer 5 per cent trade discount and another customer 3 per cent trade discount.

1 *Each retailer purchased $3500 of stock from the wholesaler in January 2008. What trade discount would each receive?*

2 *Suggest one reason for the difference in amount of trade discount.*

Mark-up

Have you ever wondered how organisations decide what price to charge for their goods and services? The price needs to be right so they can make a healthy profit without charging so much that their goods and services are no longer wanted. There are many different methods of deciding the price. Simple methods include researching what your competitors charge and then charging the same amount. We call this 'market pricing'. More often, organisations will decide on suitable prices for their goods and services by working out how much it costs to produce the goods or to provide each service. These costs will include materials, labour and any overheads (costs related to the running of the organisation, such as staff wages). They then identify the price they need to charge for those goods or services by adding a predetermined (decided in advance) percentage of the cost. This is called the **mark-up**. This means that the price charged is what it cost to make the product or to provide the service *plus* the mark-up. The mark-up represents profit to the organisation.

For example, a pair of running shoes costs \$1 to manufacture (including materials, labour costs and overheads). They are sold to sports shoe retailers in the USA for \$20. The mark-up is a huge \$19. You can calculate the mark-up percentage in the following way:

$$\text{mark-up percentage} = \frac{\text{difference between cost and price charged}}{\text{cost to make}} \times 100$$

$$= \frac{\$19}{\$1} \times 100$$

$$= 1900\% \text{ mark-up by the manufacturer}$$

In the same way that manufacturers and service providers put a mark-up on their goods or services, other traders in the distribution chain, such as retailers, will also put a mark-up on the goods they sell. For example, a sports shoe retailer buys a pair of running shoes from a manufacturer for \$20 and sells them for \$35. The mark-up is \$15. This is a mark-up percentage of:

$$\frac{\text{difference between cost to purchase and price charged}}{\text{cost to purchase}} \times 100$$

$$= \frac{\$15}{\$20} \times 100$$

$$= 75\% \text{ mark-up by the retailer}$$

Summary of main points for Unit 6

- Trade is the purchasing of goods, materials and services in exchange for money or other goods, materials and services.
- Commercial transactions are the agreements made between traders.
- Documents of trade are used by traders to record all their transactions. There are many documents of trade. You will need to know how they are used and what general details they contain.
  - Enquiry
  - Quotation
  - Catalogues and price lists
  - Order
  - Advice note
  - Delivery note
  - Invoice
  - Credit note
  - Statement of account
  - Receipt
- The terms of a commercial transaction will be agreed before any goods, materials or services are traded. The terms refer to the payment terms and the period of time that is allowed between a buyer receiving goods or services and actually paying for them. This is referred to by traders as 'trade credit'.
- Traders who are selling goods and services may offer buyers within a specific industry or trade discounts as an incentive to trade with them on a regular basis (trade discounts); or to pay immediately or within an agreed time scale (cash discounts); or to purchase goods and services in large quantities (bulk discounts).

Test your knowledge

Practice multiple choice exam questions

Look at the following statement of account for Anchor Trading prepared by Designer Fashion Wholesalers. Use it to answer questions 1 and 2 below.

Designer Fashion Wholesalers
Baker Road
London
UK

STATEMENT OF ACCOUNT

To: Anchor Trading
High Street
Birmingham

Date: 31st March 06

Terms: 28 days – 5%

Date	Details	Debits $	Credits $	Balance $
March 1st	Balance b/f			1000
March 5th	Cheque rcv		950	50
March 6th	Cash discount		50	0
March 11th	Invoice 456	1600		1600
March 18th	Invoice 624	1300		2900
March 23rd	Credit note		70	2830
March 27th	Invoice 865	600		X

1) During March 2006, Anchor Trading returned faulty goods. Which entry is a record of this transaction?
   a) Mar 5th cheque for $950
   b) Mar 6th cash discount of $50
   c) Mar 18th invoice 624 for $1300
   d) Mar 23rd credit note for $70

2) What is the balance marked X on March 27th?
   a) $3830
   b) $2230
   c) $3430
   d) $2630

3) If a retailer buys goods worth $1500 and receives 20 per cent trade discount, what price will he pay?
   a) $1350
   b) $1300
   c) $1200
   d) $1250

4) A credit note is sent to a customer for one of the following reasons. Which one?
   a) If goods were damaged during delivery.
   b) To encourage buyers to buy more.
   c) If the seller undercharged the buyer.
   d) To encourage the buyer to pay within an agreed period.

5) Trade discount is offered by organisations:
   a) To traders when goods are to be resold.
   b) To compensate for goods damaged when delivered.
   c) To encourage customers to buy in large quantities.
   d) To encourage customers to pay within an agreed period.

Test your knowledge *continued*

Practice stimulus response and structured exam questions

1) Connor Clothing Ltd sells clothing to a customer. During the course of their trading relationship the following credit note was issued.

CREDIT NOTE

CONNOR CLOTHING LTD
50 Great William Street
London W3 4MZ

To: Sharpe & Partners
116 Field Road
London SW4 5BG

Invoice No: 3492

DATE	DESCRIPTION	AMOUNT
		$
2000 6 June	Return of 6 sub-standard dresses. Cost of each dress: $15 **Less** Trade Discount of 20%	
	TOTAL CREDIT	X

   a) What is the purpose of a credit note? (*2 marks*)
   b) Calculate the total trade credit marked X on the credit note. Show your workings. (*3 marks*)
   c) Explain one other reason for issuing a credit note. (*2 marks*)
   d) Sharpe & Partners have a regular account with Connor Clothing Ltd. They owed $860 before this credit note was issued. What impact will this have on their outstanding balance? (*2 marks*)

(CIE Commerce Paper May/Jun 2000)

Make sure you double check your calculations for questions that are mathematical like question 1b.

2) A grocery food retailer offers its customers a 5 per cent cash discount.
   a) Explain what a cash discount is and why companies give them. (*2 marks*)
   b) A retailer was invoiced for $3500 of goods. What would the impact of a 5 per cent cash discount be on what he pays? Show your workings. (*2 marks*)
   c) 'Cash discounts help organisations to maintain a healthy flow of money within them.' Discuss the implications of this statement. (*6 marks*)

(Author 2006)

For a complex question such as 2c where you are asked to discuss the given statement, it can be helpful to provide examples to illustrate your answer.

3) A retailer bought 100 shirts from a wholesaler for $25 each less 20 per cent trade discount.
   a) What is meant by 'trade discount' and why is it offered by the wholesaler to the retailer? (*4 marks*)
   b) How much profit will the retailer make if they sell each shirt for $35? Show your workings. (*4 marks*)
   c) Why might the wholesaler also offer a cash discount to the retailer? (3 *marks*)

(CIE Commerce Paper Oct/Nov 2002)

4) Name four documents of home trade and explain the purpose of each. (*8 marks*)

(Author 2006)

7 International trade

What do I need to study?

- Explain the importance of international trade and the benefits it brings to a country.
- Describe what is meant by 'balance of trade' and 'balance of payments' (and how to make simple calculations relating to them).
- Identify and describe the functions of customs authorities.
- What is meant by 'free trade'?
- What is a 'trading bloc' and what advantages and disadvantages does it bring?
- Identify practices of 'protectionism' that create barriers to trade.

Introduction

In this unit we are going to examine another branch of trade: the branch usually called **international trade** (sometimes called 'foreign trade'). International trade is to do with the importing and exporting of goods and materials from one country to another.

For centuries, international trade has grown in importance; why do you think this might be?

We already understand the process by which raw materials are obtained and transformed into finished goods for customers in our home and international markets to consume. We have also examined how some countries tend to specialise in making a limited range of products in huge quantities and at very low prices, so that they can benefit from economies of scale. These countries manufacture more of these specific products than they can consume themselves and so they make a profit by selling the goods left over to buyers in other countries. This is known as **export trade**.

However, there will be a range of other products that they do not know how to manufacture or they lack the natural resources to manufacture themselves and they will have to purchase these from other countries. This is known as **import trade**.

China, for example, has become a very powerful trading nation, manufacturing and producing electronics, vehicles and textiles so efficiently and to such high quality standards that it is beginning to dominate these industries. The USA is importing increasing amounts of products made in China. The success of the Chinese manufacturers has meant that many Chinese people are now wealthier than before and can afford to travel abroad to spend their money. In response, the USA has started providing the Chinese with financial service products and tourist destinations. This is a typical example of the practice of international trade, or trade between countries.

7.1 The importance of international trade

Interdependence of countries within the global market

In the introduction to this unit, it was explained that some countries make more goods or provide more resources than they can consume themselves and so they sell the excess (left over goods) to traders in other countries at a profit. These relationships are so well established in some cases that countries have become 'interdependent' on each other. Interdependence usually means a *reliance* on people or organisations in other places for materials, goods and services. For example, the USA relies on the Arab states for much of its oil supplies and, in turn, the USA manufactures vehicles that it supplies to other countries. One country cannot possibly produce everything its inhabitants need or desire, and thus be self-sufficient (that is, not need goods from anywhere else). All countries need to trade with other countries and we see evidence of this all around us.

Theory into practice

Visit a range of different retailers and examine a variety of products to find out from their labels where they were manufactured. How many different countries did you count?

When countries trade they do so for a variety of reasons as listed below:

- Certain goods, materials or services are not available in the home country because of a lack of natural resources, human expertise or perhaps even the right climate to grow a certain type of produce.
- Goods and services may be cheaper when sourced from other countries even though they can still be obtained in the home country. This helps to explain why the nature of industry in countries is constantly changing. In Western European countries such as the UK, we can see a huge fall in the amount of manufacturing done there, because the expense of manufacturing goods such as vehicles is too high when compared to the price at which vehicles can be imported from the Far East. A large proportion of the UK's manufacturing industry is in decline but in its place we can see growth in financial services and other tertiary industries.

We refer to this process as 'comparative advantage'. This means that certain countries are better off focusing on goods and services that they can produce and provide at very low prices because of simple advantages

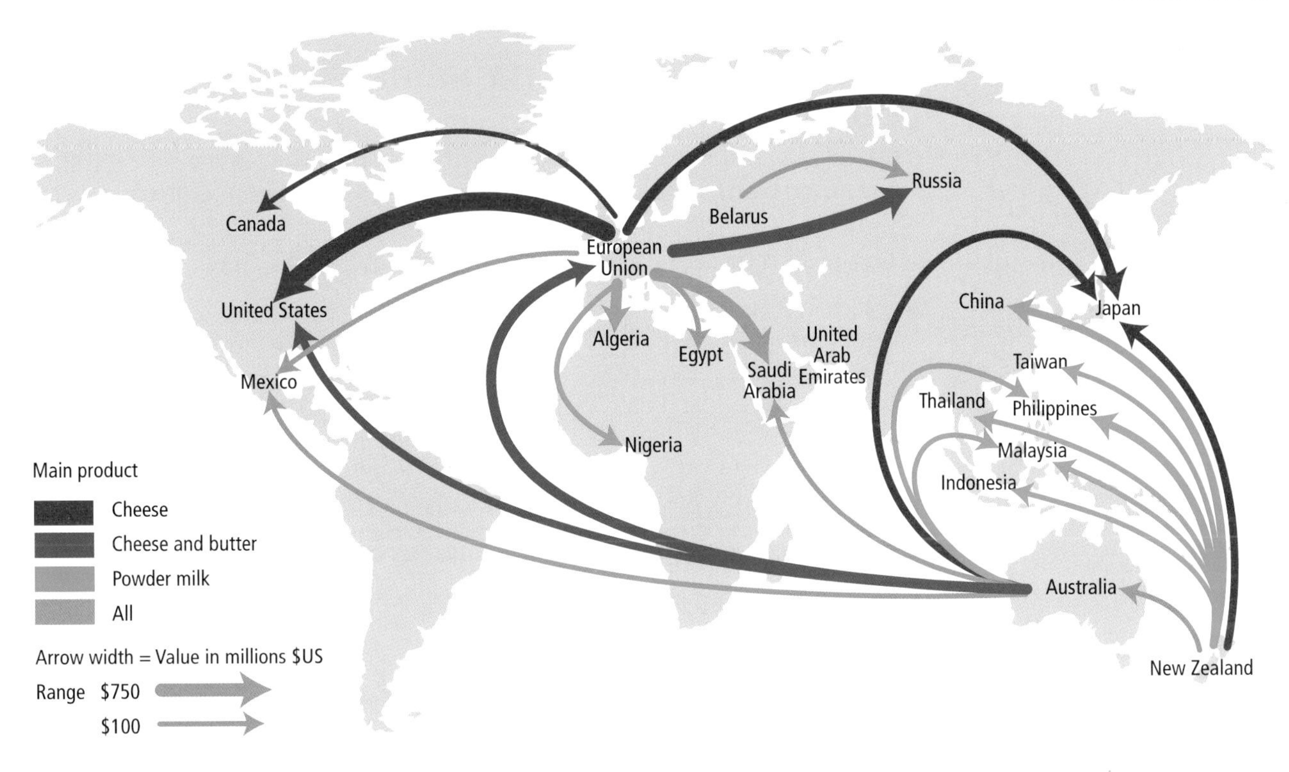

■ **Figure 7.1** *International trade flows of dairy products in 2003*

such as the availability of natural raw materials. What they export will balance what they will need to pay to import goods from other countries with different comparative advantages. Comparative advantage leads to a more efficient use of world resources because goods are made in very large quantities, using fast and efficient production processes that reduce manufacturing costs and waste of materials and energy. Goods become less expensive because of these efficiencies and so international consumers are able to consume more.

You can see from the map above that the majority of dairy produce (milk, cheese etc.) in 2003 originated from Europe and New Zealand. This is because weather and environmental conditions make it easier for dairy farmers in these regions to produce milk products in large, cost-efficient quantities and then to export them to countries where it is not possible to farm cattle in this way.

Theory into practice

Jamaica supplies the UK with exotic fruits and coffee beans because in the UK the climate makes it impossible to produce these products at the same low cost. The UK provides Jamaica with agricultural machinery that it does not have the expertise or the factories to produce itself. Investigate what goods and services are traditionally traded between your country and another. Explain why that trade exists and the benefits of that trade, giving examples where you can.

Advantages of international trade to a country

As transport and communication systems such as the Internet develop, we see increasing levels of international trade. Even small companies can now access a worldwide target audience. Increasing levels of international trade has certain benefits, as described below:

- Wider choice of goods and services available to consumers all over the world.
- Economies of scale – decreases in the cost of production or purchase price made possible when goods are produced in large quantities. This allows manufacturers to become more competitive in their markets and leads to reduced prices for consumers.
- Improved relationships between nations who trade with each other.
- Jobs are created for trade workers.
- Increased standard of living for workers and consumers.

7.2 Balance of trade and balance of payments

What are imports?

Imports are the goods that one country buys and transports from another country for use in its home market. This may be because the goods cannot be produced or are expensive to produce in that country. For example, countries with cold climates can grow bananas in greenhouses but this is a very expensive method compared to importing the goods from other countries. Every item imported by a country means money or wealth leaving that country's economy.

What are exports?

Exports are the goods, materials or services shipped or transported out of a country to another part of the world for use in commercial trade or for sale. Exported goods, materials and services are provided to foreign consumers by home producers and manufacturers. Having high imports and no exports is not good for the country's economy, which will lose money. In order to pay for imported goods or services, traders in a country export to other countries and create a flow of money back into the country's economy.

What is visible and invisible trade?

Visible imports and exports are goods that can be actually seen and touched. For example, cars manufactured in France and exported to Spain are visible exports. Bottles of wine manufactured in Italian vineyards and sold to France are a source of visible imports to France.

However, there are a variety of services sold that represent a flow of money from one country to another that cannot be actually seen or touched. These are usually referred to as invisible imports or exports. For example, a French family may visit Italy for a two-week holiday and during this time they may spend money on services such as hotels, eating out, gifts etc. These invisible forms of trade represent the flow of money from France to Italy. Common invisible forms of trade include:

- tourism
- insurance services
- banking, financial and investment services.

What is the balance of trade?

The balance of trade is the difference between a country's visible imports and exports. It is a record of the overall flow of physical goods between countries.

What is the balance of payments?

The balance of payments is a country's record of all the financial transactions (visible and invisible) between itself and the rest of the world over a given time. Every country will produce a 'current account' which shows the balance of trade and the trade in invisible services that have been imported or exported. These include the profits from organisations owned by people living in another country (where the profit will represent money flowing out of the country). For example, profits created by McDonald's outlets in Tokyo are not kept within Japan, but flow out of the country to the head office of McDonald's. This money is then redistributed to McDonald's shareholders all over the world.

The difference between total imports and total exports (visible and invisible) is known as the 'current balance' or 'balance of payments' for a country. The bar chart in Figure 7.2 shows the current account balance for Japan between 1985 and 2005 in units of 100 million Yen. As a result of its exporting success, you can see that the country had consistently positive current account balances (it was in the black) between 1985 and 2005. This means that during this 20-year period there was a constant flow of money coming into the country. Not all countries experience such success and many have negative balance of payments (are in the red) representing a period of time where there was a flow of money out of the country.

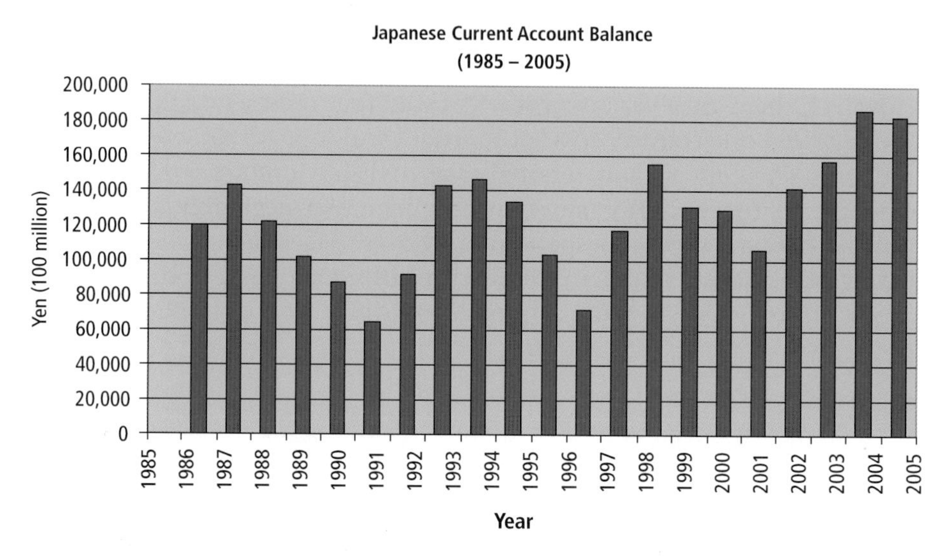

■ **Figure 7.2** *Graph of Japan's current account balance from 1985 to 2005*

(Source: Ministry of Finance – http://www.mof.go.jp)

Theory into practice

Haresh plc is a British-based, multinational company specialising in the design, manufacture and distribution of designer ethnic clothing. They have factories and distribution centres all over the world. Here is a list of some of their transactions for last year.

- As part of a sales incentive a salesperson in New Zealand was rewarded for his sales performance, and he and his family were sent on an 'all expenses paid' trip to Europe. This was paid for by the head office in London.
- The company has sold $50,000 worth of ethnic clothing to retailers in the USA from its UK-based factory.
- The company has bought shares in a fabric-manufacturing firm in India.

1. For each transaction decide whether they are examples of visible or invisible trade.
2. Draw a small flow chart to show in what direction the money is flowing. e.g. London → Italy
3. The company is based in London, England. For each flow of money identified above can you identify it as an import or export transaction?

Countries want their balance of payments to actually 'balance'; this means that the total value of a country's exports should equal its imports. If a country's balance of payments is in **deficit** (imports are greater than exports) there is more money flowing *out* of the country than *into* it. This is considered to be bad practice because the country will have to pay for the excess of purchasing through importing, possibly by borrowing money from other countries, or even selling some of its assets. If these deficits continue:

- The country will get into more debt.
- There may be a decline in industry and possible loss of jobs (because more goods are being imported rather than bought from home manufacturers).

Theory into practice

The diagram below shows the imports and exports of the fictional country Alexland.

What is the current balance of payments for Alexland?

7.3 Customs authorities

Describe what in your opinion are the three most important functions carried out by customs officials in your country. Explain clearly who or what is being protected in each case.

The importing and exporting of materials and goods is a complex process watched and controlled by customs authorities in each country. Customs authorities are usually government agencies responsible for enforcing the rules put in place to protect a country's import and export revenues.

Customs authorities perform a number of functions:

- **Collection of customs duties**
  Customs duties are taxes or levies charged on goods imported to or exported from a country. They are paid by the importer or the exporter on every item they sell. The costs of these duties are usually passed on to consumers in the form of raised prices. The customs authorities are responsible for collecting duties or taxes on imported and exported goods as detailed below:

  i. **Import tax** (also known as import duty or import tariff) is collected by customs authorities on every import that comes into a country. The amount of tax paid usually depends on the type of import. Import taxes are an important source of income for governments and can also be used by a government to restrict or encourage the import of certain goods. For example, a country may put high rates of taxes on cars imported into a country because they are trying to protect their home car manufacturers who are struggling to compete with cheaper overseas manufacturers.

  ii. **Value Added Tax (VAT)** is an additional tax currently at 17.5% on the total value of imports into the UK (which includes cost of goods, cost of transport and import tax). A lot of countries have additional taxes to be paid on top of import tax.

  iii. **Export tax** (also known as an export duty or export tariff) is collected by customs authorities and is charged on every export that leaves the country. It exists to control the goods leaving a country but is rarely used by governments today. This is because exports are usually encouraged by governments to help with the balance of payments.

- **Collection of trading statistics**
  Customs authorities for every country will produce statistical information that shows the pattern of trade, e.g. the amount and value of visible goods moving into and out of the country. This information helps the government of each country to carefully watch its own balance of payments.

Supervising bonded warehouses

In Unit 11 we shall look in detail at bonded warehouses and how they are used by importers and exporters. Customs authorities are responsible for supervising or controlling these warehouses so that goods do not enter the country unofficially and without paying customs duties.

Other functions

Customs authorities control the movement of banned goods and substances such as protected wild animals or illegal drugs into and out of countries.

They also work to control the risk of infectious diseases entering the country, by an infected animal for example, and causing a threat to public health. This is even more significant when we consider recent concerns about avian influenza (better known as 'bird flu') which represents a *possible* major threat to public health.

7.4 Free trade and protectionism

So far in this unit we have assumed that trade between countries is not restricted in any way. We refer to this as **free trade**. If trade is truly free then we will see all countries specialising and achieving huge economies of scale, and regularly exchanging goods with other countries to maintain a healthy balance of payments. For example, China might become the main producer of electrical goods, selling them to consumers all over the globe (including the USA), and the USA might specialise in selling financial services to all other countries, including China. However, it is unlikely that any country would want to specialise and become completely reliant on another country for particular goods or services, no matter how efficiently and cheaply they are produced and sold.

Despite its advantages, free trade can actually lead to some countries experiencing huge problems. As we discussed earlier, a country may experience deficits on their balance of payments every year and this would lead to it having to borrow billions. This could stop development of the country and its industries. A government will therefore choose to manage trade into and out of the country to protect their country, their industries and their people.

Protection, which we refer to as 'barriers to trade', can come in various forms and some of these are described below:

- Charging high **tariffs**, sometimes also known as taxes or duties, on imported goods, making them so expensive that local or home traders may be forced to buy from home suppliers or traders.
- Imposing **quotas** on certain imported goods so that supplies are limited, forcing traders and retailers to source them from home manufacturers.
- Using **embargoes** to completely ban import and export trade between particular countries. These types of bans, or 'sanctions', are sometimes imposed on countries for political reasons where there is disagreement over issues such as human rights or a country's involvement in wars. Some countries may use trade sanctions when they feel that another country has not been trading fairly or has been restricting their exports to that country.
- Some governments may choose to subsidise (give financial help to) home manufacturers to enable them to compete with the cheaper imports. The subsidies allow the home manufacturers to sell their products at a much lower price than normal.

Tariffs – charges or taxes applied to an imported good from another country in order to make the product more expensive in the foreign market and discourage consumers from buying that foreign product.

Quota – a legal limit imposed by a government on the amount of a particular product that can be imported into a country. When imports are limited there may be shortages, causing prices to rise. These shortages benefit the home suppliers because the consumers have no choice but to purchase their goods from them rather than going to cheaper international suppliers.

Embargo – the word used to describe a government-ordered trade restriction which completely stops the trade of particular goods or services to another country.

Think it over...

Consider your own country. Does it use any methods of trade protection?

Countries will use these barriers to trade for a number of different reasons. These may include the following:

To try to correct continuous deficits in their balance of payments by forcing a reduction of imports over a long period of time.

To try to increase local employment opportunities and reduce unemployment levels by encouraging the manufacture of goods that are easily available from abroad in their own country.

Theory into practice

Haresh plc has been manufacturing ethnic clothing in the UK and exporting about $3m-worth of textiles to the USA every year for over 20 years. There are rumours that the USA may introduce a textile import quota. Answer the following questions:

1. What is a quota and why would the USA introduce one for textiles?
2. What impact might this quota have on Haresh plc and other textile manufacturers selling to the USA?
3. 'Quotas restrict free trade.' Explain this statement.

7.5 Trading blocs

Free trade rarely exists because of the many protection policies and international trade barriers in many countries. However, there are groups of countries that have agreed to lower barriers to trade between one another in order to encourage free trade and its benefits. We call these groups 'trading blocs'. Here are a few examples:

- ASEAN (Association of South African and East Asian Nations)
- EU (European Union)
- SACU (South African Customs Union)
- NAFTA (North American Free Trade Agreement)

There are, however, many countries or states that do not belong to a trading bloc because of problems with their political systems, wars they are involved in, their size or their desire to remain self-governing.

Countries that form blocs create areas of free trade where they agree to get rid of tariffs, quotas and other barriers to trade.

The advantages of trading blocs are:

- Trading of goods and services between member states becomes easier and cheaper; the free ports or free zones created within a trading bloc lead to fewer customs restrictions and reduced taxes or duties.
- Specialisation can occur, so countries benefit from comparative advantage as a result of their natural resources, human skills or climate.
- Countries may experience an increase in income from exports.
- Consumers in the trading bloc may experience an overall increase in wealth and standards of living (as free trade reduces the prices of goods and services).

Disadvantages of trading blocs are:

- Protected or 'infant' industries in countries are no longer protected by their government. If they are unable to compete this can lead to the decline of certain industries and to increased levels of unemployment amongst people with skills that are no longer needed.
- It may take time for countries to benefit from free trade so there may be deficits in their balance of payments at the start.

7.6 Difficulties faced by exporters

As free trade tries to encourage more and more movement of visible goods and invisible services across borders, we need to consider the realities and difficulties of this for exporters. The main difficulties and barriers include:

- **Language**
  Exporting organisations need to employ staff with additional languages to help establish trading relationships in other countries.
- **Distance**
  Exporting organisations may need to transport goods or send employees great distances. This is very time-consuming and costly and can cause mistakes and problems. Organisations have to pay for expensive insurance to protect goods being transported from damage and theft.
- **Methods of payment**
  Practices may vary significantly from one country to another. This can make it difficult for exporters and importers to do even basic activities such as getting payments for goods or services that have been provided. There are many reasons for this:

  i. Exchange control regulations may make making payments very complicated where foreign buyers need permission before they can export their currency in payment for goods.

  ii. During the time it takes to agree and make a commercial transaction, currency rates may change, making goods more or less expensive to the buyer and resulting in losses to either the buyer or the seller.

- **Consumer desires**
  Organisations need to be aware that desires in different countries and communities vary a great deal and they will need to take this into consideration when designing their products if they are to export them successfully.
- **Documentation and procedures**
  Exporting is a very complex commercial activity and procedures for exporting into different countries will vary quite a lot. In addition, there is a great deal of paperwork involved in exporting goods so that they can pass freely through customs. If procedures are not correctly followed and the right paperwork is not completed and filed then it is likely that goods could be left in customs' warehouses for a long time and at great expense to the exporter and importer.

All these difficulties make trading activities by exporters more risky than home traders and, as such, trading relationships have a higher chance of failing. Some exporters may use the services of **export merchants** who have specialist knowledge of exporting activities in various countries. They help to overcome problems such as language and translation difficulties and successfully handle transactions for the exporter. Export merchants buy goods directly from an exporter in their home market for sale abroad. For the manufacturer, the transaction is almost the same as selling to the home market as it is the export merchants who are responsible for promoting and selling the goods to overseas buyers. Export merchants will request very low prices for the goods they buy as they are taking all the risk and difficulties of selling the goods to overseas markets. They are very skilled at the procedures and documentation of exporting.

Summary of main points from Unit 7

- International trade is a branch of trade sometimes called foreign trade. It is about the importing and exporting of goods between different countries.
- International trade has grown because of the interdependence that has developed between trading countries.
- International trade has led to a wider choice of goods/services available to consumers all over the world, cheaper goods and services and improved trading relationships between trading nations.
- The balance of trade is the difference in value between what a country imports and exports. It is a record of the overall flow of goods between countries. Countries whose balance of payments are in 'deficit' import more goods than they export and therefore more money is flowing out of the country than into it. This is considered to be bad practice and means that the country will need to borrow money from others to pay what it owes.
- Customs authorities control and watch the importing and exporting of goods. Their main tasks are to collect duties (taxes) charged on goods coming into or out of a country, collect trading statistics and supervise warehouses where goods are stored before duties are paid and they can be released.
- Free trade is the term used to describe a situation where traders in different countries are free to trade and experience no restrictions. This rarely happens as some countries feel they need to control trade to stop them from experiencing a balance of payment deficit.
- Barriers to trade are methods used by governments to manage trade into or out of their countries to protect their industries and citizens. Methods used include the charging of tariffs or duties, making quotas (restricting quantities) on certain goods coming into their country and finally, creating embargoes where trade with a certain country is completely restricted.
- Trading blocs are groups of countries that have agreed to lower barriers to trade between one another in order to create free trade and benefit from the advantages of free trade.

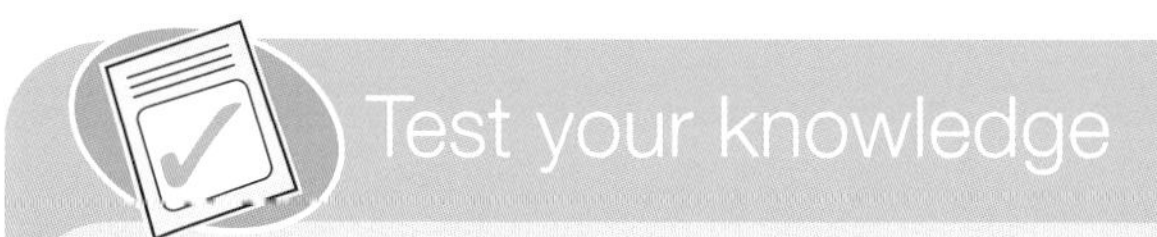

Test your knowledge

Practice multiple choice exam questions

1) The diagram below shows the imports and exports of a country in 2005.

   What is the balance of payments for this country?

Invisible imports $800m

Invisible exports $1600m

COUNTRY A

Visible imports $1320m

Visible exports $840m

   a) +$800m
   b) +$320m
   c) –$280m
   d) –$320m

2) For which of the following reasons would a country import consumer goods from other countries?
   a) To make available more of certain goods than would be available just from home producers.
   b) To benefit governments from customs duties.
   c) To create a positive balance of payments.
   d) To increase the rate of employment in that country.

3) What is the purpose of trading blocs such as the SADC (Southern African Development Community) and the EU?
   a) To restrict the flow of trade between countries who are members.
   b) To publish import and export statistics for all member countries.
   c) To protect industries in member countries from overseas competition.
   d) To generate free trade between member countries in a particular area.

4) Balance of trade is defined as:
   a) The difference between invisible imports and exports.
   b) The difference in the value of visible imports and exports.
   c) The deficit that needs to be funded when imports are greater than exports.
   d) The balance on a country's current account.

5) Which of the following is an example of a visible export?
   a) Financial services
   b) Tourism
   c) Vehicles
   d) Vehicle insurance

Test your knowledge *continued*

Practice stimulus response and structured exam questions

1) The map below shows two countries, two ports and two cities.

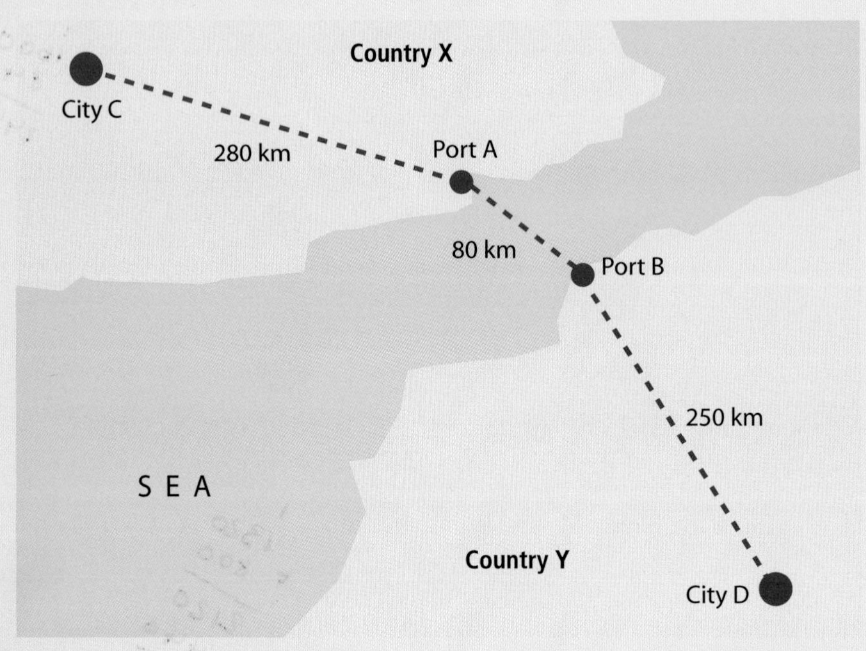

a) Country X and Y trade with one another.
   (i) Suggest two reasons why X and Y trade with one another. (*4 marks*)
   (ii) How does international trade benefit the governments of both countries? (*4 marks*)

(CIE Commerce Paper 1 May/Jun 2004)

Question 1a (i) asks you to **'suggest'** possible reasons. There are two marks for each suggestion so you would be expected to identify the reason and develop your discussion briefly to explain 'why' to get the full marks. You could use simple examples to help you explain.

2) Kobla Enterprises is a Public Limited Company (Plc) making china and pottery tableware to sell at home and abroad. State and explain four difficulties Kobla Enterprises might have when selling products abroad. (*8 marks*)

(CIE Commerce Paper May/Jun 2000)

Question 2 asks you to **'state'** and **'explain'** four difficulties. Questions that ask for explanations often have more marks allocated to them. Each difficulty you identify gets 2 marks, so the explanation need only be brief. Remember to link each difficulty back to Kobla Enterprises.

3) Customs authorities collect statistics on foreign trade and are present at most border crossings.
   a. Explain two other functions of customs authorities at border crossings. (*4 marks*)
   b. Why do customs authorities collect statistics on foreign trade? (*5 marks*)
   c. A government is concerned about the balance of trade figures of its country.
      i. Explain what is meant by balance of trade. (*2 marks*)
      ii. Explain three measures the government might take to reduce amounts of imported goods entering the country. (*6 marks*)
      iii. How might joining a trading bloc such as the ASEAN assist a country's trade? (*3 marks*)

(CIE Commerce Paper 2 Specimen 2005)

Test your knowledge *continued*

4) A country is importing large quantities of goods and making use of imported services. It has an unfavourable balance of payment.
   a. Explain what is meant by unfavourable balance of payment. (*2 marks*)
   b. Explain why imported goods/services are important to a country. (*6 marks*)
   c. i. State and explain two ways in which a country might reduce its imports. (*4 marks*)
      ii. Explain two ways in which a country might increase its exports. (*4 marks*)

(CIE Commerce Paper 1 May/Jun 2003)

Always take note of the marks given to different parts of questions. This suggests how much time you should spend on developing your answer. For example, more time should be spent on question 4c than 4a even though all the questions ask you to explain.

5) The newspaper extract below concerns foreign trade.

$2BN FOREIGN TRADE DEFICIT IN GOODS THIS MONTH

The government decides to take action to reduce the quantity of imported goods coming into the country.

Use the newspaper extract to help you answer the following:
   a. What is meant by foreign trade? (*2 marks*)
   b. The value of goods imported during the month was $18b. Calculate the value of exported goods and show your working. (*2 marks*)
   c. Explain three actions the government might take to reduce the amount of imported goods. (*9 marks*)
   d. A manufacturer of clothing has decided to use an export merchant to sell her goods abroad. What are the advantages of this instead of exporting the goods herself? (*7 marks*)

(CIE Commerce Paper 1 Oct/Nov 2003)

8 Advertising

What do I need to study?

- Describe the role of advertising.
- Explain, with examples, how advertising uses the media.
- Identify the methods of appeal used by advertising.
- Explain the difference between advertising and sales promotion.
- Identify and describe the impact of new trends in advertising.

Introduction

This unit will provide you with an in-depth understanding of the purpose of advertising and how it has become one of the most important aids to trade. In recent years, advertising has become a very successful industry used by all types of organisations to increase awareness of their goods and services, to influence groups of people in the market place and to persuade them to purchase their brands of goods and services rather than those provided by the competition.

Whether you realise it or not you already know a lot about advertising. In fact, a great deal of advertising is aimed at people just like you! There are advertisements just about everywhere you go, even in your own homes.

So, why would companies such as McDonald's spend so much money on advertising or promoting their products and services to teenagers? It may be that they have recognised that some teenagers have high disposable incomes (that is, a lot of money to spend) and, by advertising, they are hoping to persuade teenagers to purchase their goods rather than those of another company. It may also be that these companies realise that if they can attract customers when they are young, they will become loyal to the company brand and stay with it for the rest of their lives. This is referred to as **brand loyalty**.

Brand loyalty – the repeat buying of a particular product because of the value attached to its brand. Brand loyalty is created by giving the product a distinctive identity through the use of trademarks or appealing design, and by targeted advertising (advertising to a specific group of people).

■ *You will even see advertisements in your home if you watch your television*

8.1 The role of advertising

Marketing and the marketing mix

In order for a company to satisfy its customers' needs it must produce the right *products* and services, at the right *price*, in the right *place* and let consumers know about them by using the right *promotion*. This is referred to as the **marketing mix** or the **4Ps** as illustrated below.

Figure 8.1
The marketing mix

Promotion means the wide range of methods used by companies to gain new customers (perhaps from competitors) or to keep existing ones. Some examples of the wide variety of promotional methods are shown in Figure 8.2.

Figure 8.2 *Methods of promotion*

The purpose of advertising

One of the most significant and increasingly popular methods of promotion is advertising. Manufacturing and retail companies are facing the ever-increasing pressures of competition and they have realised that advertising can be an effective way to help make their products and services stand out from those of their competitors.

Advertising aims to communicate a persuasive selling message to existing or potential customers using the most-effective methods. The techniques used are aimed at influencing customer choice and buying decisions. Basically, advertising aims to raise awareness of a product or service in the hope that the **target audience** (or customer) will eventually choose to purchase it.

Target audience – those groups of potential consumers with a particular gender, age, income, status etc. that have a particular interest in and desire for a specific product or service.

Theory into practice

The aim of this activity is to get you thinking about all the different advertisements around you. Advertisements are found almost everywhere. Answer the following questions:

1 List the places you may have been exposed to advertisements today. (Think carefully, because you can be exposed to adverts even in your own bathroom through packaging.)
2 What form were the advertisements in; for example, magazine, TV, radio etc.?
3 Where would you see advertisements in your school?
4 Are there places where there are no advertisements? If so, why?

The benefits of advertising

Advertising can provide a number of benefits:

- Advertisements allow consumers to make purchasing decisions based on information. They can use them to compare products and services and select those which meet their needs and wants. They might even learn about something they never even knew existed. How else could a company making a new product make people aware of it?
- Advertising encourages competition between companies. This can lead to lower prices for consumers and better-quality products and services.
- Advertising earns money for companies such as television or radio stations, newspapers and magazines. This enables them to supply their services at a lower price.

Social aspects of advertising

Despite the many benefits of advertising, there are many people who criticise the advertising industry. Some people feel that advertising has become such a powerful communication method in their country that it has influenced their economy, their society and the cultures and traditions of their society.

Critics believe advertising convinces consumers that purchasing products makes them feel happy and therefore that a person's worth is reflected in what they own. In these societies, if you have little money and can't afford to buy the designer goods advertised on television, you might feel that you have less worth and could end up feeling very dissatisfied with your life.

Advertising can be very influential and can start to affect people's ideas about their self-image. Some women in societies where advertising is common have begun to compare themselves to the beautiful and very slim models they see on television and in magazine adverts. The adverts seem to suggest that this is what a typical woman should look like and this can result in increasing numbers of people with eating disorders, or feelings of low self-esteem, and depression in women who don't look like these models. More recently, it has been suggested that more men are also now suffering from poor self-image and eating disorders as they convince themselves that they should look like the male models they see in television adverts and in their magazines.

Other critics have argued that the power and influence of advertising could be used to reinforce negative ideas about different types of people within a society, particularly groups such as women, ethnic minorities and older people. They argue that if a negative stereotype (an over-simple idea or image that is believed to be a true description of a group of people) was shown in an advert it could influence the opinions and behaviour of other people towards that group.

The dangers of advertising

When you consider the wide range of advertisements we are exposed to on a daily basis, it becomes clear that advertising is very powerful and has an impact on all of our lives. This may be in a positive way, but it may also be in a negative way. We need to be aware of the negative aspects of advertising.

- People who are critical of advertising say that it encourages people to buy products and services they don't really need. Some advertisements encourage people to buy the latest model of a product when the old model still works perfectly well. It encourages young children to demand the latest toys from their parents and encourages young people to buy goods simply because a particular brand is in fashion. In developed countries, people are becoming too focused on consumer goods and are judging people's worth on what they have rather than who they are.
- Advertising is encouraging growing levels of consumption. We use products and replace them with newer versions more quickly than ever before. Environmentalists fear that the world's limited resources cannot sustain current levels of consumption and natural resources will become increasingly rare.
- Advertising can encourage customers to purchase and consume products which are potentially damaging to themselves, the environment and society. Car advertisements might encourage people to drive too fast; fast-food advertisements might encourage unhealthy diets, etc. This is why some countries have banned the advertising of tobacco products such as cigarettes.

- Advertising is extremely expensive and the costs are likely to be added to the price paid by customers for the products or services. If this cost could be avoided, the product or service might be cheaper for the customer, or the money could be invested in improving the quality of what is being sold.

Types of advertising

Advertising can be divided into different categories:

Informative advertising is aimed at increasing customer *awareness* of a product or service. Examples include entries in business telephone directories or newspaper advertisements letting readers know about, for example, new film releases at the local cinema. It is very common for new products and services to be launched with informative advertising campaigns to make potential customers aware of their presence in the market. For example, Sony's portable hand-held games console – the PSP – was launched internationally in 2005 and was heavily advertised in 'gaming' magazines aimed at video game fans. The advertisements clearly point out the features of the product and when it would be available and therefore they were informative.

Persuasive advertising is aimed at trying to persuade potential customers to *purchase* products or services by making them appear more desirable than others. Effective advertisements should satisfy the four stages of the **AIDA** model, which was developed by E.K. Strong in 1925. He said that for an advertisement to be effective it should:

- Attract **A**TTENTION
- Maintain **I**NTEREST
- Arouse **D**ESIRE
- Get **A**CTION

Many advertisements and advertising campaigns are good at achieving the first three stages but it is the fourth that is the most important and much more difficult to achieve. Most advertising campaigns will use a range of established techniques to enable them to achieve this.

■ **Figure 8.3** *Advertisements can inform or influence people*

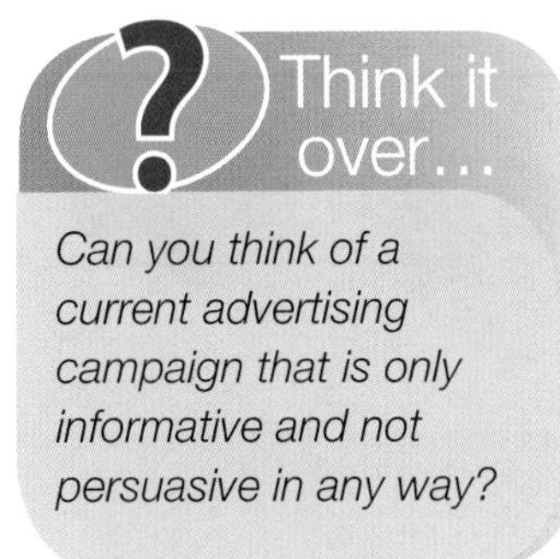

Can you think of a current advertising campaign that is only informative and not persuasive in any way?

Collective (generic) advertising is where a number of companies or independent company owners join together to advertise the same product or produce. It is very common particularly in the promotion of agricultural produce. In the USA, promotion boards collect money from farmers to fund collective advertising campaigns. Examples of such campaigns include 'Beef: It's What's For Dinner' and 'Ahh, The Power of Cheese'. Individually, the farmers or company owners could not afford such a high-profile, national campaign. Together, they can afford national advertising programmes.

Competitive (or comparative) advertising is where a company directly or indirectly compares its brands with one or more competing brands. For example, it is common among financial institutions like banks to show you that their competitors' interest rates are much higher than their own. A famous piece of competitive advertising was Pepsi's 'Taste Challenge', which filmed people on the street tasting Pepsi Cola and Coca-Cola. It showed that most people, apparently, preferred the taste of Pepsi.

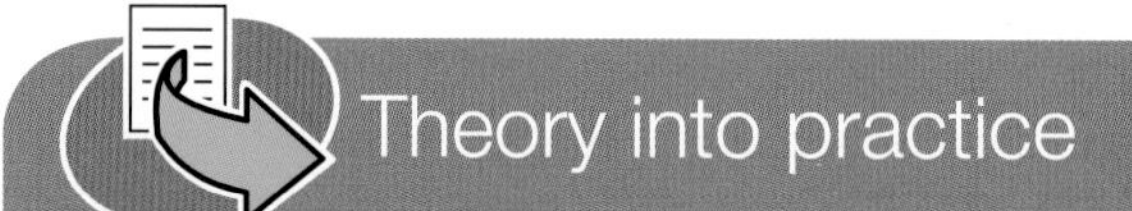

Theory into practice

Find six examples of adverts from magazines or newspapers. Use the AIDA model to analyse how effective each advert is.

8.2 Advertising media

Forms of advertising media and their advantages and disadvantages

There is an increasing amount of **advertising media** available to companies to make customers aware of their products and services.

The most common advertising media and their advantages and disadvantages are listed below.

Type of medium	Advantages	Disadvantages
Satellite & terrestrial television TV is often used by organisations marketing their products or services to a mass market. TV enables them to reach people of all ages, backgrounds and social and economic status. The arrival of recording technology and the increasing number of available channels mean that TV advertising is becoming less effective than it used to be.	■ Many different target audiences can be reached due to the large number of specialist channels now available ■ High proportion of target audience is likely to see advertising ■ Can use colour, music and movement to create desire for a product or service ■ Relatively low cost per target customer reached because of the large audiences accessible nationally and internationally	■ TV advertising messages are usually very short (approximately 30 seconds). Viewers may not remember the information and so it has to be repeated very often which is costly ■ Producing a TV advert is very costly as it requires advertising and broadcasting specialists ■ Programmes are 'saturated' (completely full) with advertisement breaks so the audience may become uninterested in new adverts unless they are particularly attention-grabbing
Radio In the last ten years there has been a growth in the number of commercial radio stations targeted to particular audiences. This has given advertisers a wider range of stations to advertise their products and services on. Most stations are regional, so smaller organisations have benefited from an increased choice of advertising media.	■ Enables creative use of sound and music ■ Most major and minority target customers can be reached through appropriate radio stations ■ Particularly good medium to target young people ■ Cheap to produce and transmit	■ It isn't a visually stimulating medium ■ Potential customers have no record of the information and so the adverts have to be repeated ■ Customers may become irritated by constant interruptions to music

Regional newspapers	■ Can reach a specific regional market place ■ Costs are reasonable and cheaper than TV campaigns ■ Adverts can be referred to again later ■ Newspaper advertising can be used to support a regional TV campaign	■ It is difficult to find newspapers that appeal to a wide audience that includes, for example, young people ■ Quality of layout and printing may be poor
National newspapers	■ Can reach a very large audience ■ Companies can benefit by building high-quality reputations and brands associated with good-quality newspapers ■ They have been proved to be a very successful medium ■ More product or service detail can be provided	■ Not very stimulating to read adverts in newspapers and usually limited to black and white printing
Magazines (regional, national, international) Magazines are targeted at specific audiences: male, female, all age groups and all interests/hobbies. It is easy for a company to select a magazine to advertise in that will enable them to reach their desired customers.	■ Interesting colour adverts are possible ■ Specialist magazines allow companies to target specific markets ■ One advert can cover international markets ■ Adverts can be linked to informative features ■ Magazines can be referred to at a later date and passed to other customers	■ There is a long time between adverts being placed and magazines being printed and distributed ■ There is usually a large quantity of high-quality competitor adverts in the same publication ■ Images have to be eye-catching to get the readers' attention
Cinema Cinema has experienced an increase in audiences in recent years and advertisers now recognise the importance of it as an advertising medium. Organisations such as Orange have developed adverts specifically for big screens so that a greater impact can be made.	■ Colour, sound and movement can be used to engage the audience ■ Adverts can be international or localised ■ The audience is 'captive', i.e. cannot switch to another channel ■ Age groups can be targeted according to the movie rating	■ Advertisers cannot control the audience numbers at a particular screening ■ The message can be short-lived in the mind of the audience, particularly if it is seen only once

continued

Type of medium	Advantages	Disadvantages
Billboards (fixed and digital), posters and transport vehicle livery This medium communicates short messages and appears in external locations. Most are seen by motorists and people walking past. To be successful, they need to be very large and attention-grabbing, and to be located on busy roads so they are visible to a large number of potential customers.	■ National and international campaigns are possible ■ Most target markets can be reached ■ Adverts are seen repeatedly ■ Excellent for short messages that remind customers of facts ■ Moving digital billboards are particularly attention-grabbing and noticeable	■ It is difficult to measure how many customers see them and how effective they are for the company ■ They can be ruined by weather and vandalism ■ They need to be located where there is a lot of passing traffic
World Wide Web The World Wide Web has provided companies with a whole new range of advertising techniques. We will examine these in more detail later in this unit.	■ Gives customers access to detailed product and service information ■ Can reach international customers ■ Sites can be targeted at specific audiences ■ Cost is relatively low, although continuous updating is necessary and expensive	■ Websites are full of pop-up banner advertisements and links to other sites which can make the site difficult to use ■ Some customers see pop-up banners as irritating and restrict them on their screen ■ Specialists are required and can be expensive to employ ■ Updating of sites and pop-up banners needs to be done regularly (usually daily)
Flyers, leaflets and handbills These are the methods of advertising most popular with smaller companies and retailers.	■ Good way to communicate important information about the product, service or selling organisation that will help consumers make their purchasing decision ■ Can easily be sent in response to an enquiry ■ Customers expect printed information and it adds to the credibility of the firm ■ Can be very cheap to produce and to post leaflets through doors ■ Cheap and easy to send via e-mail as an attachment	■ Can be expensive to employ specialists to design professional-standard materials ■ It is easy to include incorrect or out-of-date information ■ If posting through doors it may be difficult to ensure the leaflets are reaching the right people

Advertising media – this is the collective term for the many methods through which advertisements are delivered to a target audience (specific groups of customers with certain characteristics, e.g. teenage girls). Forms include broadcast media such as radio and television, print media such as magazines and websites, cinema adverts and outdoor media such as billboards or even hot air balloons.

Advertising medium – this is the singular term for one type or method of advertising. For example we can say a small retailer may only use one advertising medium, the poster outside his shop.

Factors affecting choice of medium

When companies decide that advertising is required to promote their products or services they need to ask a number of questions in order to select the most suitable advertising medium.

The questions may be as follows:

1. Does the product or service need to be demonstrated?

Products such as children's toys or household appliances like vacuum cleaners need to be demonstrated to customers in order for them to be desired. It is therefore likely that television advertising would be the most preferable media choice for toys and vacuum cleaners.

2. Do customers need a detailed explanation of the product or the service features before they make their purchasing decision?

When booking a holiday overseas many people collect brochures from travel agencies so that they can consider the hotel facilities, the attractions and the cost per person at particular times of the year. Companies selling services like holidays, and products like cars and computers, need to provide detailed printed advertisements such as those in magazines or newspapers to help consumers make the best choice for them.

3. Does the company wish to make customers more aware of their brand(s)?

Sometimes companies use advertising to put a brand name or brand image into the customer's mind. International sports shoe manufacturers such as Nike and Adidas spend a great deal of money on creating brand awareness. Common advertising media used to do this are poster/billboard campaigns and adverts in printed media such as magazines purchased by their target customers.

4. What coverage of the target audience is required?

For toothpaste manufacturers every household presents a potential sale. Their advertising coverage should be wide, covering all regions or countries in the company's target area. It is very expensive advertising to whole countries a company's products or services, so the frequency of the adverts is likely to be low. But the company then has the risk of only providing a few opportunities for the target audience to hear or see the advert.

5. How frequently do you want your target customers to see your message?

Some companies will not try to cover all of a potential target audience because they have a limited advertising budget. They will choose to target cities which have a high proportion of their target audience with frequent advertising, therefore increasing the chances that the message will be seen by potential customers.

6. What can the company afford?

Financial resources will limit how big the company's advertising campaign is. They need to select the appropriate media, audience coverage and frequency of advertising to achieve the best result within the limits of their available budget.

7. What media are the competitors using?

All companies watch what their competitors are doing. They will track changes to products and services, price increases or reductions and methods of advertising. It is very likely that if one competitor is using a particular advertising medium effectively, others will do the same.

8. Is there more than one medium required?

Most companies will not rely on one medium for their entire advertising campaign. They will have a selection of methods designed to support each other in helping the company achieve its objectives. For example, a single campaign could use cinema, TV, billboard and web advertising to name just a few media. This reinforces the message of the advert.

8.3 Methods of appeal

What are devices of 'appeal' and why are they important?

People who work in advertising need to have the creativity and skills to persuade customers that there is something particularly attractive about a certain brand of products that will not be found in any of the rivals' products. In doing this, the advertiser attempts to create 'appeal'.

Methods of appeal

There are many methods used in advertising to create appeal. We will look at four of them:

Using music

One of the best ways to make an advertisement on television or radio memorable is by using music. Carefully selected music can create an emotion such as happiness, sadness, excitement or fear which will make the advertisement harder to forget. The type of music used can totally change the message that is being given. Lively music with a fast beat can make something seem exciting, while slow, classical music can give a sense of peacefulness, which can be perfect for a product that is meant to be relaxing or luxurious. Many advertisers will use well-known music by popular bands to give the product or service more appeal for a particular audience.

Using colour

Selecting colours to appear in advertisements is an important decision. There is a psychological element to colour that subconsciously (without the consumer being aware of it) communicates something about the product or service to the target consumer. For example:

Colour	Psychological impact
Yellow and blue	Makes products/services seem modern, bright, sunny and light. For example, many fabric conditioners are packaged and advertised using yellows and blues.
Black	Reflects drama, luxury and is used in important messages. For example, some mobile phones are sleek and dark, aimed at stylish, young and technology-aware people.
Silver	This colour is often used to reflect masculinity. For example, Gillette razors for men are masculine in design and colour and are totally different from Gillette's range of ladies' razors.

Using successful and famous people

Many adverts appeal to a person's desire to be successful in their lives. Advertisements with this appeal may show a successful person using a particular product or service. The advertiser hopes that the customer will believe that if they own the brand of product advertised they too will be successful. For example, one car manufacturer recently used this appeal when advertising their latest executive car. The advert focuses on three executives who are keen to impress their boss. One executive pays for lunch, but the boss still gets his name wrong; another executive offers to carry the boss's luggage, but still the name is wrong. However, when the third drives the boss to the airport in the car manufacturer's executive model the boss is impressed, and remembers this executive's name correctly. The advertisement is clearly stating that there is a link between driving this car and success at work.

Advertisers pay celebrities and highly successful sports people huge quantities of money to use and recommend particular products and services. The belief is that because the target audience admire the celebrity or sports star they will want to be like them and use the product or service. This is sometimes referred to as a 'hero worship' appeal. Film and sports stars regularly appear in advertisements and are paid large sums to wear a particular company's clothing or use their equipment, or they can be sponsored by a company to wear its logo on their sports kit. This can sometimes cause difficulties. In 2004, a major telecommunications company sponsored the West Indies cricket series against South Africa. Unfortunately, some of the West Indies players had their own contracts with another telecommunications company. So they refused to play!

Theory into practice

1. Make a list of all the advertisements you can find which use famous people to promote goods or services.
2. Explain why the famous person used might be particularly successful in promoting these particular goods or services.
3. Can you think of any famous person whose promotion of goods or services might make you more likely to buy?

Using emotional appeals

Advertisements can be designed to create different emotions in their potential customers, which may then cause the viewer to react in a particular way. Some advertisers, especially charities, use emotional appeals to get their message across. Viewers may feel sorry for people in a particular situation, and that will cause them to make a donation (give money). Or their sympathy may be aroused because of a particular character that is shown. Advertisers also use anger, frustration or, in particular, humour as a way of making their advertisements memorable.

Romance is an emotional appeal that is also very widely used. It is usually aimed at the younger audience. In advertisements using emotional romance the advertisers try to link the characters' success in romance with the use of a product or service. Common images are of happy, attractive young men and women together. The advertiser hopes that target customers will buy the products or services because they see a link between owning them and being lucky in love.

One cosmetics company uses the romance appeal in a humorous way to advertise its deodorant. In the advertisement a very ordinary young man walks into a bar and starts to dance. He is not a particularly good dancer but suddenly he is surrounded by beautiful young women. The reason? He is using a fantastic deodorant! There are some people who do really think that if they wear this company's deodorant they may be as lucky in love as the character on the screen.

Theory into practice

Consider an advertisement (TV or printed) which you have particularly enjoyed.

1 What was the appeal?
2 How effectively did the advertiser use music, colour and emotional content?
3 In your opinion, was the advertisement successful? (Use the AIDA model studied earlier to help you explain.)

8.4 Sales promotion

The distinction between advertising and sales promotion

It is easy to assume that advertising and sales promotion are the same thing, but they are very different and are used to achieve different results. Advertising tries to make a product or service appealing, giving customers a reason to buy it. Sales promotion is a type of promotional strategy that gives customers reasons to buy *now*.

Sales promotions are short-term incentives to encourage the purchase of a product or service.

There has been a rapid growth in the use of sales promotions, particularly in consumer markets where over 75 per cent of all marketing expenditure is used on sales promotion.

■ **Figure 8.4** *Sales promotion objectives*

Methods of sales promotion

Free samples

These may be given to customers in retail outlets, sent by mail or attached to another product. This is an expensive but effective way to promote a new product and increase consumers' awareness of it. For example, when the fruit drink range 'Sunny D' was introduced to international markets a large part of its promotional campaign consisted of giving potential customers in stores samples of the new drink.

Coupons offering 'money off'

These are normally found in newspapers and leaflets and offer consumers the option to buy a particular product at a reduced price. Coupons can be used to promote a newly launched product or to help the sales of an established brand. Consumers are rewarded with price reductions and retailers/manufacturers get increased sales.

Premium packs

This is a common technique used by manufacturers to increase sales of an old product or to introduce a new product. Customers are encouraged to swap brands as this incentive gives the customer more of a product for their money. The company hopes that they will then keep the consumer if they prefer the new brand. Established brands of shampoo quite often offer extra free to encourage customers to swap brands.

Free gifts

Companies have offered free gifts in packs as an incentive for many years, but children's breakfast cereal manufacturers have made the technique their own. Manufacturers realise that if children desire the gift inside, they will put huge pressure on their parents to purchase that specific cereal brand. Other companies that have mastered how to influence children include McDonald's and their 'Happy Meals' with free toy!

Point-of-sale promotions

These displays and promotions are found in the retail outlet and at the point of sale (till). Techniques include huge cardboard cut-outs, signs, posters and branded shelving systems. Manufacturers are helping retailers to present their products in an eye-catching and desirable way so that they both benefit from increased sales levels.

Loyalty cards

Competition is extremely tough in retail, particularly food retail. In order to encourage customers to return to a particular retailer some have introduced 'loyalty cards' on which points are awarded for every $1 spent. Customers are encouraged to repeatedly use the same retailer to collect points which they can later exchange for money off purchases or free products.

Multiple buy offers (buy-one-get-one-free or BOGOF)

This kind of promotional offer is becoming very common. Customers are encouraged to buy products they did not intend to buy because they see an unmissable offer that may not be repeated. Customers will try new products because they feel they are getting good value for money.

.5 Trends in advertising

The Internet

The most important development in advertising in recent years is the Internet. The World Wide Web has given companies the opportunity to connect to millions of people who are online. In 2007, it was estimated that over 1.3 billion people had access to the Internet worldwide and this number is continuing to grow. This represents a massive potential market to online organisations.

The Internet allows companies to reach customers without the costs and overheads of running retail outlets. Also, retail outlets are restricted to a geographical location and therefore can only be accessed by customers in that area. In turn, their cost savings can be passed on to customers in the form of reduced prices. This is why you can quite often purchase products online more cheaply than in your local stores.

Advertising and promotion on the Internet use the same principles as in other media. They have to be designed to catch the attention of the audience and create desire for the product or service. The following are involved in Internet advertising:

- **Banner advertisements** – These are advertisements placed at the top of a web page, often with some animation and pictures, to catch the users' attention. Companies will pay the website owners to place their advertisement there. If visitors to the website click on it they will find themselves on the advertiser's website. This is known as a 'click-through'. The banners will be placed on sites where advertisers feel their potential customers may possibly visit.
- **E-mail advertising** – Every day over 4 billion e-mail messages are sent. Modern companies can benefit from this communication method. Dell Computers is believed to have received more than $1 million per week in revenue through e-mail advertising campaigns in 2001. E-mails can be targeted specifically at potential or existing customers and, although they can be deleted, they are not easily ignored as the person receiving them will always see the message header. Companies will build up a database of customer details and use this to send promotional 'blanket' e-mails (e-mails sent to a huge number of people). Some Internet users do not like to receive unsolicited e-mails (e-mails they have not asked for) and can block them.

Summary of the benefits and limitations of Internet advertising

Benefits	Limitations
■ Inexpensive	■ Competing with millions of other websites and banner adverts appearing every day
■ Reaches a worldwide audience	■ Hard to target a small specific audience. Product cannot be easily demonstrated
■ Provides detailed information	■ The domain name you want may not be available
■ Can get consumer feedback	■ Requires expertise
■ E-mail advertising can be very effective	■ It is difficult to get your website to appear ranked highly (one of the first to appear) on a search engine search

Digital billboards

Digital billboards are a modern version of the old-fashioned billboards. They are entirely digitised using projection and computer technology that allows information on the board to change effortlessly (e.g. rotating adverts) and to make use of the highest quality animations. In some countries amazing holographic (three-dimensional) billboards have been developed and are in use.

Digital billboards offer a type of interaction that traditional billboards could never have done. In Piccadilly Circus in London you will find the Coca-Cola digital billboard. It responds to the weather and even has the technology to detect when passers-by wave at it, responding with an animated wave on its screen. London movie theatres are developing digital billboards which contain computer chip technology and can interact with the web browsers found in many mobile phones so that the billboard can provide more information on what is playing at the theatre. The true potential of digital billboards has yet to be fully realised.

Summary of main points from Unit 8

- Advertising has become in recent years an important aid to trade, creating awareness and interest in an organisation's goods and services and persuading customers to desire and purchase them rather than those offered by the competition.
- Brand loyalty is the repeated buying of a particular product because of the value attached to the brand through the use of logos, trade marks etc.
- The marketing mix or '4Ps' is a model used by organisations to help them sell their products and services successfully. Companies must aim to provide the right products, at the right price, in the right place and let consumers know about them by using the right promotional methods.
- Target audience is the term used by companies and advertisers to describe the groups of potential consumers that have a particular interest or desire for a specific product or service. This information is used to create advertising campaigns that specifically appeal to and reach these groups of people.
- Advertising offers the benefits that consumers are more aware of their choices and are able to make informed decisions. However, critics of advertising feel that it encourages unnecessary consumption of the earth's resources, creating desire for new products all the time when our existing versions have not been consumed or worn out.
- There are many different types of advertising. Each one has its own objective. They include informative, persuasive, collective and competitive advertising.
- Advertising media is the collective term which refers to the many methods by which adverts are delivered to a target audience. They include broadcast media (radio and TV), printed media (magazines and websites) and outdoor media (billboards). Each medium has its own benefits and limitations. Advertisers will select the medium that best communicates the benefits of the product or service being advertised, that reaches the desired target audience most successfully and, of course, that the company which is advertising its products and services can afford.
- Advertising uses a range of methods to create 'appeal' for products and services being advertised. There are many appeals but the most commonly used include using music, using colour, using famous and successful people and using emotional appeals.
- Sales promotions are different to advertising in that they are 'incentives' used in the short term to encourage the purchase of a specific product or service. There are many methods of sales promotion but the most commonly used include 'buy-one-get-one-free' offers and free gifts.

Test your knowledge

Practice multiple choice exam questions

1) Which of the following types of advertising is used when many organisations work together to advertise the same product, e.g. milk?
   a) Informative
   b) Competitive
   c) Collective
   d) Persuasive

2) Which of the following four options is used in advertisements as a method of appeal?
   a) Poster
   b) Film
   c) Television
   d) Music

3) Which of the following sales promotion methods is the most suitable for quickly increasing the sales of a particular brand of shampoo?
   a) Shelf display of shampoo containers.
   b) Demonstration of how to use the product.
   c) A 'buy-one-get-one-free' campaign.
   d) A famous person endorsing the shampoo.

4) Which of the following is NOT an objective of sales promotion?
   a) To increase long-term sales.
   b) To encourage customers to try a new product.
   c) To lure customers away from competitors.
   d) To move ageing or old stock.

5) Which of the following aspects of Internet advertising requires organisations to make payments to other website owners?
   a) Domain names
   b) Search engines
   c) Banner adverts
   d) E-mail marketing

Practice stimulus response and structured exam questions

1) Samuel Moyo is a sole trader running a general hardware shop in a small town. Below is a list of advertising media that he could use to promote his business. Select the **two** advertising media that you think are the most suitable giving **two** reasons for each choice. (*6 marks*)
   a. Television campaign
   b. Leaflet with special offer
   c. Large signs outside his shop
   d. Newspaper and magazine advertising

(CIE Commerce Paper 2 Specimen 2005)

Test your knowledge *continued*

Remember, where questions like 2 to 5 below are based on a business scenario that has been given, you must refer to that business scenario in your answer.

2) Kamwengo Ltd is a successful multinational company specialising in manufacturing and selling breakfast cereals in a number of countries. Should it use the Internet to extend its markets? Explain your answer. (*4 marks*)

(CIE Commerce Paper 2 Specimen 2005)

3) Ubongo (Pvt) Ltd is a large private limited company growing sugar cane and processing it for sale. The company has recently developed a new sugar product and wishes to introduce it to the market. Select three advertising media it might use for this project giving, in each case, a reason for each. (*6 marks*)

(CIE Commerce Paper May/Jun 2000)

4) Pricebuy is a well-known supermarket chain operating in many parts of a country. Explain what is meant by each of the following and show how they might contribute to the commercial success of Pricebuy:
   a. Pricebuy's website on the Internet (*4 marks*)
   b. Point-of-sale advertising (*4 marks*)
   c. A national TV campaign (*4 marks*)
   d. Sales promotion such as buy-one-get-one free. (*4 marks*)

(CIE Commerce Paper 1 May/Jun 2004)

5) Solomon Ltd has developed a new brand of soap.
   a. (i) Explain what is meant by a brand. (*2 marks*)
      (ii) Explain two reasons why companies brand their products. (*4 marks*)
   b. (i) Why would Solomon Ltd need to advertise its new brand of soap? (*6 marks*)
      (ii) What are the benefits of television advertising for Solomon Ltd? (*4 marks*)
   c. Explain why advertising the new brand of soap may lead to lower prices for the consumer. (*4 marks*)

(CIE Commerce Paper 1 May/Jun 2004)

9 Communications

What do I need to study?

- Explain why communications are so important to the global economy.
- Identify the range of communication methods available to organisations.
- Explain the role of the Post Office and Telecom organisations and the communication services they provide.

Introduction

This unit will provide you with an understanding of how important communication is to the process of trade. Communication is commonly defined as the exchange of information between people or organisations. When a buyer wishes to purchase goods from a manufacturer they will have to communicate their needs and requirements, whether that is in writing on a purchase order document or a spoken request over the phone. Trade would be extremely difficult without some form of communication between organisations.

Communication is therefore one of the most important aids to trade, and in fact indirectly links all the traders that exist within the chain of production. In all the stages of trade, from an enquiry sent by a buyer to a seller through to the final payment for the goods or services received, contact between buyers and sellers is essential.

Communication is in fact totally necessary to trade. For example, consider a paint manufacturer that has just received the biggest order in its trading history but has just found out two of its mixing machines have broken down. A quick telephone call can organise the urgent repair of the machines within hours and means the order deadline does not have to be delayed.

In this unit, we will investigate in detail the importance of all the many types of communication that exist to ensure transactions take place successfully. In all stages of trading there needs to be effective communication between companies, their customers, their suppliers and their staff. This is why communication is so important. Some people say that communication is making the world smaller. It is as easy to trade with someone in America, for example, as it is in your own country.

9.1 The importance of communications in the global economy

Trade between countries is not a modern trend. We have evidence that global trade has existed for centuries. If we go back to the 13th century, we know that the majority of trade was in grown produce or building materials and, more commonly, knowledge. We know there were large markets where traders and customers would travel long distances to carry out their trading activities.

However, trade between world economies has grown dramatically in the last 50 years. This is because of our many improved systems of communication and of course, the Internet. These new systems mean that there is no need for traders to meet in a market place any more, so the nature of trade in the global economy is very different from how it used to be.

What has led to the increase in global trade?

- **Transport technology** – New, improved and varied forms of transport now exist and they are quicker than they have ever been. This allows certain countries to buy food produce that would otherwise have become rotten by the time they reached their destination. For example, it is difficult and expensive to grow tropical fruits such as bananas in the UK because the weather is not warm enough. Transport technology such as refrigerated transport containers has made it possible to harvest bananas and transport them halfway across the world to be eaten and enjoyed in Britain.
- **Changing tastes** – We desire ever-increasing varieties of goods at the lowest prices possible. Societies demand traditional products from their own country as well as produce from other nations. Also, customers recognise that they can buy certain goods for far less money in other countries.
- **Relationships between governments** – This has made it easier for organisations to trade with many different suppliers globally.
- **Improvements in communication** – Developments such as the Internet and mobile telecoms, which allow organisations to instantly communicate with each other from nearly anywhere in the world. Technology has reduced human error and sped up the process of communication and decision making.

So, why is communication so important? Communication is all about how effectively information is sent within and between organisations. It is a two-way process enabling information to be passed from one person or organisation to another. As organisations now deal with suppliers and customers who could be based anywhere in the world, effective communication has become even more important.

You have a relative who lives in another country. You would like to tell them all about what you are learning in your new 'commerce' course and how much you are enjoying it. Write down as many methods of communication you could use to achieve this. Try to consider a wide variety of traditional and modern methods of communication. What would this list have looked like 20 years ago?

Without effective communication, traders are unlikely to be successful in our increasingly complicated world. Successful traders will use communications to:

- **Manage staff** – by giving them clear instructions and performance targets to achieve so that the company can successfully carry out its activities.
- **Keep staff informed of changes** – so that they can perform their duties more effectively.
- **Get information from employees and customers** – on ways to improve their products and services.
- **Instantly communicate with suppliers, customers, banks and other service providers** – the essential people when carrying out their business activities. In order to survive and be profitable organisations need to:
  - i. Send the latest product and service information to existing and potential customers
  - ii. Receive, process and supply orders from customers in the shortest time possible
  - iii. Receive goods and materials from suppliers in time to meet their customer orders
  - iv. Arrange prompt payments to suppliers and from customers so that there is enough money within the company for it to continue trading
  - v. Respond quickly to possible mistakes that may lead to incorrect products or materials being received from suppliers, made by manufacturers or sent to customers, all of which can be expensive
  - vi. Know exactly where products and materials are during global transport so that they are kept in good condition and secure.

In the global economy none of these things can be done effectively without the fast and accurate transmission of information. All organisations need quick and reliable forms of communication in order to operate efficiently and experience trading success.

This means that communications need to have three characteristics. They need to be:

- ***RAPID***
- ***ACCURATE***
- Suitable for ***GLOBAL TRANSMISSION***

We will look at the many forms of communication available to organisations and when they might be used in the next section of the unit.

9.2 Methods of communication: internal and external

You will need to work in groups for this activity. Get two large pieces of paper and write down as many methods of communication used within an organisation (internally) and methods used to communicate with people outside an organisation (externally) as you can think of. Are there any methods of communication that appear on both lists?

All business communication can be grouped into either **internal** or **external** forms of communication.

Internal communication

This is the range of communications that take place within an organisation. These may include the exchange of telephone messages and e-mails or spoken instructions given by a manager to their team. It could also include a memo (note) sent to a company's maintenance department requesting that essential maintenance work be carried out in a particular department.

External communication

This is the range of communications that take place between the employees of a company and customers or companies outside. For example, a letter of enquiry may be received from a potential customer requesting details and prices of products or services. If the customer were then to purchase the goods or services they would be sent external documents such as invoices and statements of account. All these processes would be described as external communication.

All communications, whether they are internal or external to the company, can take place in a variety of different ways. This is demonstrated in the diagram below.

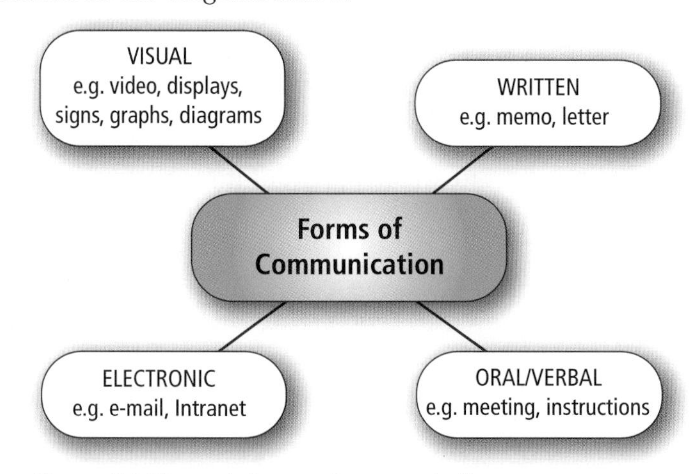

■ **Figure 9.1** *The main forms of communication*

Communications may also be a mix of the above methods. For example, an e-mail sent to a customer is an electronic written form of communication. A product manager presenting a new product to potential customers may use oral/verbal (spoken) communication and also slides and a video as an exciting visual form of communication.

Oral forms of communication

Much of our daily communication is oral, also known as verbal communication. You may turn to somcone in your class and ask them where the text books are kept. You didn't need to write a letter or an e-mail to get that information.

Oral communication can take place in two ways:

- **Direct oral communication** – This is face-to-face communication and examples may include *team briefings, meetings, interviews* or even a *conversation* in a corridor or *instructions* given by a manager to an employee.

Advantages	Disadvantages
Sharing new ideas by talking to your classmates or colleagues can lead to better solutions to problems	Meetings can sometimes be lengthy with a lot of talking but little actually achieved
You can get immediate feedback on oral comments	Some people in the meeting may not be willing to participate and share their views
It encourages cooperation	Some people can be very controlling and dominant in meetings
You have the opportunity to ask questions to make sure you understand the message being communicated	People who do not want to be at the meeting may have a negative effect on the other people
Detailed information can be shared and understood quickly	
Written records may be kept if minutes of a meeting are taken	

Table 9.1 *Advantages and disadvantages of direct oral communication*

- **Indirect oral communication** – This is where oral communication takes place but there is no direct face-to-face contact, for example, a conversation over the telephone. This is particularly useful where people who need to communicate are far away from one another.
- **Teleconferencing** – This is an example of indirect oral communication where two or more people who are based in different places have a meeting across a telecommunications link. This is sometimes called audio-conferencing.

Advantages	Disadvantages
Sharing new ideas by talking to your colleagues by telephone can lead to better solutions to problems	Can be an impersonal way of communicating particularly if discussing sensitive issues
In conversation you can get immediate feedback to oral comments	There is no written evidence of what has been discussed. Many people will confirm in writing after the conversation
It encourages cooperation	You can't see the other person's body language
You have the opportunity to ask questions to make sure you understand the message being communicated	Usually the communication can only occur between a few people
Detailed information can be shared and understood quickly	
If people are far away, you can save time and cost of travel to meetings by speaking to them by telephone	
Very quick method to get a response to an urgent problem	

■ **Table 9.2** *Advantages and disadvantages of teleconferencing*

When are oral communication methods the most suitable means of communication in commercial activity?

Oral methods of communication are most suitable where it is essential that information is communicated quickly either in person (face to face) or verbally at a distance using telephones or other distant communication methods such as teleconferencing. They can be a very cheap means of communication and can encourage almost immediate feedback on issues and ideas, leading to faster decision making and therefore faster commercial activity overall. In the exam you may be asked to consider a method of communication and explain its suitability to a given circumstance or you may be given a particular circumstance and asked to suggest with reasons what communication method(s) would be suitable. Below, to help you with your revision are a couple of examples of commercial activities where a particular type of oral communication would be suitable, with an explanation for its use.

- **Meeting between a customer and supplier to discuss the design and specifications of a one-off piece of machinery designed to order** – Oral communication in a meeting is suitable here because it allows detailed and technical information to be shared, discussed and understood quickly by everyone at the meeting.

Any issues regarding the design can be raised immediately and possibly resolved immediately because of the quick two-way communication that is taking place. If the communication were to be carried out by written forms of communication, such as letters and e-mail, it may take weeks or even months of correspondence to reach the same point. Meetings provide the additional benefit of being able to see the body language and facial expressions of the people attending. It would be easy to see immediately if the customers were pleased with the designs that were being presented to them!

- **International teleconference of all managing directors within an international organisation to discuss the sale of one of its companies** – Oral communication by teleconferencing is suitable here because it allows the sensitive issue to be discussed quickly without waiting for everyone who needs to participate to be in the same location (involving much travel and expense). In this circumstance it is probably the case that a decision needs to be made quickly because of media attention and the impact on employees of the company being discussed of any decisions being made. Detailed information can be communicated quickly and questions or objections can be raised before a final decision is made. Alternatives can be suggested which may influence the overall decision made.

Written communication

A large amount of communication between and within organisations is in written form. When using written forms of communication the communicator must make sure:

- it is suitable for the person they are sending their communication to
- it is presented and written using the proper professional format.

Reports

These are used for many reasons in organisations. They provide a very detailed form of written communication. A report is a type of document written by one person or a group of people in an organisation. It is generally an account of an event, or results from an investigation where recommendations are made.

A common example of a report would be a 'market research report'. These reports provide a summary of the market research findings in the particular market that a company works in. It would also provide information about current and potential customers for that company as well as recommendations on how products and services could be designed, changed and marketed. Another common report is a financial report. These reports provide details of the financial performance of a company on a regular basis. Table 9.3 shows the benefits and limitations of reports.

Their uses	Advantages	Disadvantages
Excellent for providing detailed information that can be referred to regularly E.g. Research findings reports, project results, financial reports, incident reports	■ Provide structured, logical and detailed information presented in an easy-to-use and accessible format	■ May be difficult for some people to use if there is a lot of specialist language ■ If very long, they may never be read or referred to by busy employees

■ **Table 9.3** *Benefits and limitations of reports*

Memos

Sometimes known as memorandums, memos are used internally within organisations as formal messages between employees. Some organisations still use them but where they have the technology they have been replaced by e-mail.

Their uses	Advantages	Disadvantages
They are a quick internal form of communication used to ask for information, request specific actions or to give instructions. Memos usually only contain the names of the people communicating, the subject of the message and the date it was sent	■ Provide the person receiving the memo with a permanent record that can be kept and referred to ■ It is a fairly quick way of communicating, depending on how efficient the mail room is	■ They have to be delivered by someone and could get lost or delivered to the wrong person ■ Much slower than the electronic alternative of e-mail

■ **Table 9.4** *Benefits and limitations of memos*

Theory into practice

Your commerce teacher will be away for the next two weeks attending a course to update their business knowledge. In their absence, the class will be held by a substitute teacher, Mrs Bhatti. Produce an internal memo to be sent to all the students in your class to communicate this information to them.

Letters

These are very widely used by companies to communicate with each other and with their own employees, for example to inform them of a change to their terms and conditions of employment.

Their uses	Advantages	Disadvantages
Letters are more detailed and formal than memos. They are usually produced on headed paper with the company's business details and logo at the top so it is clear who is sending the letter. They are used to provide important information or business proposals, or to respond to customer enquiries or complaints	■ They provide a permanent written record that can be referred to at a later date (particularly when there is a disagreement) ■ They are a confidential way of communicating with a customer, supplier or employee	■ It can be expensive to produce and send letters, particularly to a large number of customers ■ They may take a lot longer to produce because they are usually typed by secretarial staff

■ **Table 9.5** *Advantages and disadvantages of letters*

Delicious Pastries
12 Jamnalal Bajaj Road, PO Box 11333,
Nariman Point, Mumbai 400021.
22 66582236
www.deliciouspastries.in

18th April 2008

Dear Ms Tandon,

RE: Notification of promotion

I am writing to confirm that, with effect from 01 May 2008, you will be promoted to Sales Manager at the regional head office.

All other terms and conditions outlined in your Contract of Employment remain the same and you should treat this letter as an addendum to your original contract.

May I take this opportunity to congratulate you on your new role and wish you well at your new location.

Yours sincerely,

N. Jogalekar

N. Jogalekar
Business Development Manager

■ **Figure 9.3** *An example of a business letter*

Theory into practice

You work in the customer services department of a luxurious 5-star hotel called 'The Palace' in Mumbai. Yesterday, a valued and wealthy customer, Mrs Shetty, booked into the hotel and was taken to her usual room. To her shock, as she was settling into her room she noticed that someone else's belongings were in the wardrobe, the bed had been slept in and the bathroom was full of used towels. Mrs Shetty was very upset. She complained to the hotel reception, then collected her bags and went to stay at another hotel nearby. Mrs Shetty is a regular client, and her loss to your hotel might also lead to the loss of other valued customers if she tells them about her experience.

Write a letter to Mrs Shetty, apologising for the error and explaining what might have happened to cause it. Try to offer Mrs Shetty an incentive to return, so that you don't lose her business. Remember that your letter will need a logo and details of the hotel at the top. Make sure that you use appropriate language and the correct letter format. Mrs Shetty's address is: 12 Central Road, Bangalore 560 002, INDIA.

Notices

These are large, eye-catching displays of information aimed at all people using the area where they are displayed. All companies have display boards near offices or canteen areas and employees will look at these boards for any information that is relevant to them.

Their uses	Advantages	Disadvantages
They are used to catch people's attention and to provide information. They are usually the size of a small poster or A4 sheet of paper, but can be much bigger	■ Colour and pictures can be used to make the display more eye-catching and effective ■ A cheap, successful method of communicating to large groups of people particularly if they do not have access to e-mail	■ They can take a long time to produce and display ■ You will usually need to get the notice approved before displaying it on the notice board

■ **Table 9.6** *Advantages and disadvantages of notices*

Theory into practice

Produce an eye-catching and effective notice, to be pinned on a notice board near your school's canteen, telling the students that there will be a special, themed food week next week. Decide what the theme of food will be, what meals will be on offer and how much each will cost. Remember to make use of colour and pictures to encourage students to try the new range of meals.

When are written communication methods the most suitable means of communication in commercial activity?

Written methods of communication are most suitable when it is essential to have a written record of information that has been discussed or that is being communicated so it can be referred back to at a later point in time. For instance, a written agreement or contract for services that are to be provided by one company to another. Sometimes, while oral communication is faster and allows decision making to be carried out quickly, there still needs to be a written record of what was discussed in case there is a disagreement in the future. In addition, when there is a lot of information to consider it is almost impossible to expect people to remember everything so again, a written record is important here. In the exam you may be asked to consider a method of communication and explain its suitability to a given circumstance, or you may be given a particular circumstance and asked to suggest with reasons what communication method(s) would be suitable. Below, to help you with your revision, are a couple of examples of commercial activities where a particular type of written communication would be suitable, with an explanation of its use.

- **Confirmation in writing of an order for goods given to a seller by a buyer over the phone** – Written communication in the form of a purchase order document sent to the buyer by mail is suitable here because it allows the detail of the order to be recorded and documented for transaction records (both seller's and buyer's records). It is unlikely that the purchase order would be sent in the form of an e-mail because of how easy it is for e-mails to be left unread and deleted. When the document is received the buyer can confirm that it does reflect what they requested on the phone and that all other details such as price and quantity are correct. The document would then be used by the warehousing staff to ensure the correct goods are sent and received by the customer by the correct day.
- **An important message regarding a potentially faulty and dangerous product that needs to be recalled sent to all customers** – Written communication in the form of a formal letter would be sent in this situation because there is a higher chance it will reach its recipients than an e-mail etc. where customers are likely to regularly change their e-mail address. The letter will be formal in its appearance so communicating the seriousness with which it is dealing with the situation. It would be very costly to contact every customer by phone due to the cost of the call and the cost of staff to call all the customers, which could be in the region of hundreds of thousands of people. Such letters are usually produced on headed paper with the company's business details and logo at the top so it is clear who is sending the letter and to whom the customers will need to respond. The letter will contain important reference details that the customer will need to ensure their item is checked and returned to them in a safe condition.

Visual forms of communication

Visual communication is an effective, memorable and easy-to-understand form of communication. Some examples of visual communication are discussed below.

Signs, symbols and images

These are used regularly by all companies and are a common way of communicating general messages that may affect everyone, for example about health and safety at work.

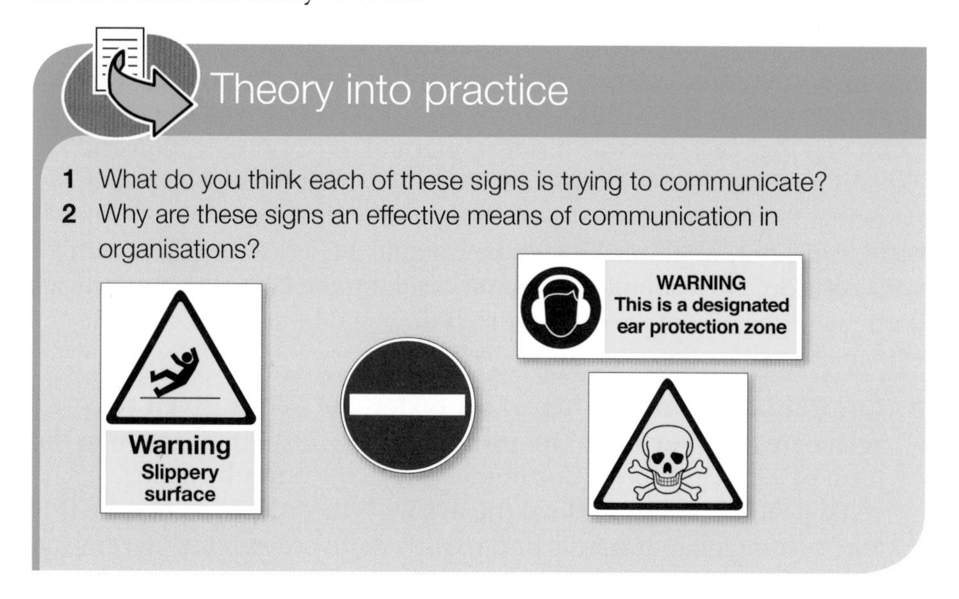

Graphs

These are used to show trends or general information about a particular issue so that all readers can understand them. Because graphs look interesting, and communicate their message quickly and efficiently, they may be used instead of tables of numbers and statistics. See page 102 in Unit 7 for an example of a bar graph showing the current account balance for Japan.

Diagrams or flowcharts

These are used to show the sequence of a particular activity or process, or how products and services are provided. See page 51 in Unit 3 for an example of a flowchart that shows how credit cards work.

When are visual forms of communication the most suitable means of communication in commercial activity?

Visual methods of communication are most suitable when a visual impact is required and where it is most suitable for information to be communicated simply with the use of a diagram, image or even a symbol. For example, it is much easier to display an organisational chart which shows all the employees within an organisation and their levels of authority than to describe in words everyone who works for an organisation and for whom and to whom they are responsible. There is a famous expression which says a picture is worth 1000 words! The added benefit is that these methods of communicating can also be far more memorable and easy to understand, particularly if it is a brief message being communicated about, for example, the beliefs and values of a company. In the exam you may be asked to consider a method of communication and explain its suitability to a given circumstance, or you may be given a particular circumstance and asked to suggest with reasons what communication method(s) would be suitable. Below, to help you with your revision are a couple of examples of commercial activities where a particular type of visual communication would be suitable, with an explanation of its use.

- **Communicating the monthly sales performance of the sales team by the use of a graph (bar chart)** – Visual communication in the form of a bar chart is suitable here because it is an instant visual representation of the performance of the team which is easy to read and understand by most people. Trends in sales compared to previous months or expected sales can be shown easily so that the reader can quickly judge the performance of the team. They can be presented in an interesting and colourful way, with each colour possibly showing a particular line of products or even a particular member of the sales team. When communicating number data this is usually a preferable means of communication rather than a difficult and hard to interpret table of figures and statistics. In addition, because it is a written form of communication it can be stored and referred back to at a later date if the data is needed for a different purpose, such as deciding to stop manufacturing a line of products or when making members of staff redundant.
- **A flowchart describing the stages in the construction of a new school** – A site manager responsible for building a new school by a deadline will need to plan what he wants his staff to do at certain points within the project and by when. A flowchart diagram is an easy to understand visual form of communication that can be used by most people to understand the sequence of activities involved in such a large project. The site manager can use it to check that his staff are doing their jobs by the deadlines given. The staff can easily use it to see what their responsibilities are and what the consequences of not carrying them out are. It is far easier to understand than a technical list of written instructions or a report. At a glance it is easy to see how the project is progressing.

Electronic forms of communication

Electronic forms of communication have become possibly the most important form of communication in modern businesses. Electronic communication has led to:

- An increase in the speed and efficiency of communication within and between companies.
- Reduced cost of communication because less money needs to be spent on postage and printing costs.

Fax

Documents can be sent instantly from one fax machine to another. A fax machine, which is short for facsimile machine, is a telecommunications technology system that can transfer copies of documents containing written communication, diagrams and pictures etc. using very affordable devices that operate over telephone networks. They can be accessed just like when making a phone call by inserting a phone number into the fax machine that corresponds with the number of another fax machine. Faxes are widely used by organisations, particularly when a document is only available on paper and there is no electronic version (because in that form it could be easily transmitted by e-mail). Faxes are a fast way of communicating which gives exact copies 24 hours a day.

There are limitations to faxes:

- The machine can run out of paper and the message isn't received if someone doesn't keep the machine supplied with paper.
- Fax machines are openly available to everyone within the company and are not suitable for sending confidential documents because anyone could see the document and read it (unless they are the newly developed password protected fax machines which can only be accessed by authorised people).
- Faxes can be picked up accidentally and may not then be received by the person who the document was intended for if security around the machine is bad.

Faxes are gradually being replaced by e-mails as written or printed documents can now be scanned and attached to the e-mail in electronic form.

E-mail

This has become a popular method of communication at work (and at home). E-mail users can send messages by a computer to other users on a network (that may exist within the company or through the Internet). As long as you have an e-mail address, you can send and receive messages from anyone else with an e-mail address, inside or outside of your company. An e-mail address is a user's electronic mailbox name or address, which is needed for linking the sender of the e-mail and the person who is intended to receive it. An e-mail address is usually a series of characters, such as 'raj@school.ed', that identifies the electronic mailbox of a person who can send and receive e-mail. The e-mail address includes the person's name (for example, raj) followed by an @ and then an Internet domain name (school.ed) which indicates the computer on which the e-mail account is registered. You may have a personal or school e-mail address.

Messages sent by e-mail are almost instantly delivered and are very secure – only the person using the e-mail address to which you sent the message can access it 24 hours a day – with the use of a password. The recipient can respond quickly and easily without even needing to look up the person's details because the e-mail address is attached to the message.

We can also send large quantities of attached data with our e-mail messages by attaching files or pictures to our messages. It is easy and fast to copy or forward an e-mail to someone else but you must consider if this is correct and if the person who sent it to you would wish it. Some people may receive hundreds of e-mails every day and so to keep them organised they can delete the ones they do not need to keep, store and save the important ones and print out the ones they may need to refer to or have a printed record of.

Most employees have their e-mail services open all the time so they can view and respond to messages very quickly.

There are limitations to e-mail communication:

- You cannot guarantee that the e-mail will be read or even accessed.
- There are so many e-mails now being sent that an that an important e-mail could be accidentally deleted.
- An e-mail could contain a harmful electronic virus which might damage your computer system. This means that companies need to install security devices, and e-mail users need to be aware of the threat all the time when opening messages.

Videoconferencing

Videoconferencing is very like teleconferencing which we discussed earlier, but as well as hearing others who may be located on the opposite side of the world, you can also see them. It allows people in organisations to hold face-to-face discussions with others without being

You can use videoconferencing to communicate face-to-face with people in another location

in the same room. It reduces the cost, time and inconvenience of travelling to a common meeting place. All that is needed is a special studio room which is linked to another. A lot of international organisations have studio rooms in their building, but specialist conferencing centres also offer videoconferencing services. They are very expensive to set up but, over time, they will probably be worth the money because of the savings that organisations will make – no longer having to send employees to expensive meetings overseas. As computer technology develops employees may be able to videoconference with others over the Internet more easily, without specialist studio equipment and facilities.

Internet/Intranet

The Internet or, as it is more commonly known, the **World Wide Web**, is a worldwide interconnected group of computers that has completely changed communications. It is the Internet that has made it possible for organisations to send and receive e-mails, download files and contact customers all over the world. Organisations can also set up their own simple website. This will enable them to access a worldwide market place and provides their customers with an alternative way to find out about them and their products. For example, a company that specialises in selling jewellery may receive orders and designs for manufacture from places ranging from America to Nairobi to Bangkok.

Here is an example of a screenshot from the home page of Heinemann's website; the publishing company that has produced this book for you.

■ **Figure 9.2** *The Heinemann website*

The Intranet is for internal company use. It is a private network inside an organisation that uses the same kind of software which would also be found on the Internet. Companies will use an Intranet to make their internal communications efficient and to protect them from the viruses on the World Wide Web.

The ***World Wide Web*** (often referred to as the Web) – an electronic source of millions, probably billions, of pages of information available via the Internet that can be easily accessed with software called 'browsers'. Companies can publish information about their products on the Web. This information is usually accessed via their 'home page' or 'website'.

When are electronic forms of communication the most suitable means of communication in commercial activity?

Electronic methods of communication are the most suitable choice of communication when there is a need for a high-speed and possible long-distance communication (that is virtually immediate) that is relatively inexpensive to achieve. With technological advancements in communications moving quickly, we have a whole range of technological devices at decreasing costs that we can use, including mobile phones and mobile laptop computers to name just two. As our economies become increasingly global electronic forms of communication are growing in importance. They are allowing organisations on opposite sides of the earth to communicate with each other almost immediately, carrying out transactions and building effective business relationships. In the exam you may be asked to consider a method of communication and explain its suitability to a given circumstance, or you may be given a particular circumstance and asked to suggest with reasons what communication method(s) would be suitable. Below, to help you with your revision are a couple of examples of commercial activities where a particular type of electronic form of communication would be suitable, with an explanation of its use.

- **Distribution of new price lists and product specifications quickly to sales people across the globe** – The electronic form of communication, e-mail, is suitable here because it is an instant and virtually cost-free way of communicating a lot of information to people across the globe. If this information were sent by post it would be expensive and could take weeks to reach its intended recipient, by which time a great number of orders may have been taken at the incorrect price levels. The recipient can print off a copy of the information so that they have a written document that they can refer to when dealing with clients. The quality of this print would be far greater than if the document had been faxed, which is also an expensive means of communication compared to e-mail.
- **Communicating product development and new product launches**
  Again, as a company becomes more well known, so too will their website. An organisation will feel that it is an effective means of communicating developments in products and new product launches because it has a great number of customers accessing its Web pages daily. It is cheap and cost-free to communicate in this way (although setting up and maintaining the website might cost a great deal of money). Using computing technology a company can make

communication through its website exciting, stimulating and interesting using graphics and interactive options. It still may choose to produce written forms of communication in the form of leaflets or flyers to send directly to its customers using the postal service as it cannot guarantee that all its customers regularly access the website.

Factors affecting the choice of communication method you may wish to consider

When an employee decides that they need to communicate with another person or company they will consider several factors before choosing their method of communication:

1. **The nature of the communication**
   a. An instruction from a manager to an employee may be given verbally.
   b. A warning from a manager to an employee about their poor performance may take place in a formal meeting and be confirmed in a letter which will be kept for reference.
   c. A customer requesting details about a company's products may be sent a letter of introduction and a catalogue of products. They may then be contacted by phone or even visited by a sales representative to see if they are interested in placing an order.

2. **The number of people that need to be communicated with**
   a. A message to be sent to all staff about changes planned within the company may be sent by e-mail or communicated by a team briefing.
   b. A request from a manager to a member of staff to do something may be agreed during a meeting or requested by e-mail.
   c. A new catalogue and price list for products offered may be sent to all customers on a database by post or e-mailed with an attached file to save money.

3. **Whether speed of delivery is important**
   a. In an emergency, such as the breakdown of equipment or injury of a member of staff, the communication has to be instant. In these cases direct contact by phone with the desired person would be the best method.
   b. A request for information that is needed in two weeks can be sent by mail, memo or letter.

4. **Whether cost is significant**
   Some communication methods, such as sending letters and catalogues in the post to customers, can be very expensive. If a company needs to cut costs it may consider cheaper alternatives such as sending the catalogue to customers via e-mail.

5. Length of message/detail of information
Some information that needs to be communicated may contain a lot of detail, data or technical instructions. In this case a written form of communication like a letter or report is required so that it can be referred to again as necessary.

6. Whether a record is needed
For some transactions it is important to have a record of what was agreed. You may take minutes at a meeting as a record of what was said or confirm in a letter or e-mail a conversation that you just had by telephone. Very formal arrangements may be recorded in a written **contract** which is signed by both parties to say they agree with the contents.

7. The importance of visual appeal
If the communication is aimed at a large audience and the sender wants the message to be seen and remembered they may use colour and images to make an impact. This could be in a written form of communication like a notice, or even electronic images and animation in an e-mail.

Contract – an agreement between two or more people or organisations which represents a commitment to do or not to do a particular thing, e.g. supply goods or services in return for a payment. They are legal agreements and can be made verbally or in writing.

9.3 Post Office and telecoms

The Post Office

Every country has its own national postal service. They operate in similar ways and provide similar services. In the UK the postal service is called Royal Mail. In Pakistan it is called Pakistan Post.

Letters and parcels are still essential to companies and private individuals. Postal service providers have developed a range of services for people to make use of.

We look at the type of services provided below:

- **Business reply service**
  This allows customers to send orders or other documents to a company without having to pay for postage. Customers are more likely to contact a company for further information on products or services if they don't have to pay any postage costs. Companies therefore use this free reply service as part of their marketing. Companies do have to pay to use this service, plus the cost of postage, but it is a low cost compared to the potential sales they may be able to generate.
- **Freepost**
  Companies using this service can send customers pre-printed envelopes with the word 'FREEPOST' appearing in the address. Banks and credit card companies use these special envelopes to encourage customers to make payments. Mail order or catalogue organisations may also provide freepost envelopes to encourage customers to make orders without needing to buy a stamp. The organisation will pay the postal charge for the customer plus a small additional charge for the use of the service.
- **Certificates of posting**
  When a company posts an important or valuable item of mail they are advised to get a certificate of posting from the postal service as proof that the package was sent. If the item of mail is damaged or lost then the certificate acts as insurance and, depending on the postal service used, a small damages payment may be paid to the sender. If items of post are very valuable, senders may pay additional charges to insure the high value of the item should it get lost, stolen or damaged in the postal system.
- **Recorded delivery**
  This service allows companies to get evidence that a letter or parcel was received by someone at the address it was sent to. The recipient is asked to provide their signature as proof of its delivery. Recorded delivery is commonly used by companies sending important documents such as contracts.

- **Registered service**
  Some postal services give their customers the opportunity to track their item of mail through the Internet so that they know exactly when the item has been delivered. The registered item of mail is pre-paid with the normal postage rate and an additional charge known as a registration fee. The sender is given a receipt and a registration label with a unique number which is stuck to the letter. The sender can input this number on the postal company's website and check whether the item has been delivered or not. If an item is not received then the sending company will know to send it again. Recently, registered delivery services have been replaced by what is now referred to as 'special delivery' but the service offered is essentially the same.

Theory into practice

A friend has just told you they are starting up an Internet company specialising in buying and selling baseball cards, some of which are very valuable collector's items.

Considering the value of the cards she is selling and sending through the post, give her a brief explanation of which of the above postal services she should use.

Telecommunications (telecoms)

Telecommunications, and mobile telecommunications in particular, is a growing industry. The level of communications we are able to use today is incredible compared to just 30 years ago. There are not many companies which do not use some form of telephone service, whether they are land lines, digital or mobile telephones. Telephone services provided include:

- **Freephone numbers** – This is where a company will pay for the calls made to them by customers. Companies will use freephone numbers to encourage customers to call them instead of other companies, particularly when customers have a large range of different suppliers to choose from. This helps companies to get ahead of their competitors and is very common among insurance companies, for example. Companies with freephone numbers have to pay the cost of the call plus a small additional charge for the service. This is a small cost compared to the potential sales they stand to make.
- **Radio paging** – This is where an employee can be provided with a pager which will bleep when someone who wants to contact them dials a special number. The telephone number of the person trying to contact the pager holder will appear on the pager. Mobile phones have reduced the use of pagers because they allow people to be contacted directly when needed. Doctors still use pagers because they do not use radio waves that may interfere with medical equipment in hospitals.

- **Directory enquiries/printed directories** – Some telecommunication companies provide a service that allows people to call a fee-paying number and request the telephone number of a specific company or person. This is very good for organisations that are looking for suppliers and also for customers who may be looking for the number of a particular company. In addition, the same telecommunication companies will put the contact details of certain organisations in printed directories. These are distributed to almost every home and company so that potential customers can contact organisations directly.
- **Redirected calls or call routing** – This service helps to stop companies from missing urgent calls. It does this by automatically transferring all calls to a particular telephone number, where the company owner or a call service is ready to take the call. For example, a website designer working on his own may find that he has to attend regular meetings during which he is unable to take calls from customers. He may choose to redirect his calls to a friend or member of his family or to a professional messaging service where he has to pay for someone to answer his calls and take messages on his behalf.
- **Teleconferencing** – This is a service that allows more than two people to participate in a group call over the phone. We talked about this method in detail on pages 142–3.
- **Mobile telecommunications** – Mobile phones (also known as 'cell phones') allow organisations and their customers to contact employees at all times, even outside business hours. The employee does not have to stay in the house or office near to a landline. They have the freedom to carry on with life without the fear of missing an important or emergency phone call. One disadvantage of mobiles is that they will not work if they are in a weak signal area or if they have run out of batteries.

  Mobile phone technology is developing fast and users can now communicate in writing through text messages, take and send pictures, receive and send e-mails and also access the Internet.

Summary of main points from Unit 9

- Communications and methods of communication are some of the most important aids to trade as they provide the links that exist between traders in the chain of production and distribution.
- Developments in communication in recent years have contributed greatly to the increase in global trade we see today.
- Methods of communication can be split into internal and external. Internal communications take place within an organisation between employees. External communications take place between the employees of an organisation and people outside (customers and employees of other organisations).
- Communication methods can be split into four main types: written, verbal, visual and electronic. Each communication method is used for different situations. In exams you may be asked to suggest suitable communication methods and give reasons for your suggestions.
- Factors which influence the choice of communication method used by someone in an organisation include the type of message that is to be communicated, the number of people that need to receive the message, how quickly the message needs to reach its target audience, whether the message has to be transmitted cheaply, the amount of detail the message contains, whether a record of the message needs to be kept and if the message needs to be visually appealing.
- There are a number of industries and organisations whose only purpose is to provide communications services. These include traditional postal services and telecommunications organisations.

Test your knowledge

Practice multiple choice exam questions

1) Which communication method would most likely be used to confirm orders for goods and services that were taken over the phone or left as a phone message on an answering machine?
   a) Memo
   b) Internet
   c) Letter
   d) E-mail

2) A shoe company wishes to have an urgent sales meeting including sales managers at home and overseas. Which form of communication method should save travel time and expenses?
   a) Mobile phone
   b) Teleconferencing
   c) E-mail
   d) Fax

Test your knowledge *continued*

3) To send a message to all workers within a company it is usual to:
   a) Telephone each individual.
   b) Meet with everyone personally.
   c) Send a letter to each person.
   d) Send a memo to each person.

4) Which of the following is a non-verbal method of communication?
   a) Business meeting
   b) Journal or newsletter
   c) Telephone
   d) Interview

5) Which of the following are informal methods of communication?
   i. Social events
   ii. Staff notice boards
   iii. Reports

   a) Only (i) is informal
   b) Only (iii) is informal
   c) (i) and (ii) are informal
   d) (i), (ii) and (iii) are informal

Practice stimulus response and structured exam questions

1) A company uses the following means of communications: e-mail, fax, letter, telephone and teleconferencing).
   a) Name three features of communication by fax. (*3 marks*)
   b) When would a company use:
      (i) Letters rather than the other methods? (*3 marks*)
      (ii) Telephone rather than e-mail? (*3 marks*)
   c) What are the benefits of teleconferencing to the business? (*6 marks*)
   d) Why is e-mail important as a means of communication in many companies? (*5 marks*)

   (CIE Commerce Paper 1 Oct/Nov 2003)

2) a) Explain why communication is important for an international company working in world markets. (*5 marks*)
   b) Name three methods of communication which an international company might use in its operations and show in what circumstances they might be used. (*9 marks*)

   (CIE Commerce Paper 1 Oct/Nov 2004)

3) Name two methods of communication and describe how each might be used by a manufacturer of electronics selling in world markets. (*10 marks*)

   (CIE Commerce Paper May/Jun 2000)

4) Profiles Ltd is a multinational corporation manufacturing and selling car tyres in many parts of the world. Explain three methods of communication they might use for rapid communication with their sales offices and representatives in other countries. (*9 marks*)

   (CIE Commerce Paper May/Jun 2002)

10 Transport

What do I need to study?

- Explain and illustrate the importance of transport in the chain of distribution.
- What factors affect the choice of transport method selected by organisations?
- List the benefits to organisations of owning their own vehicles for the transport of goods.
- Define what is meant by containerisation. Why are containers used and what are their advantages?
- Describe the modern trends and developments in transport.
- Identify the features of various transport documents and describe how they are used.
- Describe the range of services offered at seaports and airports to assist international transport of goods or cargo.

Introduction

In this unit we aim to investigate another important aid to trade: transport. Transport means the movement of raw materials, products and people from one location to another. It is a central function of all commercial and trading activity.

We are seeing increasing amounts of international trade in our global economy, and this makes efficient and effective, quality transport increasingly important. In this unit we will look at the importance of transport and the many methods of transport available to companies trading domestically (within their home country) and internationally (with organisations in other countries).

10.1 Transport

Importance of transport in the chain of distribution

Transport involves the movement of raw materials, products and people from one location to another. It is a central function of all commercial and trading activity. Raw materials need to be transported from where they are extracted, grown or produced to factories where they are used in the production of finished goods or in the provision of services. Many raw materials are only available in certain regions of the world and tonnes of material may need to be transported across continents or overseas. For example, diamonds are mainly mined in South Africa from where they are transported to jewellers across the globe.

Finished products made in factories then need to be transported directly to consumers or national retailers or, more traditionally, to wholesalers to be redistributed.

Finally, transport is also concerned with the movement of people, whether they are moving between home and work, shopping or even going on holiday.

As systems of transport improve, the target market of each organisation grows. The more customers or organisations can be reached, the more successful a company becomes. As companies become more successful, they produce more, and therefore the more goods and services there are for consumers to enjoy.

Transport plays a significant role in the chain of distribution. We discussed this in Units 2 and 5. If transport systems are efficient it means that there is less money tied up in stock sitting on shelves in warehouses. If delivery of goods can be made quickly, regularly and when needed, this means that manufacturers can produce just enough to satisfy orders.

Methods of transport

There are a number of transport methods for companies to choose between. First we shall look at the different methods available and the benefits and limitations of each one. Later in the unit we shall investigate the things that may influence a company's choice of transport.

Road

This is the central transport method on which all other transport methods rely. We see evidence all around us of developing road networks with new and faster motorways, ring roads reducing city centre traffic, and the widening of busy roads. Road transport, or haulage, is probably the most important and most used method of transport within a country (internally).

The building of new roads and the upkeep of existing road networks are usually paid for by governments out of tax payments made on fuel, new cars sold and, sometimes, road licence tax.

Advantages of road transport

- A convenient and direct form of transport of goods from manufacturers to wholesalers or retailers.
- Goods can be moved when required, using a selected route.
- Regarded as a speedy form of transport, particularly when motorways or toll roads (roads you pay to use) are used.
- No restriction to fixed timetables, as in rail transport.
- Haulage prices are quite low due to high levels of competition.
- Transport is direct so there is a reduced chance of theft and damage to goods.
- Companies can own their own vehicles for extra flexibility and cost-effectiveness. In addition, they can use the vehicles to raise awareness of their organisation through the use of advertisements and logos which are placed on the side of their vehicles (normally known as vehicle 'livery').

Disadvantages of road transport

- Roads are becoming more and more congested (busy), making road transport slower because of traffic delays.
- If oil prices increase so does the cost of fuel, which could make road transport an expensive method of transport.
- When heavy goods vehicles are used only for deliveries there is a point in a journey where the vehicle is empty, making the transport less cost-effective.
- Road transport is not suitable for all materials and products such as the transport of bulky raw materials like coal or steel.
- For safety reasons road haulage is a very regulated industry with guidelines on weight of goods and length of driving time.
- Road transport is leading to increasing levels of congestion and therefore pollution.

Rail

Rail travel first started in 1825. Raw materials and goods with a short shelf life, such as fruit and vegetables grown in particular regions, became available across whole nations and countries because of trains. As the decades have passed, rail has become the preferred transport method for bulky commodities and goods such as coal, steel, fuels like petrol, and building materials. In addition, many national postal services use rail services to speed up delivery of parcels and letters. In most countries the postal service uses trains to transport parcels from one side of the country to another. In some countries, like in the USA until very recently, parcels and letters were sorted by postal workers during the rail journey.

The convenience of road haulage has reduced the demand for rail transport because, regardless of speed, there still needs to be some other form of transport to get the goods to and from the rail terminal. The main aim of all rail activities is the provision of fast and comfortable passenger travel.

Advantages of rail transport

- Suitable for transporting bulky goods such as coal or steel.
- Rail travel can be faster, more efficient and more cost-effective over long distances than other forms of transport over land.
- There are stations and rail terminals in all cities and in most towns, allowing quick transport of goods into towns and centres.
- It is a cheap way of transporting containers of goods and materials.
- In the future rail travel will play a significant role in trying to reduce the ever increasing problem of congestion (too much traffic on the roads) experienced in highly populated countries.

Disadvantages of rail transport

- It isn't a cost-effective means of transport for small loads transported short distances.
- Routes are fixed and so there will also be a need for an additional form of transport to and from the terminal, which could lead to delays and damage to goods and materials and possibly an increased threat of theft.
- Trains are timetabled and so companies using them are limited by these schedules.
- It is an expensive means of transport due to the high maintenance costs of keeping the system safe and working.
- Unusual loads like vehicles or construction equipment cannot be transported by rail because of their size and shape.

Air

This is a developing method of transport and is growing in importance as globalisation of trading activities increases. We even see the use of helicopters to deliver essential supplies and medicine to remote regions. Air cargo services now transport goods and materials to most parts of the world. Despite this, the core (main) activity of air travel remains the transport of passengers. However, air cargo shipments are growing in size due to the availability of larger aircraft and excellent warehousing facilities at airports. It is still an expensive means of transport with charges based on the value, weight and destination of goods. It is for this reason that sea travel remains the most popular international transport method.

■ *Air freight is growing in importance*

Advantages of air transport

- It is the quickest form of long-distance transport.
- Larger aircraft now available can accommodate containers of products which are easier to load and very secure.
- There is less documentation involved in air freight compared to sea transport.
- Insurance costs of goods being transported is less, due to the reduced time of transport leading to a reduced chance of theft or damage.
- Less protection is required than for sea transport because goods or materials are not exposed to the elements as they are on ships.
- It is a suitable and cost-effective method for small, light and very valuable items such as precious metals, medicines and perishable goods (goods that have a short shelf life).

Disadvantages of air transport

- It is an extremely expensive transport method due to the cost of air travel.
- Flights are at a high risk of being cancelled due to poor weather conditions.
- Additional transport is required to transport goods or materials to and from airports, which are usually located quite far away from cities or towns.

■ *Bulk carriers are purpose-built transporting ships*

Sea

For countries like the UK and Hong Kong, surrounded by water, the importance of sea transport is very high. There is more reliance on sea transport to bring materials, foods and goods to satisfy a whole nation demanding a variety of goods from across the world. On the other hand, island nations must export produce from their own countries to others to pay for the goods they receive. Sea transport is also central to this trade.

There are many types of shipping transport available to exporting and importing organisations:

- **Bulk carriers (OBO – Oil/Bulk/Oil ships)** – purpose-built transporting ships designed for specific produce, such as oil, transported in tankers or perishable goods on refrigerated ships.
- **Liners and roll-on/roll-off ferries** – these have a dual purpose, carrying passengers for tourism purposes and cargo at the same time.
- **Tramp ships (chartered)** – are hired by companies to carry goods and materials on a charter basis.
- **Coastal shipping** – carry goods and materials around a country's coast and between ports.

Advantages of sea transport

- It is a relatively cheap form of transport over long distances compared to air freight.
- Containers can be easily used to transport goods and materials safely and securely on ships.
- It is a method that can bring and take goods and materials to and from ports all over the globe.
- It is a very suitable method for transporting heavy and bulky products and materials like coal and steel.
- Specialist ships can be built to transport specific produce like oil in tankers or perishable goods in refrigerated ships.

Disadvantages of sea transport

- Sea transport is extremely slow and is therefore unsuitable for perishable goods with a short shelf life.
- There is still a need for additional transport to and from ships docked at port.
- There is a very high likelihood of damage to goods and materials due to extreme temperature variations and salt from sea air.

Inland waterways (canals)

These are a very cheap form of transport. They are an under-used form of transport in some countries today, because of the development of faster air, road and rail travel. Canal barges are vessels used to carry freight on canals, but are now often converted to passenger use for leisure cruising. Barges are a very slow method of transport with very limited routes and networks available. As air, road and rail transport costs rise, and with increasing amounts of pollution and congestion, we may see an increase in the use of canals in the future.

Pipelines

There are some substances which are unsuitable to be transported by rail, road or air, such as drinking water, gas, petrol or oil. These substances are commonly transported by pipelines. According to the Association of Oil Pipelines, in 2005 in the USA, pipelines moved nearly two-thirds (66 per cent) of the ton-miles of oil transported. The rest was transported via water carriers (28 per cent), trucks (4 per cent) and rail (2 per cent).

Theory into practice

For each of the following products identify a suitable means of transport domestically (within their home country) and internationally (overseas and across borders). Give reasons for your suggestions.

1. Luxury sports cars
2. Designer watches
3. Microwaves
4. Textbooks

Factors affecting choice of transport

Organisations have a wide variety of transport methods that they can use. The method they choose will depend on a number of factors:

1. **The goods being transported**
   Perishable goods and fragile products need to be transported in controlled and secure environments such as refrigerated vehicles and rail containers. Bulky goods like coal can be poured into rail trucks with little worry about the effects of the weather.
2. **The value of goods being transported**
   Precious items and metals need to be secure and transported quickly to reduce risk of theft and loss. When precious stones are being transported long distances or internationally the preferred form of transport is likely to be by air.
3. **The size and weight of goods being transported**
   Bulky and extremely heavy materials like steel can only be transported in large quantities by ship from overseas, or by rail within the country. Deliveries of lighter products, such as clothing, that are being transported short distances, are likely to be made by road.
4. **The timescale of delivery and frequency of deliveries**
   Most companies and, in particular, Internet retailers, are under pressure because of high levels of competition to deliver goods in the fastest time possible. This helps organisations to stock fewer goods, so less of their money is tied up in stock and less storage space is needed.
5. **The need for door-to-door delivery**
   Some companies offer their customers – as an incentive to trade with them – quick, efficient delivery straight to their doors to make the transactions as convenient as possible. For example, Delice de France offer daily fresh deliveries of continental savoury and sweet pastries to their retail customers.
6. **The distance goods and materials need to be transported**
   For longer distances there is more need for cheaper and faster transport such as by air, ship or rail. Shorter journeys are more economical using road transport.

For most countries, road transport is the most common and preferred method of transport for 'inland' transport. For the transport of goods to and from other countries, shipping is the most commonly used, as it is the cheapest method.

Benefits to a business of having its own transport

The road haulage industry in most countries is made up of a large number of smaller hauliers (companies that own lorries for road transport). Companies can choose between having their own fleet of vehicles or paying private hauliers for their delivery services. Each has its own advantages and disadvantages which we will investigate below:

Advantages of businesses having their own transport

- Companies can plan their own journeys to suit their own requirements and to provide tailor-made (made for the particular company) delivery services for their customers.
- Companies are not restricted by the fixed timetables and routes involved in rail transport.
- Where a great deal of transport is required it can be cheaper for a company to own and operate its own fleet of vehicles rather than pay the expensive rates charged by a haulage company.
- If an employee drives the company van, for example in firms such as plumbers, then equipment can be delivered and installed at the same time.
- Other employees can act as replacement drivers if regular drivers are not available.

Disadvantages of businesses having their own transportation

- The haulage industry is highly regulated and only drivers with special licences can drive heavy goods vehicles.
- It is very expensive to purchase fleets of vehicles and to maintain, tax and insure them. A company must have regular deliveries and collections to justify the cost of setting up and running its own fleet of vehicles.

10.2 Containerisation

Containerisation is probably the biggest development in transport in recent years. Technological advances in container design have made it possible to quickly and conveniently ship materials and products thousands of miles to reach their final destination in perfect condition. Containers are large metal storage cases in which products or materials are packaged and stored; they are then locked and secured and sent to their destination by road, rail, air or sea. Different types of goods can be contained in one storage case.

Goods or materials packaged into containers are delivered directly to the customers in the same condition as when they left the manufacturer. At rail terminals, airports and seaports, the movement of goods is made easier by a range of cranes and vehicles designed to move and transport containers to and from trains, ships, vehicles and aircraft.

Benefits of using containers

- They save time. A crane needs to make only one lifting movement to shift a large heavy load, compared to having to lift and move lots of smaller pallets (storage platforms) of goods or materials.
- They reduce handling costs because it is easier to lift a container than several pallets of goods or materials.
- They are very secure and can be locked to avoid loss and theft of goods or materials.
- Containers are very robust (strong), therefore reducing the chance of damage to goods and materials.

Containers, therefore, enable organisations to transport large quantities of goods and materials quickly, cheaply, securely and reliably.

Containers are most commonly used for goods and materials going to and from other countries. They are very convenient, can be easily checked by customs officials and then sealed securely.

10.3 Other trends in transport

When we investigated the main methods of transport, we discussed developments in each area. In this section we will summarise the main modern developments and trends in transport relating to the handling of goods and passenger transport.

- **Charter transport** – This is where a company hires the transport services of a rail, air or sea transport provider. It means that they have flexibility and control over where the transport method goes and when (to a certain degree).
- **Growth of air freight** – The increasing size of aircraft and increasing number of air terminals is making it possible to transport larger quantities, so the cost of air transport for goods, materials and passengers is becoming less expensive (although it is still a very expensive means of transport).
- **Express road routes** – More extensive motorway networks and pay-to-use toll roads are speeding up travelling by road by helping transporters avoid congestion around towns and cities.
- **Changes in the use of rail transport** – Tilting trains and high-speed trains, such as the TGV (Train à Grande Vitesse/high-speed train) in France, are leading to faster journey times, making it possible for passengers to commute longer distances to work. There is increasing use of tunnels to by-pass difficult routes, such as the Channel Tunnel between England and France, and the Seikan Tunnel in Japan.

Can you think of an example of a company or group of people that would benefit from each of the trends in transport identified here?

10.4 Transport documents

We investigated a wide range of documents involved in transactions in Unit 6. In addition to these, there is a range of documents used by organisations involved in trade between different countries. These documents are:

Delivery note

This document is normally associated with the transport of goods by road or rail. It accompanies the goods or materials and a copy of it is given to the receiver of the goods, with a signature being taken as proof of delivery. If there are any problems with the delivery, such as missing or damaged packages, these are noted on the kept copy of the delivery note and damaged packages are returned.

The note contains the following information:

- Description of goods
- Number of packages in the consignment (batch of goods)
- Weight of the packages being delivered
- Sender's address
- Delivery address
- Whether the carriage cost is paid on delivery or by the sender.

'Consignment' notes are similar to delivery notes, but are the documents used when a company uses a private delivery organisation to ship goods to a customer rather than delivering them themselves. The sender will complete the consignment note (provided by the delivery organisation) and when the goods are delivered the recipient will sign the note to say the goods have been received.

Bill of lading

This document is used when goods and materials are transported by sea. It is completed by the owner of the goods or cargo being exported, and given to the shipper. The document contains the following details:

- Sender's details
- Description of goods/cargo being exported
- Name of port from which the goods/cargo are being exported
- Name of ship transporting the goods/cargo
- Destination of goods/cargo (both the port and customer)
- Charge to be paid to shipping company
- Customs number.

When the goods/cargo arrive at their planned destination a copy of the bill of lading is given to the person receiving or collecting the goods (the importer) so that they can claim their goods. The other important function of the bill is that it is a legal 'document of title' or proof of ownership.

Air waybill

This document is used when goods are transported by air. It has the same function as the bill of lading document and contains the following details:

- Sender's details
- Description of goods/cargo being exported
- Name of airport from which the goods/cargo are being exported
- Identity number of plane transporting the goods/cargo
- Destination of goods/cargo (both airport and customer)
- Charge to be paid to air transporters
- Customs number.

Unlike bills of lading, air waybills *do not* provide any legal proof of ownership and so are not considered as documents of title.

All documents form an extremely important means of communication between a company and its customers and suppliers. Information technology developments, such as the Internet, have made it easier and quicker to record, track and pay for transactions. Organisations sending goods and materials overseas by ship or air now have access to Web-based software packages that allow them to interact with the shipper's systems. This means that they can track their own cargo or consignments of products so that they always know where their goods are. They can therefore inform their customers when to expect their goods or materials, or if there is a chance that they may be delayed.

10.5 International transport

Shipping by sea and air is essential to international trade. There is a range of services offered at seaports and airports that are more than the standard transport of goods, cargo or materials from one port to another. These are shown in the spider diagram below.

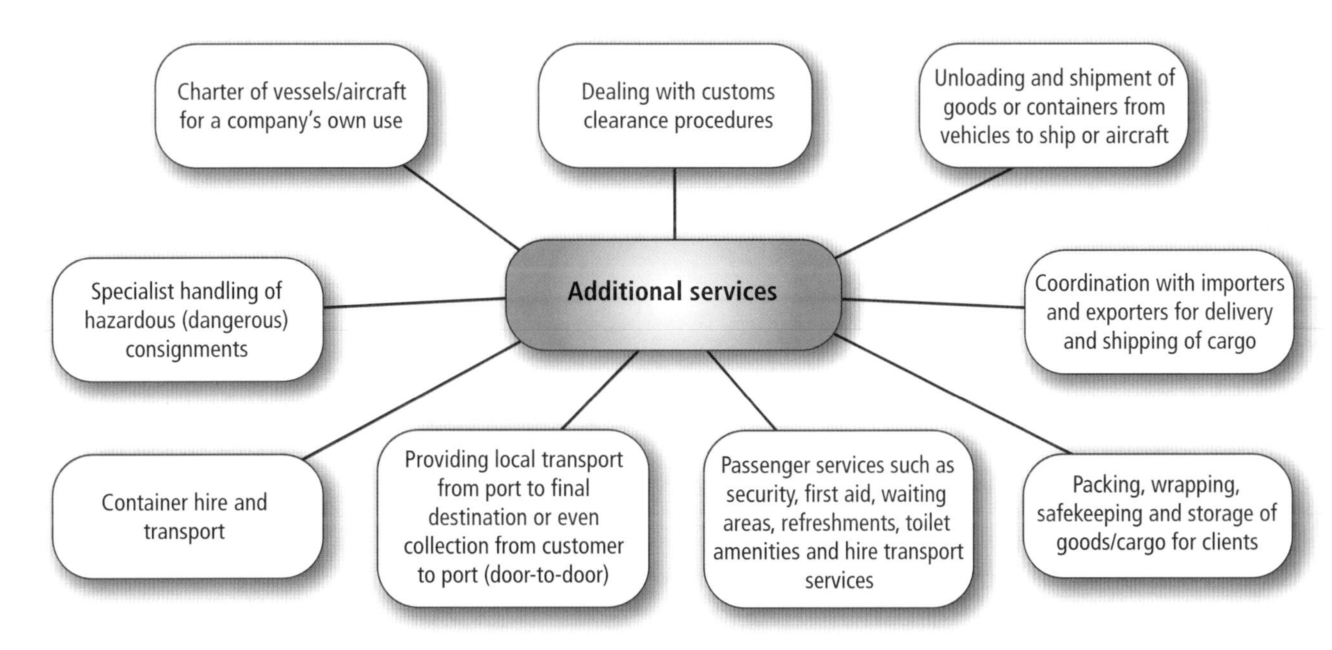

■ **Figure 10.1** *The range of additional services offered at seaports and airports*

Theory into practice

Using resources available to you, research the services offered by your nearest airport or seaport to companies using them to transport goods internationally. Make an attractive and informative information sheet that could be used by the port you investigate to promote their services to companies in your country.

Summary of main points from Unit 10

- Transport is an important aid to trade. It is defined as the movement of raw materials, products and people from one location to another. It has become extremely important because of growing international trade.
- Methods of transport include road, rail, air, sea, inland waterways and pipelines.
- Things which influence choice of transport include what type of products are being transported, their value, their weight and size, how quickly and often they need to be delivered, whether door-to-door delivery is needed and how far away the final destination is.
- Some organisations have their own transport. This provides them with increased flexibility but can be extremely expensive to set up and maintain.
- Containers are large metal storage cases in which goods are packaged and stored. They are locked and secured and can be transported by road, rail, air or sea. They offer many benefits and are increasingly used due to international trade growth.
- When goods are transported, particularly overseas, there are important and necessary documents that accompany the goods, including delivery notes, bills of lading and airway bills. You will need to know the function of each.

Test your knowledge

Practice multiple choice exam questions

1) By which of the following are bulk materials, such as coal, commonly exported?
   a) OBO ships
   b) Cargo liners
   c) Air transport
   d) Passenger liners

2) Which group of factors would influence the choice of transport for a manufacturer who delivers milk directly to retailers?

	Capacity	Speed	Reliability	Flexibility
a)	X		X	X
b)		X	X	X
c)	X	X		X
d)	X	X	X	X

3) What is the main function of the document called a bill of lading for goods which are transported over sea?
   a) To provide dutiable and non-dutiable details of goods.
   b) To show the value of goods being transported.
   c) To act as a document of title to the goods.
   d) To show that there is a contract for the hire of a ship.

Test your knowledge *continued*

4) Which of the following is not an advantage of rail transport?
   a) Unlimited loads
   b) Use of containers
   c) Door-to-door service
   d) High-speed, long-distance services

5) Which of the following is not an advantage of sea transport?
   a) Suitable for bulky goods
   b) Access to all parts of the world
   c) Relatively cheap
   d) Fast delivery

Practice stimulus response and structured exam questions

1)

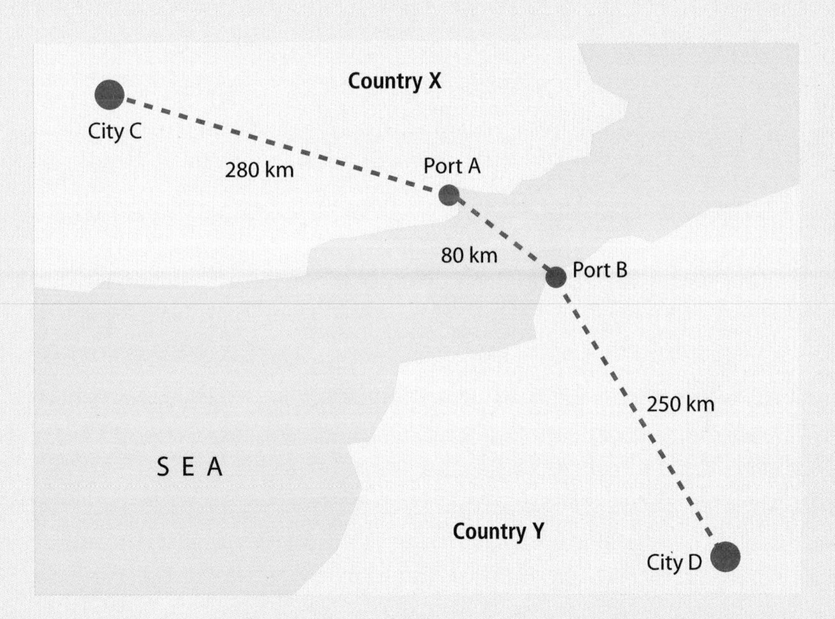

a. A trader in City C wishes to send a consignment of shoes to a trader in City D.
   (i) Advise the trader of *two* methods of transport he might use. Give reasons for your answer. (*8 marks*)
   (ii) How does the port authority in Port B assist the trader? (*4 marks*)

(CIE Commerce Paper 1 May/Jun 2004)

2) Soyo Logistics Ltd is a transport company based in a port in the UK. It specialises in moving bulk cargoes all over the world. It owns several ships, hires other ships and has a fleet of lorries for transporting goods within the UK.
   a) Explain the functions of each of the following documents and give the circumstances when Soyo Logistics Ltd might use each of them.
      i. Bill of lading (*4 marks*)
      ii. Delivery/consignment note. (*4 marks*)
   b) Explain two advantages to Soyo Logistics Ltd of owning and operating its own fleet of lorries. (*4 marks*)

(CIE Commerce Paper 1 May/Jun 2004)

Test your knowledge *continued*

3) Mr Manyere owns an export business in South Africa growing and selling tomatoes for the European market.
   a) Name two methods of transport he might use for his business. Give reasons for the suitability of each choice. (*8 marks*)
   b) He will need to complete several documents when he exports a consignment of tomatoes to Europe. Name two documents and explain how Mr Manyere will use them. (*6 marks*)
   c) State and explain three reasons why it would be easier for Mr Manyere to sell his tomatoes in his own country rather to the European market. (*6 marks*)

(CIE Commerce Paper Oct/Nov 2002)

4) Airports offer many facilities for air cargo and passengers.
   a) Name two services provided at airports for passengers. (*2 marks*)
   b) List three facilities provided at airports for the handling of cargo. (*2 marks*)
   c) Give three reasons why firms are more encouraged to use air transport and explain your reasons. (*2 marks*)

(CIE Commerce Paper 1 May/Jun 2003)

Question 4b asks you to **'list'** three facilities. This question only gives two marks. Keep answers to these types of question short. Do not be tempted to waste time by providing a more detailed answer.

5 a) Containerisation continues to assist all forms of transport. Explain the benefits of containerisation for the transport of many types of goods. (*10 marks*)
  b) Rail transport is becoming less important in some countries than it used to be. Explain the reasons for this trend. (*10 marks*)

(CIE Commerce Paper May/Jun 2002)

Question 5 asks you to **'explain'** and there are 10 marks available. Your answer here must be well developed. You will need to explain at least four separate points for each type of transport. You should also try to use commercial examples to illustrate your answer.

11 Warehousing

What do I need to study?

- What is the role of warehousing?
- List and describe the many functions of warehousing.
- Explain the importance of warehousing to trade, particularly where there is seasonal production and demand for goods and materials.
- List the types of warehousing available to organisations and private individuals.
- Describe the importance of each type of warehousing in either home or international trade.

Introduction

The aim of this unit is to introduce you to another aid to trade, warehousing. Without warehousing much home and international trade would be extremely difficult to carry out. Warehousing is defined as the **storage** of goods. Warehouses are used by commercial organisations such as manufacturers, importers, exporters, wholesalers, transporters, customs authorities and many more. They are usually large buildings equipped with loading docks to load and unload vehicles containing large quantities of goods and materials.

The need for the right sort of storage is essential to all organisations. In the case of the UK's ice-cream makers, there is an additional problem in that the product is seasonal in nature (there is high demand in warmer months and low demand in colder months). A great deal of produce therefore has to be stockpiled over the winter months to accommodate the increase in demand during the summer months. So storage – or warehousing, as it is often called – is of very high importance. In this unit, we will investigate the role of warehousing and the types of warehousing available to a wide variety of companies to store materials and goods in the short and long term.

11.1 The role of warehousing

Organisations and consumers demand a variety of goods on a daily basis. In order to ensure a ready supply of goods for retail or manufacture, organisations may choose to buy goods or materials in large quantities, known as 'bulk', and store them in warehouses. Warehousing allows organisations to purchase goods and materials for use at a later date. For example, in the UK, summer fruits such as strawberries may not be available all the time. Some manufacturers, such as ice-cream or yoghurt manufacturers, will need these ingredients all through the year, and the only way this is possible is by importing berries from overseas or freezing berries in the summer and storing them for use throughout the year. Storage of the raw materials for strawberry ice cream or yoghurt involves proper preservation from the time of purchase until they are actually used. In business we rarely use the word 'storage' these days, preferring to use the term 'warehousing'.

So what is warehousing? It is the storage or holding of properly preserved goods or materials in large quantities, from the time they are purchased or received until they are used in the production process or sold on to other customers.

Figure 11.1 shows the typical function of warehouses in traditional production firms. Parts and materials are received from suppliers and 'booked in' to the warehouse in the form of stock. When they are needed, these components or materials are then 'booked out' of the warehouse and into the production facility, where they are used in the production of finished goods. Finished goods at the end of the production process are then booked back into the warehouse until they are purchased by customers, at which time the goods are loaded on to delivery trucks and despatched. The components, materials and finished goods are moved around the warehousing facility usually by fork lift trucks – three- or four-wheeled mechanical trucks with prongs ('forks') at the front, designed for lifting and carrying large loads, often on pallets.

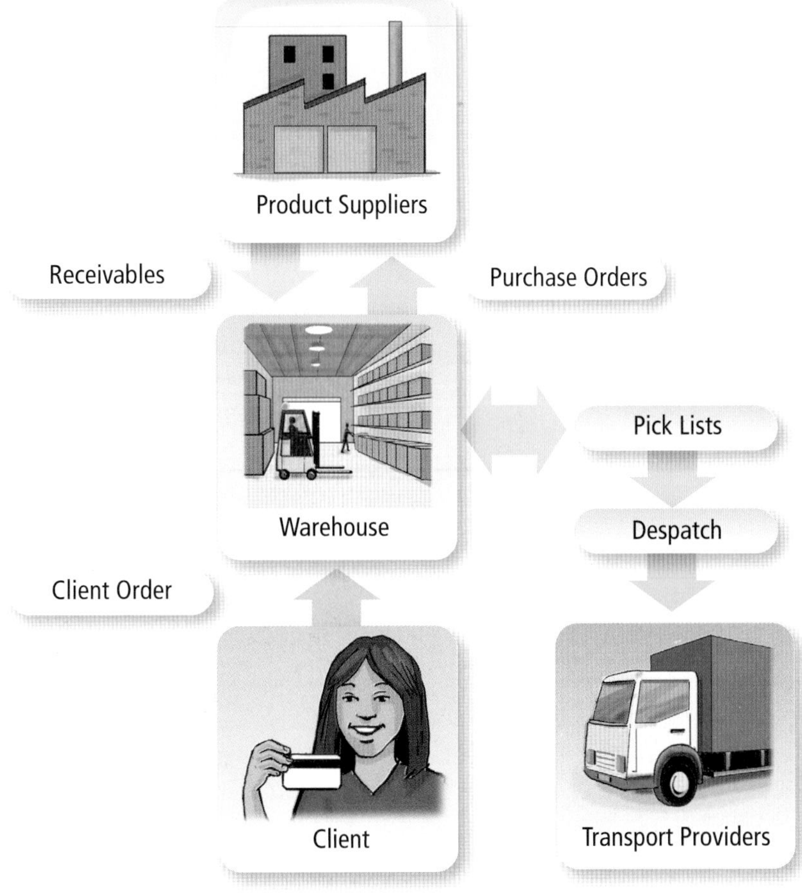

■ **Figure 11.1** *The role of the warehouse in transporting goods*

The functions of warehousing

We know that the basic functions of warehouses are to preserve goods in large quantities and protect them from the elements, so that the goods are not spoiled or wasted. Additionally, warehouses carry out other functions as described below:

- Storage of large stocks of goods from the time of purchase until their sale or use.
- Protection from loss or damage caused by extreme environmental conditions.
- Providing conditions suitable for the preservation of certain types of products or materials.
- Receiving goods or materials from suppliers.
- Processing and picking orders received from customers.
- Packing and despatching orders to customers.
- Checking the quality of goods and materials for use in the manufacturing process or selling on to retailers or final consumers.

The importance of warehousing to trade

Warehousing offers many advantages to organisations, including the following:

- Protection and security of goods and materials through careful storage, handling and use of security systems.
- Regular flow of goods and materials that can be consumed or used throughout the year.
- Possibility of continuous production because raw materials are always readily available. For example, some manufacturers will operate their production facilities 24 hours a day. Warehousing allows them to store enough materials and components to maintain production even over holiday periods (when suppliers may not be open or able to make deliveries).
- Organisations can have their own warehousing facilities, although smaller companies may find it less expensive to hire space in a larger warehouse. These self-storage facilities are growing in number. They are popular because they allow companies to be flexible – they can rent space as and when it is needed. Owning their own warehouse would require massive financial investment as land and building costs are extremely expensive.

Of the four advantages discussed above, the most important are that they offer organisations the security of a regular flow of goods and materials that can be consumed or used throughout a typical year, and therefore the main activities of the organisation need not be affected.

■ *Inside a manufacturer's warehouse*

This is extremely important when we consider the following four main reasons for warehousing:

- **Seasonal production** – Agricultural produce is affected by the seasons and most crops are harvested once or twice a year, but they are in demand the whole year round. Therefore proper storage and warehousing of these products is essential to keep them in a useable state for as long as possible.
- **Seasonal demand** – There are certain manufacturers and retailers of goods that are in demand only at certain times of the year. For example, swimming costumes and sun hats in the summer, and coats and umbrellas in the autumn. Demand varies significantly over the year, so manufacturers and retailers will build up a large stock of these goods in a warehouse. This is called 'stockpiling', and means that the goods are readily available when the seasons change.
- **Future demand** – Manufacturers produce goods to meet estimated future demand for their products. For example, when Nike plan to launch a new pair of designer sport shoes they spend months manufacturing and stockpiling millions of pairs in preparation for the forecasted demand.
- **Price stability** – It is not in the interests of organisations and their customers for prices of goods and materials to change significantly. However, this may happen if stocks of a particular product or material run low and supply becomes limited, which can lead to an increase in market price. If excessive amounts of stock or materials are available,

this will lead to a lowering in market price because supply is greater than demand. Warehouses allow organisations to maintain sufficient stock levels so that there is price stability of goods and materials in the market.

Because of the importance of warehousing to trade (discussed above) we are seeing a growth in international warehousing activity. The table below from the US Department of Commerce shows that the number of warehousing establishments in the USA almost doubled between 1997 and 2002 and the number of people employed in warehousing grew by over 600 per cent. This was mostly because of the fact that goods need to be stored to accommodate larger and more cost-efficient production runs. Also, as Internet sales increase, companies such as Amazon Books hire the services of warehousing organisations to fulfil book orders directly without actually having to have their own warehousing facilities or staff.

Growth of Warehousing 1997–2002				
Warehousing and storage				
	Establishments	Revenue	Annual payroll ($,000)	Paid employees
1997	6,497	10,657,925	2,926,119	109,760
2002	12,637	17,924,787	18,689,122	639,174

■ **Table 11.1** *The growth of warehousing in the USA 1997–2002. (Source: US Department of Commerce: Department of the Census: Economic Census)*

11.2 Types of warehousing

Warehousing is carefully designed for the different goods and materials that are being stored. There is a wide variety of warehouse types.

Private warehouses

These warehouses include those used by manufacturers and retailers as well as regional distribution centres. They are built, owned and managed by the company owners themselves:

- **Manufacturers' warehouses** – These are located close to the company's production facilities and, possibly, their customers, particularly if their products are very large and difficult to transport.
- **Regional distribution centres** – These are used by large retailers. They are usually centrally located in a country, near to good systems of transport, so that it is convenient and cheap to transport goods to their retail outlets and therefore their customers.

  Regional distribution centres are very common among supermarket retailers and other chain stores. These types of organisations buy huge quantities of goods directly from manufacturers at low prices and need somewhere to store all these products (normally stored by wholesalers). We discussed this in Unit 5 in detail. Regional distribution centres provide retailers with a network of warehouses that can easily and efficiently supply their retail outlets on a daily basis with goods and, more importantly for supermarkets, fresh foods.

  ASDA's regional distribution centre for the north of England is in Skelmersdale. It cost the company £11m (about US $19m) to build and took only 24 weeks to complete. It is a state-of-the-art (very modern) facility offering multi-temperature and fully refrigerated warehousing and distribution facilities.
- **Retail warehouses** – No matter how big or small, all retail outlets will have some sort of storage facilities or warehouse nearby. This means they always have reserve stock nearby and are therefore able to minimise the chance that they will run out of popular products. This helps them to satisfy their customers.
- **Giant barns** These 'warehouses' are used by farmers who will locate them near to their fields.

All the warehousing facilities discussed in this section are *privately owned*. It is likely that they will be built to suit the nature of the goods or materials that are stored in them. For example, the ASDA distribution centre is fully refrigerated because a large amount of goods stored there will be perishable. However, warehouses can be very expensive to build, maintain and manage. Companies considering building their own warehousing facilities need to weigh up the benefits of such an investment against its cost.

Public warehouses

These are built and managed by specialist organisations to offer organisations and private individuals warehousing facilities in exchange for rent payments. They are used by manufacturers, wholesalers, exporters and importers, and private individuals who do not have their own warehousing facilities. They can be expensive, but are a cheaper alternative to building private warehouses.

*Other than needing more storage space, why would a small **Italian** manufacturer of ski clothing, snow boards and ski equipment need a rented storage space in a public warehouse in Val d'Isère, one of the locations for the Winter Olympics in **France**?*

- **Bonded warehouses** – These are used to store goods or materials that have been imported by a company and on which 'import duty' (a form of tax) is paid. Importers will leave their goods in bonded warehouses until they sell them and they only have to pay import duty when they take the goods out of these bonded warehouses. Bonded warehouses are found near ports. Goods may be stored at a bonded warehouse for a short period of time and then shipped to another overseas location. In this case, import duties are not paid at the first bonded warehouse but will be paid at the next warehouse once the goods leave it and are sent to buyers.

  While goods or materials are in the bonded warehouse they may be packaged, processed or changed in some way. For example, fine cooking oils like olive oil may be received in large containers and then repackaged into smaller more attractive bottles. This means that the importer avoids paying the duty for as long as possible, therefore avoiding having a large sum of their money tied up in duty while the goods are still being processed. Some importers will sell the goods and as part of the arrangement the customer will agree to pay the duty.

  If goods are to be released from a bonded warehouse, a 'warrant' has to be drawn up with the details of goods to be released and to whom. To satisfy customs requirements and to ensure the correct import duties have been paid other documents need to be produced and signed by customs officials to show that duty has been paid and the goods are ready for collection from the warehouse. These are:

  i. **Customs warrant** – received from customs officials authorising the warehouse to release the goods as confirmation that the correct duty has been paid (more information on this can be found in Unit 7.3 – Customs authorities)

  ii. **Memorandum** – showing what duty was payable on the goods being released and given to the person collecting the goods

  iii. **Warehouse keeper's order** – instructs warehouse managers to release the goods because duty has been paid and ownership of the goods has been confirmed by the original warrant.

A company exporting boxes of mixed spices to food retailers across the globe imports spices from their countries of origin, in containers, by the tonne. What are the benefits of bonded warehouses and how would they apply to this particular company?

- **Cold-storage warehouses** – A great deal of fresh and processed food has to be kept in cool or freezing conditions so that it remains edible for as long as possible. Goods may be refrigerated or frozen. Some warehouses are built with refrigeration systems specifically for this reason.

- **Cash and carry warehouses** – Cash and carry wholesalers are trying to make it as cheap as possible for small independent retailers to compete with large retailers by offering goods at the lowest prices they can. Cash and carry wholesalers are able to do this because they do not send out sales people to collect orders or deliver stock to their customers. This means that the costs of running their wholesale organisation are kept as low as possible. Small retailers have to go to the cash and carry wholesaler themselves, pick their own items, put them on to a trolley and pay for them with cash as they leave. Cash and carry warehouses are a cost-free warehousing facility to small home-based retailers, who use them as their main source of retail supplies. They can collect as much or as little of what they need without being concerned about whether or not they have enough storage space themselves.

Summary of main points from Unit 11

- Warehousing is an important aid to trade, and if it was not available a lot of home and international trade would be extremely difficult.
- Warehousing means the storage of goods, and it is used by most organisations in the chain of production and distribution. Warehouses, in addition to providing storage, also protect goods from loss or damage, provide services where they receive goods on behalf of other organisations and of course will process, pick, pack and despatch orders.
- There are many types of warehousing. Each has its own purpose and function.
- Some organisations decide to have their own private warehousing facilities. Manufacturers will have warehouses for storing materials and finished goods, retailers will have small warehouses for goods before they go on the shelves and farmers have giant barns. National and international retailers often have regional distribution centres where goods are stored and then despatched to retail outlets in a certain region.
- Some organisations choose to use the specialised warehousing facilities of warehousing specialists and avoid the cost of purchasing and maintaining their own. Examples of warehouses like this include bonded warehouses, cold-storage warehouses and cash and carry warehouses.

Test your knowledge

Practice multiple choice exam questions

1) John Jones is a manufacturer of Christmas decorations. 95% of his sales are made between October and November each year. What do you think will be his most important reason for warehousing his decorations?
   a) To enable him to offer cash and carry facilities.
   b) To allow production to be ahead of seasonal demand.
   c) To store the decorations in preparation for export.
   d) To keep his decorations secure.

Test your knowledge *continued*

2) In which of the following would goods from overseas, which duties are payable on, be held until customs duties have been fully paid?
   a) Cold stores
   b) Bonded warehouses
   c) Wholesale warehouses
   d) Dockyard warehouses

3) Which of the four reasons for warehousing listed below describes the function that allows manufacturers to stockpile a new product prior to its launch?
   a) Future demand
   b) Seasonal demand
   c) Price stability
   d) Seasonal production

4) Which of the following describes the central function of warehousing?
   a) Checking the quality of goods or materials before use or sale.
   b) Picking orders (selecting goods ordered by customers off shelves so that they can be packaged and despatched to them).
   c) Despatching orders made by customers.
   d) Ensuring large quantities of goods and materials are kept secure and in saleable condition.

5) Which type of warehouse does not involve rental of storage space?
   a) Private warehouses
   b) Cold-storage warehouses
   c) Public warehouses
   d) Bonded warehouses

Practice stimulus response and structured exam questions

1) There are three kinds of warehouses in the industrial area of a large seaport, cash and carry, traditional and bonded.
   a) Describe three general functions of warehouses. (*6 marks*)
   b) Explain the importance of bonded warehouses to:
      (i) An importer of coffee who plans to sell it in the home market (*6 marks*)
      (ii) An exporter of locally produced computer software (*4 marks*) ***(CIE Commerce Paper 1 Oct/Nov 2003)***

2) a) Explain why warehousing is important to the following:
      i. A manufacturer of seasonal products (*3 marks*)
      ii. An importer of tea who then re-exports it (*3 marks*)
   b) Why should a supermarket operating in a shopping centre have a small warehouse as part of the premises? (*4 marks*) ***(CIE Commerce Paper 1 Oct/Nov 2004)***

3) Warehousing is necessary for the storage of goods.
   a) Explain two reasons why goods need to be stored. (*4 marks*)
   b) Mrs Boah owns a cash and carry warehouse. What are the benefits of this kind of warehouse for Mrs Boah and the retailers she supplies? (*6 marks*)
   c) Advise the owners of a large-scale retailing business on the importance of warehousing for their business. (*6 marks*) ***(CIE Commerce Paper 2 Specimen Paper 2005)***

4) Why do many large-scale retailers have small storage areas on their premises? (*4 marks*)
   (CIE Commerce Paper Oct/Nov 2002)

5) A furniture manufacturer has been selling to wholesalers and retailers and is considering selling directly to consumers. How will a warehouse assist this furniture manufacturer's business? (*6 marks*)
   (CIE Commerce Paper May/Jun 2002)

12 Insurance

What do I need to study?

- Describe the purposes of insurance.
- What is the statistical basis of insurance?
- Why is the 'pooling of risk' important in the insurance market?
- Identify the range of possible risks that organisations and private individuals may wish to insure against.
- Explain the basic principles of insurance.
- Explain how organisations and private individuals obtain insurance cover.
- Define the role of the insurance broker.
- How do organisations and private individuals make claims on their insurance?

Introduction

On 29 August 2005, one of the biggest hurricanes, 'Hurricane Katrina' hit the coast of America and caused a level of devastation that had never been seen before by those who lived and worked in the city of New Orleans. The whole city's population had to leave the region, not knowing whether they would ever return and, if so, what they would return to. Some buildings were knocked down and damaged beyond repair by the force of the floods caused. Nothing escaped the destructive forces of the water.

Much of New Orleans' business is tourism related with many hotels, bars and restaurants, and many people wondered if this industry would ever recover. Yet, within months of the hurricane hitting the city, company owners had returned and started to operate again, focusing on attracting tourists into the region once again. How was this possible and were all owners so lucky?

The answer to this question is that the lucky ones *were* able to recover from this devastating blow with the aid of **insurance**, the subject of this unit. Insurance is a very important aid to home and international (or foreign) trade because trade is not without risk.

Insurance – A form of agreement between an insurance company and private individuals and/or organisations. In exchange for a payment of a sum of money (called an insurance premium), private individuals or organisations are guaranteed compensation for losses to them resulting from certain events such a fire, flood or theft.

Organisations and private individuals all over the globe face a variety of risks on a daily basis that could influence the way they operate or live. Careful people insure against certain risks, so that these risks will not affect them financially if the worst happened. Those people who do not take out insurance could be left with nothing, which was the case for hundreds of thousands of people and organisations in New Orleans.

In this unit, we will investigate the role that insurance plays in making sure operations can continue after important activities have been affected by a range of factors including fire, accident and many others.

12.1 Purposes of insurance and the statistical basis of insurance

Compensation, financial protection, confidence and insurance as an investment

Organisations and private individuals take out insurance to protect them against possible financial losses caused by a range of causes or unexpected factors. This means that, should the worst happen and these losses occur, they will receive financial *compensation* from their insurance company. Therefore, insurance provides companies with *financial protection* in the event of a loss that could influence their operations.

For example, Raphael Detouri has just opened a small Italian restaurant that offers a pizza delivery service. He has two delivery vehicles which are in constant use at the weekend. During a delivery to some apartments one of the cars is broken into and stolen. Raphael tells the police but the vehicle is never found or recovered. He is a very careful company owner and has taken out a variety of different insurance policies to provide him with financial protection in such circumstances. His loss was insured, so he was fully compensated, and within a week he purchased a replacement vehicle. Although the theft caused Raphael many difficulties, he was protected by his insurance policy, which also provided him with a temporary vehicle until he was able to purchase another one with the compensation money.

Research a recent natural or man-made disaster in your own country. How were organisations and private individuals affected? You might find it useful to access newspaper articles from the library and/or from the Internet. Select two companies that are featured in the articles and describe the impact of the disaster on each one. Did they have insurance? If yes, explain what this meant to the company's recovery. If no, explain what this meant for the company's future.

Properly insured organisations can continue carrying out their daily activities knowing that – if their property was damaged by fire, flood or theft; if an employee or customer was injured accidentally and claimed compensation; or if a business partner were to suddenly die – financial compensation would be received, so that business could continue. Therefore insurance provides organisations and individuals with *confidence* and, even though insurance policies can be very costly to take out, they are regarded as an *investment*.

How insurance works

Organisations wishing to insure themselves against possible losses will take out an insurance policy with an insurance company. We will describe this process in more detail in section 12.4. Almost every company has some form of insurance and pays the insurance company a small amount every month in return for the protection they receive. This is called an **insurance premium**. The payments for insurance premiums are collected from a huge number of organisations and private individuals. It is these payments that allow the insurance companies to pay claims for compensation (as described above). This process is more commonly known as the 'pooling of risk' and is demonstrated by Figure 12.1.

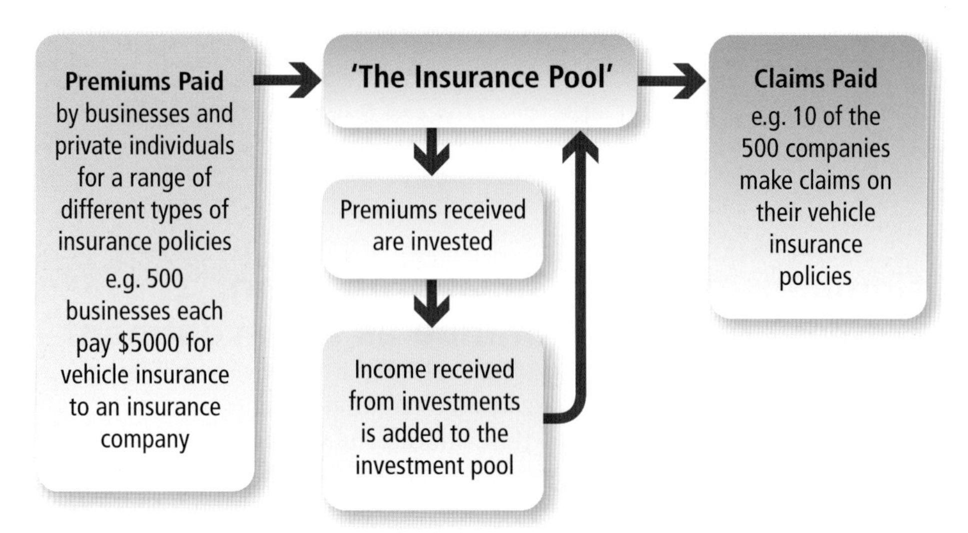

■ **Figure 12.1** *The insurance pool*

The importance of pooling of risk

Insurance companies rely on a high number of organisations and private individuals paying small premiums to cover themselves for losses that may never happen. In the unlucky minority of cases, losses do happen, and the insurance company has to compensate those policy holders, paying much more than they have actually paid in premiums. The 'pooling of risk' principle that underpins insurance means that we accept we may make payments and never need to claim on a policy. The problem with risk is that no one knows who the unlucky ones will be. It's a case of 'better safe than sorry'.

Premium prices will vary on a daily basis, depending on the quantity of premiums being paid and how many claims are being made. If fewer people pay for insurance against certain risks, but more claims are being made, this will result in a rise in premium prices. The higher the risk (or likelihood) of something happening, the higher the rate of premiums that will be charged. For example, a 55-year-old driver with 30 years' experience who has had no accidents for 15 years will pay much lower premiums than an 18-year-old driver who has just passed their driving test. Can you think why this is?

Insurance companies are like any other organisation; they provide an important service but want to make a profit. They attempt to collect premium payments with a higher value than the value of what they have to pay out in compensation claims. The premiums they collect are also invested for a financial return, so that the shareholders of the insurance company are rewarded in the form of high **dividend** payments. Dividends are covered in more detail on pages 245–6.

Any organisations or private individuals wishing to take out insurance will always be advised to obtain a number of **quotations** from a variety of different insurers so that the most cost-effective choice can be made.

Features (or benefits) of policies can vary dramatically as well. For example, vehicle insurance policies may include the use of a free hire car until your car is repaired or replaced, but not all insurance policies offer this benefit.

Theory into practice

A manufacturer wishes to insure his factory for $400,000 and its contents for $200,000. If the premium he pays for buildings insurance is $40 per $10,000 and for contents insurance it is $50 per $10,000, how much will he pay for a year's worth of buildings and contents insurance cover?

12.2 Business and personal risks

There is a range of risks, common to most commercial activities, for which insurance cover should be taken out. These risks are:

- Fire
- Theft
- Accidental damage to the property of the company
- Accidental damage to the property of others, including customers and the general public
- Accidental injury to employees, customers and the general public
- Health crises and the need for expensive medical attention
- Death.

Insurable risks

There are many risks which commercial organisations can insure themselves against. We will consider each type and the insurances available to them.

Fire, theft and natural disaster risks insurances

Insurance policies will cover policy holders for a combination of these risks. It is unlikely that they will need a separate policy for each risk.

- **Buildings and contents insurance** – This is taken out by organisations and private individuals who own their own property, to protect it and its contents from loss due to fire, flood, theft and any other natural disasters. Claims made against these policies allow property owners to rebuild, repair or, in extreme situations, replace their buildings and their contents.
- **Consequential loss insurance** – This is also a very important form of insurance, particularly to companies. This type of insurance covers, for example, loss of earnings following fire or other damage to property. It may also cover the cost of setting up another property to operate from until their usual property is habitable again.

Marine risks and insurances

- **Hull insurance** – This protects ship owners from accidental damage to their ships.
- **Ship owners' liability insurance** – This covers ship owners for possible damage to other ships or quaysides, and also for injury to passengers or crew members.
- **Cargo insurance** – This protects owners of cargo being transported by ship from the financial impact of damage to cargo or loss of cargo

when being transported. This is a very important category of insurance to importers and exporters of goods and materials by sea.

- **Freight insurance** – This provides ship owners with compensation if they are not paid for their transport services when delivering cargo.

There is a range of similar insurances related to air freight risks which are equally as important to importers, exporters (international traders) and air freight organisations.

Accident risks insurances

This category covers a wide range of possible accidental risks that could happen in the workplace or at home, while driving a vehicle, or while overseas or on holiday.

- **Employers' liability insurance** – This protects organisations against, sometimes large, compensation claims made by staff who have been hurt in an accident while carrying out the duties of their job.
- **Public liability insurance** – This protects organisations against, usually very large, compensation claims made by anyone who may have been accidentally injured while on the company premises.
- **Motor vehicle insurance** – This protects the owners and drivers of company or private vehicles if they are involved in road traffic accidents. The insurance will generally pay for car repairs or car replacements and for compensation to injured drivers and passengers.
- **Accident and health insurance** – This provides policy holders who experience accidental injury, accidental death or serious sickness, with benefits such as paid hospital expenses, medical or surgical expenses, and income payments to cover a period when they are unable to work.
- **Travel insurance** – This protects a traveller's holiday cost against possible cancellation and interruptions (e.g. flight cancellations), and also provides medical cover and cover for loss of, or damage to, property.

Business risks and insurances

There are additional commercial risks that organisations may wish to protect themselves against, for example:

- **Bad debt insurance** – This protects companies from losses caused by customers failing to pay for goods that they have accepted and received on trade credit terms.
- **Goods in transit insurance** – This protects organisations against the cost of theft or damage to goods that may be in transit (transported) to a warehouse or customer.
- **Fidelity guarantee insurance** – This protects organisations from dishonest employees who may steal cash or goods or try to defraud the company.

- **Stock insurance** – This is similar to buildings and contents insurance but specifically protects stock of a very high value in warehouses.
- **Machinery and equipment insurance** – This is similar to buildings and contents insurance but protects high-value and specialist machinery, and equipment that may have been built specifically for it, that is owned by an organisation.

Life assurance

Life assurance and life insurance – are general terms used to describe the different types of personal protection policy that exist to provide payment in the event of the death of an insured person.

We have looked at a variety of risks that organisations and private individuals can insure or protect themselves against financially. However, what would happen if one of the partners or directors died? Companies and private individuals may choose to insure (or **assure**) the life of an important individual within a firm, or the family income earner. They do this so that, if that person dies, the company or family of that individual will receive a large sum of money (and possibly a regular income) so that they are not put in financial difficulty.

Non-insurable risks

It is not possible to insure against every possible risk. Running your own organisation is a risk that may not work out. The main risks that you cannot insure against include:

- Making a trading loss
- Becoming insolvent (going out of business)
- Stock going out of date and becoming unusable.

The reasons for a company making a loss or becoming insolvent may be because it has been poorly managed or run inefficiently, or its goods or services may have become unfashionable. These factors are impossible for insurance companies to calculate and so are regarded as *uninsurable risks*.

12.3 Insurance principles

The concept of insurance will only work if a number of principles are upheld. We will investigate each one in turn:

Indemnity

This principle simply assumes to compensate (also called indemnify) the insured organisation or private individual so that their financial position is not affected by the loss. This principle means that someone seeking to take out insurance should not be able to profit from a loss incurred.

For example, if an office fire ruins computers and printers which were eight months old, the insurance company will only compensate the company for the value of the equipment. It will not necessarily buy it brand new equipment because that would mean the company has profited from the fire.

Contribution

This principle prevents an organisation or private individual from insuring against the same loss with more than one insurance company and then claiming full compensation for this loss from each company. If the risk *is* insured with several insurance companies, they will each make a contribution to the insured person or company.

For example, a laptop stolen from a sales person's car may be covered by motor insurance *and* buildings *and* contents insurance. The insurance companies that provide each type of insurance will split the compensation payment between themselves.

Subrogation

This principle assumes that once an organisation or private individual receives compensation payments against an item, such as a car which has been stolen, they do not have any ownership rights if the vehicle is recovered at a later date.

For example, imagine that a person has lost a valuable piece of jewellery and claimed compensation for its value from their insurance company, but later the jewellery is found and returned to them. They will now be required either to repay the compensation or hand over the item to the insurance company, as it is considered the property of that company.

Insurable interest

This principle assumes that any organisation or private individual wishing to insure themselves must be in a position to suffer the possible loss which they are insuring against. The company or private individual must legally own what is being insured. This principle stops organisations and private individuals from trying to gain from insurance and other people's misfortune.

For example, a shoe shop owner on a high street cannot insure the butcher's shop next door against fire or theft, because in the event of fire or theft the shoe shop owner would not actually suffer any financial loss. And why would they want to insure a company that was unrelated to them – unless they were planning to obtain insurance money illegally (by insuring premises and arranging for them to be burned down or robbed).

Similarly, an organisation can only insure a person's life if their death would be a financial problem (for example if it would be very difficult to find a suitable replacement).

Utmost good faith

Any insurance policy represents a contract between the insurer and the customer taking out the insurance. All insurance contracts are taken out under the principle of 'utmost good faith' (honesty). This means that both parties in the contract must act with utmost good faith towards one another during the negotiations before an insurance contract is agreed, and in the handling of claims afterwards.

The most important principle that arises from utmost good faith is the 'duty of disclosure'. When acting in good faith, each party to the contract has a duty to disclose (make known) during negotiations anything that they are aware of that will influence the insurance relationship or affect whether the insurer is willing to take the risk associated with the insurance policy proposed.

Customers must disclose on their insurance proposal form anything which they reasonably understand would influence the insurance company's decision in accepting the risk of providing insurance. For example, if a person wishes to take out a $2m life insurance policy but they know they have a life-threatening illness which they do not disclose this would be an example of 'non-disclosure'. If the insurance company became aware of this non-disclosure, the policy would be declared null and void (not valid) as it was not secured under the principles of utmost good faith. If an organisation insured the contents of a warehouse for $100,000 when they were actually worth only $10,000, then that non-disclosure would make the policy invalid too.

The principle also requires that the insurance company clearly states the terms and conditions of the policy, so that the company or individual can make the best choice for their requirements and understand the conditions of their policy before they make a claim.

12.4 Arranging insurance cover

Procedures

There are four main stages involved in obtaining insurance as described in the figure below.

Request for an Insurance Quotation
(usually from a number of insurance companies)

Complete an Insurance Proposal Form
Businesses and private individuals wishing to take out insurance against losses must fill in a **proposal form**. It is an application for insurance that requires the applicant to provide details about the business or themselves and what risks they wish to insure against. This information forms the basis of the contract between the policy holder and the insurance company.

Receive Cover Note
The insurance company will assess the application/proposal received and the risk associated with it. Once it has been accepted and the first premium (payment) paid, a **cover note** is issued and sent to the business or private individual who requested the insurance. A cover note is a temporary policy for use while the final policy is being prepared.

Receive Insurance Policy & Certificate of Insurance
The insurance company then issues a **final policy document** that details all the terms and conditions of the insurance agreement. A **certificate of insurance**, attached to the policy, is used if proof that the insured party has insurance is needed. For example, in the UK, to tax your vehicle you need to provide evidence that you are insured to drive.

■ **Figure 12.2** *Stages when obtaining insurance*

The role of the insurance broker

Organisations and private individuals can apply for insurance in a variety of different ways. They may arrange it:

- In person at an insurance company's local branch (office)
- Through the mail or postal service
- By phone with a call operator at the insurance company's central office
- Online through the company's Internet website.

Quite often, organisations and private individuals will use an **insurance broker**, who works on behalf of several insurance companies. The broker offers clients a range of suitable policies from these companies.

Insurance broker – A person who works on behalf of the person or organisation that requires insurance and who negotiates the terms and cover provided by the insurer in the insurance policy.

Insurance brokers can also give specialised advice on which policy will best suit the needs of a company or individual and which is most cost-effective (each insurance company will give different insurance quotations).

The broker operates as a 'middleman' between the insurance company and the people requiring insurance. For every policy they finalise with a customer they will receive a commission (money) from the insurance company issuing the policy. Some people question whether the advice they get from brokers is truly in the interests of the customer, because the broker will be motivated by the commission they receive from insurance companies, and this may vary considerably. However, the insurance industry does have a 'code of conduct' that all brokers must follow and this basically says they must act in 'good faith' – that is, honestly.

12.5 Making a claim

Procedures

There are two main stages involved in making an insurance claim, as described in the figure below.

Claim Form

If a loss happens, the insurance company is informed and it will send the insured business or private individual a **claim form** to complete. This contains the details of the claim on which the insurance company will base the compensation payments it will make to the insured party.

Compensation Received

As long as the claim and policy satisfy all the principles of insurance the insurance company will pay compensation.

■ **Figure 12.3** *The two main stages involved in making a claim*

Summary of main points from Unit 12

- Insurance is a very important aid to home and international trade because trade is not without risk.
- Insurance is defined as a form of agreement between an insurance company and private individuals and/or organisations. In exchange for a payment of a sum of money (called an insurance premium), private individuals or organisations are guaranteed compensation for losses to them because of certain events such as fire, flood or theft.
- Insurance companies collect premiums and place them in a fund called an 'insurance pool'. This money is invested by the insurance company to make the pool larger. When an organisation or individual experiences a loss they make a claim and they are financially compensated from the insurance pool. The number of people who claim is far lower than the number of people who pay premiums. The insurance company relies on this and it is referred to as 'pooling of risk'.
- There are a wide range of different insurance policies offered by insurance companies depending on the type of loss that is being insured against. These include:
  - Fire, theft and natural disaster risks and insurances, e.g. buildings and contents insurance
  - Marine risks and insurances, e.g. cargo insurance

Summary *continued*

- ☐ Accident risks and insurances, e.g. employers' liability insurances
- ☐ Business risks and insurances, e.g. goods in transit insurance
- ☐ Life assurance.

- Organisations cannot insure against making a trading loss, becoming insolvent or against stock going out of date.
- Insurance is founded on a number of key principles which you must be familiar with and may be asked to explain and give examples of. These are the principles of indemnity, contribution, subrogation, insurable interest and utmost good faith.
- There are procedures for arranging insurance cover and for making claims in the event of loss that must be followed by organisations and individuals who wish to have the security of being insured.

Test your knowledge

Practice multiple choice exam questions

1) The diagram below illustrates the 'pooling of risk' in the insurance industry. What does Y represent?

Y → Insurance Company → Compensation paid to claimants, costs of running the insurance company and profit

a) Interest
b) Premiums
c) Commission
d) Policies

2) The 'insurer' is the name given to the:
a) Insurance company providing insurance
b) Documents of insurance produced
c) Buildings or land covered by the insurance
d) Person who has requested the insurance

3) A clothes retailer insured her shop and its contents against fire and flood for $350,000 in 2004. In 2005 it was worth $370,000 and in 2006 it was worth $320,000 because less stock was being held on her premises. In 2006 the shop and its contents were destroyed by flood. How much compensation would the retailer receive from the insurance company?
a) $300,000
b) $370,000
c) $350,000
d) $320,000

Test your knowledge *continued*

4) Insurance premiums are calculated according to which of the following?
   a) The risks involved
   b) The costs involved
   c) The profits required
   d) Government laws

5) What does the insurance term 'indemnity' mean?
   a) You can only insure something you have an interest in.
   b) The risk is too high to be insurable.
   c) Insured people and organisations cannot profit from a loss.
   d) The risk carries a higher premium charge.

Practice stimulus response and structured exam questions

1) The diagram below shows the pooling of risk in insurance

   a) Explain the benefits of the pooling of risk to the 500 companies. (*3 marks*)
   b) (i) Calculate the total premiums paid to the insurance company for fire insurance. Show your workings. (*2 marks*)
      (ii) Apart from paying claims, state two other reasons for taking out insurance. (*2 marks*)
   c) Explain how the principle of insurable interest applies to each of the 500 companies. (*4 marks*)
   d) (i) Name three other business risks against which businesses may insure. (*3 marks*)
      (ii) Explain why it is important that businesses insure against these risks. (*6 marks*)

(CIE Commerce Paper 1 May/Jun 2003)

2) Mr Joseph wishes to insure his new factory.
   a) Explain why insurance is important to Mr Joseph. (*4 marks*)
   b) State two risks against which his factory should be insured. (*2 marks*)
   c) What is the difference between employers' liability insurance and public liability insurance and explain why Mr Joseph will need both types. (*6 marks*)
   d) Show how the following insurance principles will apply in relation to a valid contract of insurance for the factory:
      i. Utmost good faith (*4 marks*)
      ii. Indemnity. (*4 marks*)

(CIE Commerce Paper Oct/Nov 2002)

To address Question 2c you need to identify and describe each type of insurance, explain their main purpose, and then relate your commercial knowledge back to the fact that Mr Joseph owns a new factory.

continued ▶

Test your knowledge *continued*

3) Mr and Mrs Phiri own a warehouse.
   a) State two reasons why they should insure their warehouse. (*2 marks*)
   b) Explain the functions of this insurance of:
      i. A proposal form (*2 marks*)
      ii. A policy (*2 marks*)
   c) Their warehouse is valued at $1 million but they wish to insure for $750,000.
      i. Why would they do this? (*2 marks*)
      ii. Why is it not advisable for them to do this? (*2 marks*)
      iii. Explain how consequential loss insurance might assist them if the warehouse were to burn down. (4 marks)

(CIE Commerce Paper May/Jun 2002)

4) Mr Mohammed owns a small shop selling electrical goods. He is experiencing theft of cash by one of his employees.
   a) Name the insurance cover he should have to protect himself against dishonest employees. (*1 mark*)
   b) Describe the procedure for taking out such insurance cover. (*6 marks*)

(CIE Commerce Paper 1 Oct/Nov 2004)

5) Mr Ahmed and Mrs Singh are sole traders owning shops of equal size in the same street.
   a) Explain why Mr Ahmed may have to pay larger insurance premiums to protect against fire than Mrs Singh. (*6 marks*)
   b) Explain two business risks apart from fire against which Mr Ahmed and Mrs Singh should insure. (*4 marks*)
   c) Explain why they cannot insure their shops against the risk of bad management. (*4 marks*)
   d) Name one insurance principle and explain how it might apply to a fire insurance policy. (*6 marks*)

(CIE Commerce Paper 1 Oct/Nov 2003)

In Questions 3, 4 and 5, remember to relate your answers back to the individual case studies described in the question. This will demonstrate to the examiner that you can apply your commercial knowledge to a real situation.

13 Banking

What do I need to study?

- List and describe the range of services that banks offer to organisations.
- What methods of payment are available to organisations and private customers?
- Explain how recent trends in banking make a difference to the service received by organisations and private customers.

Introduction

Bank – This is an institution or company that provides banking services to organisations and private customers for a profit. Banks generate their profits from charging fees on each financial service or transaction they provide and from the interest they charge on money they have lent to organisations and private customers.

This unit looks at the important and wide range of services offered to organisations by banking institutions. These services include lending organisations money, possibly to buy new machinery or buildings, or providing general financial advice. Banks and the services they provide are essential services because without them new and existing companies would struggle to survive, do well and grow.

Think back to the last time you made a purchase. Did you pay with cash or by some other method? Now, consider the last time a parent or relative made a purchase. What method of payment did they use? Paying for our purchases is getting easier as we have an increasing number of different methods to choose from. It is thought that in the future we will not have any need for cash or even credit or debit cards. We will all have mobile communication devices that we can use to buy things, make telephone calls, receive e-mails and organise our daily lives. All this is made possible by advances in technology and banking services.

Organisations are no different. As they become larger the number of their transactions increases. They use a variety of banking services to ensure their transactions (payments and receipts) are made quickly, accurately and efficiently. In this unit we will look at the methods of payment available to organisations and customers and the role played by banks in providing these services. We will also look at the implications of recent trends that have influenced banking services.

13.1 Banking services

Banking services are probably the most important services a company will use. Banks provide their private and business customers with a variety of services. Some of these services are listed as follows:

- Keeping **money deposited** by customers secure
- **Making and receiving payments** on behalf of their customers
- **Loaning money** to customers
- Providing **financial advice on commercial activities** such as what sources of money or finance would be most suitable to an organisation or how it can improve the flow of cash through the business or how it can keep the company going during difficult trading periods etc.
- Offering a wide variety of **financial services** such as insurance.

Look at the following diagram. It illustrates the range of services offered by banks to businesses.

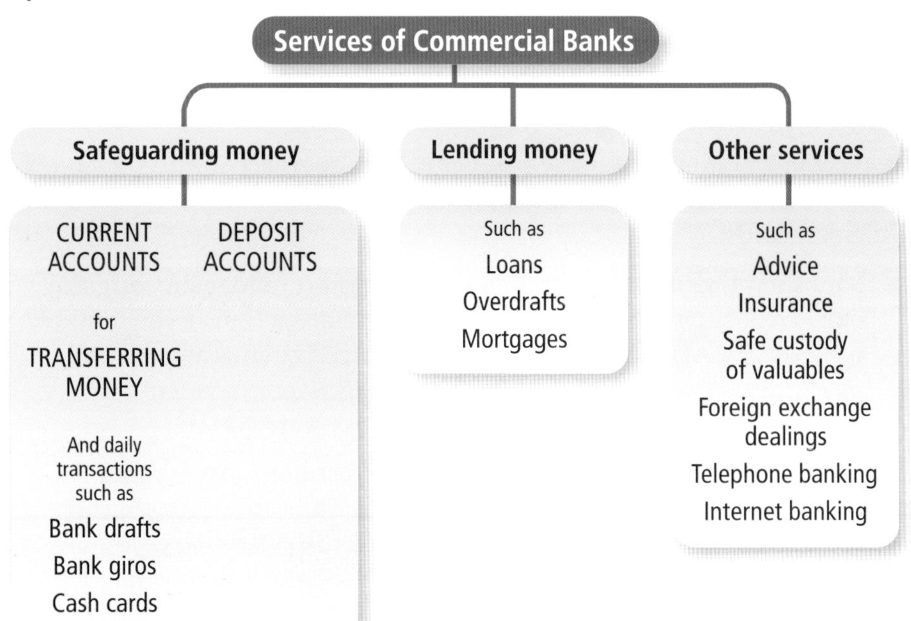

Figure 13.1 *Services offered to businesses by banks*

Think it over…

You are considering starting your own small company retailing personal computers and computer accessories from a high street retail outlet. Consider Figure 13.1 which details all the services offered by commercial banks. Select three services and briefly explain why they would be of particular interest to you and your new business opportunity.

Types of bank account

Bank accounts offered to both private and business customers can be put into two main categories.

Current or cheque accounts

These are very important to both private and business customers. Current accounts allow the customer to access their money with no delay on a daily basis. A customer who opens a current account will receive a cheque book and debit cards which they can use to make payments for goods or services or to withdraw cash at banks or cash machines (automatic teller machines or 'ATMs').

Becoming overdrawn – happens to an account holder who withdraws more money from the account than it actually holds at that time. If you are overdrawn, you will probably have to pay an interest charge. This charge will be based on the amount that you are overdrawn by.

Business account holders usually pay charges for each business account they have and for the transactions they make. This is how the bank covers its running costs and makes profits. In general, private account holders do not have to pay any charges for their accounts unless they **become overdrawn** or choose to access other services.

Benefits of current accounts to their users

- Their money is safe. Money kept at home or in an office might be stolen or lost.
- It is easy to open a current account. The individual or business customer will need to fill out an application form and then provide proof of identification, the signature of the person responsible for the account and, sometimes, an amount of money to be deposited.
- Account holders can make payments from their accounts in a variety of ways, using cash withdrawn from ATMs, by cheque or by debit or credit cards.
- Banks send regular statements to each account holder showing the balance of their account and details of all transactions (when money has been moved into or out of the account). Statements are very important as they allow account holders to watch payments and receipts and to check that all the transactions are correct.
- Banks can provide overdraft facilities to customers. An overdraft allows the customer to spend more money than they have in their account for a short period of time. The overdraft limit is set by the bank so that the customer does not go above a reasonable amount. Customers have to pay interest on the amount they are overdrawn by. This interest is charged daily for the time their account is overdrawn. Overdrafts are important to business account holders who may need to make payments to suppliers before they have received money owed to them by customers. The organisations can use their overdrafts until the money they are waiting for has been received. This means that they can pay their suppliers on time and receive any discounts that the suppliers may be offering for early payment.

- Banking services make it easier for organisations to pay their employees' wages. Organisations can use 'credit transfer' services to automatically move money from the business's account to the accounts of their employees. This and other forms of payment will be covered later in this unit.

Theory into practice

Visit your local bank and ask for leaflets or information on the accounts they offer to business customers. Identify three benefits of a business **current account** that are likely to be useful to a small restaurant owner, who serves about 50 customers a night over the summer season but has to close the restaurant over the winter months and has seven members of staff to pay. Make sure you explain your answer fully.

Deposit or savings accounts

Some individual or business customers may have money left over after their regular outgoings or expenses have been paid. They may choose to put these savings in a deposit or savings account. Money is deposited with the bank and in return the customer may receive some **interest** on the balance of the account.

Interest – the amount of money received by an account holder from the bank for letting them use (invest) your money while it is in their care. The bank will pay an agreed interest rate, which is the same for all savings account holders.

Interest is the main reason why customers would choose to have their money in a deposit or savings account rather than a current account. Most current accounts do not receive any interest payments, although competition has meant that a lot of banks have begun offering interest to try to attract customers from other banks.

The money in savings accounts can be withdrawn whenever customers want, although if they wish to withdraw a large amount they sometimes need to give the bank advance warning. These accounts are used for storage or deposit of money, unlike current or cheque accounts.

Theory into practice

Sheridan Industries Ltd is having a very successful trading period. The accountant, Miss Sidhu, has noticed that there is a large amount of money sitting in the business's current account. You have advised her that the money would be better off in a deposit or savings account.

1 What benefits might a savings or deposit account bring to Sheridan Industries Ltd?

Documents and forms used by deposit and current account holders

Paying-in slips

When a customer wishes to pay cash or cheques into a deposit or current account, they will have to complete a 'paying-in-slip'. Account holders are usually given a paying-in book full of these slips and they may also find paying-in slips at the back of their cheque book. The paying-in slip will include the following information:

- The date that the deposit was made
- The name of the account holder
- The name of the person paying the money or cheques in
- The account number to which the payments will be made
- The sort code of the account holding bank
- Details of what is being paid in, e.g. how many $10 bills
- The name of the bank where the account is held.

The person making the payment fills in the slip. They then take it and the money to the bank cashier, who checks that the details on the paying-in slip are correct and agree with the amount being paid in. The cashier stamps and initials the paying-in slip, which has two parts: the main slip and the counterfoil. You will recognise the counterfoil because it is divided from the main paying-in slip by a line of perforations (tiny holes). If you tear gently down this line the counterfoil can be easily removed. The cashier then gives the counterfoil back to the person making the payment. This is proof for their records that the payment was made.

Theory into practice

Look at the blank paying-in slip below.

Using the following details, complete the paying-in slip as if you were making a deposit:

- Name of account holder is Alex James
- Name of person making the payment is your name
- Account to which the payment is being made is 098776544
- Name of bank is Security Bank Plc
- Branch sort code is 34-09-76
- The following is being paid in:
  - cheque for $253
  - notes ($10 x 2, $5 x 8)

Date

Cashier's stamp

Paying-in slip

Paid in by

TheMoneyBank

Reference:

No. of Chqs/POs

Account

Sort Code

Account Number

$50 Bills	
$20 Bills	
$10 Bills	
$5 Bills	
$2 Coins	
$1 Coins	
25¢	
10¢ and 5¢	
1¢	
Total Cash	
Total Chqs	

Please do not write or mark below this line or fold this voucher

TOTAL $

Bank statements

The bank will keep a record of every transaction made in each customer's bank account, whether it is money coming into the account or going out. The bank will then send all customers a bank statement which lists all this information, usually monthly. Account holders should check all the transactions on the statement against their own records to make sure they are accurate.

The Money Bank

PO Box 49368, New Delhi

Mr Mukherjee,
PO Box 360773,
New Delhi

Account Number: 10045321
Sort Code: 90-99-19

Statement Number: 17
Page: 1 of 1

TRANSACTION DETAILS

DATE	DESCRIPTION		DEBITS	CREDITS	BALANCE
Balance brought forward					35.00
6 May	CD07	Silk Supplies Ltd	10.00		25.00
8 May	DC07	Kapoor Industries	3.00		22.00
11 May	BACS	Cutting edge Fashions		46.50	68.50
19 May	DD	Wages	16.50		40.30
22 May	SO	Kapoor Industries	21.00		19.30

■ **Figure 13.2** *A bank statement*

Theory into practice

Enter the following details and transactions in the blank bank statement below. Calculate the closing balance of the account on 31st July 2005.

TheMoneyBank

PO Box 49368, New Delhi

Account Number:
Sort Code:

Statement Number:
Page:

TRANSACTION DETAILS

DATE	DESCRIPTION		DEBITS	CREDITS	BALANCE
Balance brought forward					

- Name of account holder is Sri. Prakash Joshi
- Account to which the statement relates is 098776544
- Name of bank is Bank of India Plc and its address is 84, Rajaji Salai, Chennai, Tamil Nadu
- Branch sort code is 34-09-76
- Balance brought forward from 1/7/05 is $34.50
- Transactions are:

2/7/05	Cheque 115234 drawn	$23.50
6/7/05	Cheque 115235 drawn	$54.00
10/7/05	Deposit 6543 (cheque 78654)	$345.00
12/7/05	Cash dispensed – 84 Rajaji Salai	$60.00
15/7/05	Direct Debit paid	$46.70
19/7/05	Deposit 6544 (cheque 678946)	$42.00
29/7/05	Bank charges	$6.80

13.2 Means of payment for home and international trade activities

The most common methods that private individuals and organisations use to pay for goods and services are cash, debit card payments and cheques, although there are many other methods of payment that could be used. In this section of the unit we will investigate the features, purpose and documents of each method of payment.

Cash

These are the notes and coins that circulate between customers, organisations and banks. They are referred to as 'legal tender' and represent guaranteed payment to whoever receives the money. Cash is a suitable method for immediate payment of small amounts, for example, when you are buying a newspaper or paying a bus fare. Some companies still pay wages using cash, which they place in pay packets with a payslip. Organisations will also keep small amounts of cash in their offices called 'petty cash'. They will use this for small transactions, for example, if an office printer needs a new ink cartridge and they have to buy one from a local shop.

Cheque

A cheque is a written instruction from an account holder to a bank requesting that the bank pay an amount of money from the customer's account to another person's account. Customers are given cheque books when they open their account. Each cheque book contains a set of printed forms to be filled in, signed and then given out as cheques. Each cheque has a counterfoil which is kept by the account holder so they can check it against their bank statements. Cheques can be **crossed** or **open**.

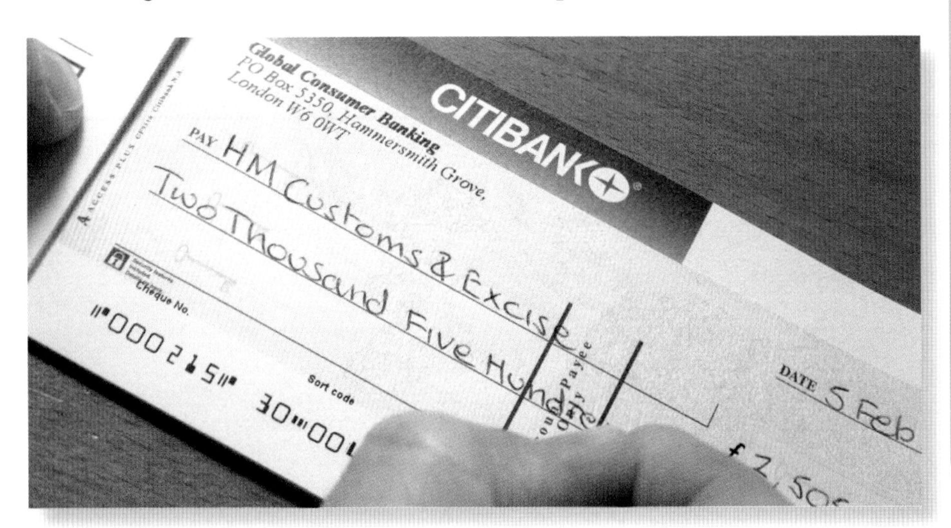

■ *An example of a crossed cheque*

Crossed cheque – a cheque that must only be paid into the account of the person named on the cheque. It is clearly marked with two parallel lines drawn across the cheque, usually with the words 'not negotiable' or 'Account Payee' written between them. This means that the cheque cannot be passed on to anyone else as payment.

Open cheque – a cheque that has not been crossed and which is considered to be 'negotiable'. This means that it can be changed for cash at a bank and does not necessarily need to be paid into a bank account. Some organisations may sign over or **endorse** open cheques to other traders as payment.

Endorsing – is when the person who has received an open cheque signs the back of it and gives it to someone else as a payment. This doesn't happen very often these days because open cheques are not very secure. There is no guarantee that there will be any money in the bank account when the cheque is presented to the cashier at the bank.

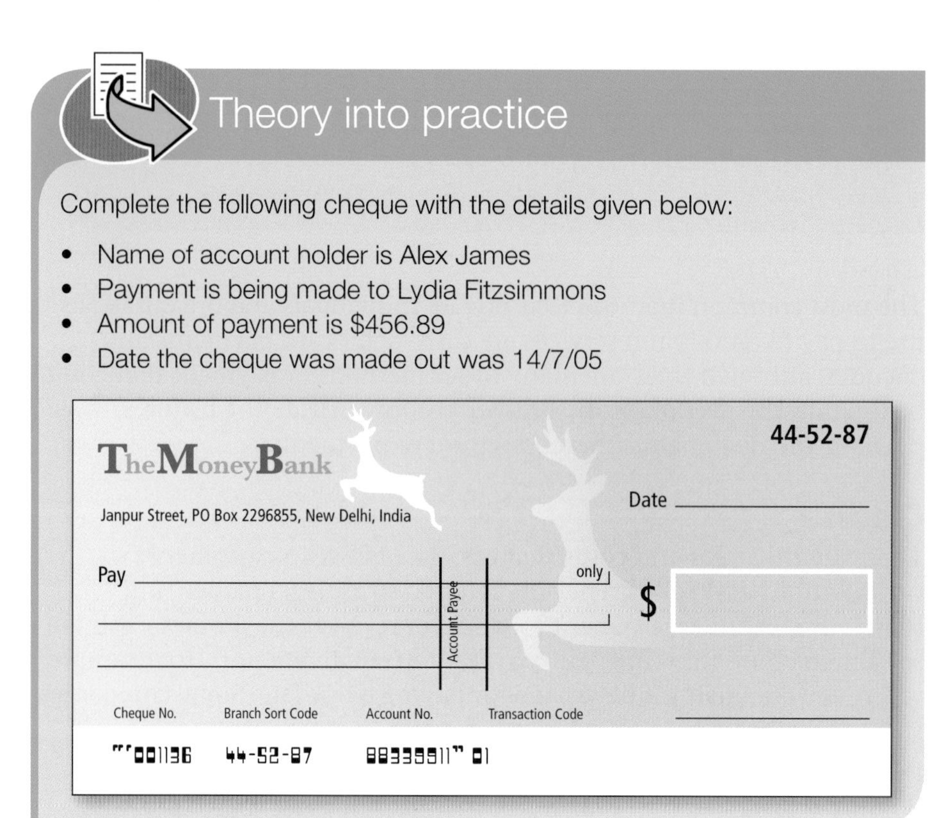

Advantages of cheques to business

- They are more secure than cash, which can be lost or stolen. If a cheque is lost it can be cancelled and a new cheque sent by the customer.

Disadvantages of cheques to business

- A cheque has 'cleared' when you receive notification that the money has gone into your account. Sometimes cheques can take a great deal of time to clear.
- Cheques may 'bounce'. This happens when the person who wrote the cheque does not have enough money in their account to cover the amount of the cheque. The cheque is usually crossed through and the letters R/D written through the lines, which means 'refer to drawer' which is a phrase used by banks to mean a cheque has been dishonoured or 'bounced'.
- If a cheque is not paid in within 6 months, it becomes unusable.

Standing orders (SO)

Private or business account holders may ask their banks to make regular payments automatically on their behalf for fixed amounts of money. The bank will make these payments until they are told by the account holder to stop them. These payments are known as standing orders (SO). They are used to pay for long-term loans such as mortgages, for regular bills like rent and rates, or to make payments to insurance companies.

Direct debits (DD)

Direct debits are similar to standing orders but instead of asking the bank to make a payment on your behalf, the direct debit gives an organisation or an individual permission to withdraw money directly from your account for a set period of time. The account holder completes a document called a 'Direct Debit Mandate' which is given to the bank as proof that they have given permission for an amount of money to be taken from their account at regular times. Payments by direct debit are regular payments of variable amounts and are usually used for utility bills such as electricity, gas or telephone bills which have to be paid regularly but the amount of money owed may vary.

Standing orders and direct debits are convenient because once the forms have been filled out the payments are automatic. This means that the account holder doesn't have to remember to make payments or post cheques every week or month.

Theory into practice

A friend of yours wants to start their own shoe retail business. They have found the perfect premises and are in the process of purchasing them. They can pay their mortgage by standing order or direct debit.

Explain to your friend how the two payment types differ and the advantages of each to their business.

Consider what you have told your friend about these different payment types and describe when a payment by standing order would be generally used instead of direct debit?

Credit transfer (CT)/bank giro credit

Credit transfers are automatic transfers between bank accounts. They are used for making single payments and when large numbers of different payments are being made at the same time; for example, paying salaries or wages from the bank account of an organisation into the bank accounts of its employees. Credit transfers can take place between different banks. Organisations will collect the bank account details of their employees and on 'payday' they will calculate what the employee is owed, provide them with a detailed payslip (showing how their pay has been made up) and using credit transfer, automatically pay the sum of money owed straight into the employees' bank accounts. It is a very simple method of payment and more secure than handing out cash pay packets. Credit transfer also reduces the possibility of mistakes in counting out cash.

Credit card

Most, if not all, banks issue credit cards to organisations and private individuals. A credit card holder can buy goods or services from organisations that accept payment by credit card. Using credit cards allows private individuals or organisations to purchase goods or services immediately and to pay for them later (unlike debit cards which we will discuss later).

Every month, the holder of a credit card receives a credit card statement detailing all the items they have bought up to a specified date, any interest they need to pay and the total balance that should be paid to the credit card company. The business or individual can choose to pay the whole balance or make just a minimum payment. However, if they only make a minimum payment then they will have to pay interest on the amount that is left. Using a credit card in this way is like having a very short-term loan. However, if the whole of the credit card account balance is not paid off at the end of each month, it is likely the credit card holder will have to pay a very high interest rate (also known as the Annual Percentage Rate or APR). In fact, APRs for credit cards are usually much higher than the rates for a medium- or long-term loan from a bank. If someone needs to take out a loan but will not be able to pay it back in less than six months, they may be better off getting a bank loan rather than building up a large credit card debt.

Credit card companies offer interest-free periods and free gifts to get organisations or private individuals to apply for a card with them. They know that each card holder could potentially earn them a great deal of money in interest charged.

Advantages to businesses of using credit cards

- Businesses may use credit cards to purchase goods and services now and pay for them later when they have money available to them. But remember, this may cost more money in interest payments.
- Businesses accepting credit cards as a payment method may find customers are more likely to buy expensive goods and services like new furniture or a holiday than if they had to pay by debit card straight from their own bank account. If they had to save the cash first they might never save enough to pay for these expensive goods and services. Businesses accept credit cards to encourage customers to spend more.

Disadvantages to businesses of using credit cards

- Businesses that choose to accept credit cards have to agree to pay their credit card company between 1 and 3 per cent of the sales value made by credit card by customers. This is a charge for the privilege of using the credit service to enable them to sell a product or service to a customer.

Theory into practice

Give one advantage and one disadvantage to a credit card holder of purchasing goods and services with their card. Give one advantage and one disadvantage to a retailer of accepting credit cards.

Debit card and electronic transfer

A debit card looks very similar to a credit card but it works in a totally different way. Debit cards have almost replaced the need to use cheques in retail outlets. All bank current account holders are given a debit card to use as an alternative to cash or cheques when paying for goods or services.

A debit card is very convenient to use. Customers are able to go into almost any retail outlet and pay for an item using their bank debit card. This is because there is a computer system in place all over the world known as the 'Electronic Funds Transfer at the Point of Sale' (EFTPOS) system. When the customer uses their debit card in a shop, the system automatically transfers money from the purchaser's bank account to the account of the retailer. This means that customers do not need to carry large amounts of cash around with them.

A debit card is different from a credit card because the transaction is *instant*. The money is taken out of the card user's bank account and put straight into the bank account of the business or retailer at the time of the transaction. If the customer chose to pay with a credit card, they would not have to pay for the item until the end of the month when they receive their credit card statement.

Advantages of debit cards to customers

Debit cards are a very secure way of paying for goods and services. The payments are very fast and there is no longer any need to carry large quantities of cash around.

Recently, there has been a new development in the way debit card payments are made. We call it 'chip and PIN'. It has made it even easier to make payments by debit card. Customers no longer need to sign receipts to prove that a card is theirs. All they need to do is enter a secret, personal number code called a PIN (Personal Identification Number) into a key pad in the shop. This has also meant that retailers have been able to speed up the process of serving customers and taking payments.

Chip and PIN – is a banking scheme designed to make debit and credit card payments more secure. When a customer pays for goods with their debit or credit card, they authorise the sale by typing a Personal Identification Number (PIN) into a special device instead of signing the receipt. This prevents crime by people who used to steal bank cards and then forge the card holder's signature on the receipt.

■ *Some debit cards now have chip and PIN technology*

Theory into practice

David's martial arts company has been operating very successfully. In fact he has decided to expand his company and offer private security services to a range of customers, from local celebrities to retailers, transporting large quantities of cash to their banks at the end of the working day. David's clients prefer not to make cash payments for his services. He has employed two full-time security staff to cope with the demand for his new services.

1 Suggest ways that his clients may prefer to make payments for his services. List the advantages and disadvantages of these payment methods.

2 Why is it safer to use credit or debit cards for payments than to use cash?

3 David has been paying his staff with cash. Can you suggest an alternative to him and describe the advantages of that approach?

Documentary credit

Documentary credits are sometimes known as 'letters of credit', 'documentary letters of credit' and 'commercial letters of credit'. They are used by organisations who import goods to pay their exporting suppliers. The whole payment process is carried out by document and not by electronic transfer of funds. The importer will ask their bank to draw up a documentary credit. This is then given to the exporter who can use it to get payment from a particular bank as long as they provide documentary evidence to show that the goods they wish to receive payment for have definitely been sent. This speeds up payment. These documents are very formal and must be prepared by specialists. They usually contain the following details:

- How much will be paid
- When the money can be paid
- What goods are being exported and where are they being shipped from
- What documents need to be shown to the bank before payment can be received such as:
  i. packing list
  ii. signed invoice
  iii. bill of lading
  iv. relevant insurance relating to the goods being shipped.

The exporter will not be paid until they have provided evidence that the goods have been despatched as set out in the original agreement of sale.

Banker's draft

A draft is a bank's own cheque and is accepted by all organisations because they know that payment is guaranteed by the bank. As we discussed earlier, a personal cheque received from a customer in exchange for goods or services could 'bounce' if the customer does not have enough money in their account to pay the cheque. This would mean that the organisation does not receive the cash they are owed. If a company is selling an expensive item like a car they will ask to be paid by cash, credit card or a banker's draft before letting the customer drive it away. It is unlikely they will accept a cheque.

13.3 Trends in banking

Automatic teller machines (ATMs)

Most banks have a variety of ATMs inside and outside their buildings to allow account holders to withdraw cash 24 hours a day. To provide an even better service banks are putting ATMs in town centres, outside petrol stations and outside supermarkets, to name just a few locations.

To withdraw money, account holders must put their cash card (which is almost always a debit card) into the ATM and enter their unique personal identification number (PIN). The ATM will provide the money required by the account holder if the PIN is correct and the account holder has not requested more money than they have in their account.

Customers can also use the ATMs to print out statements of their recent transactions, to make requests for cheque books or paying-in books and, in some cases, to make deposits into their account. Some ATMs even allow customers to top up the limit on their mobile phones. Who knows what else we will be able to do through ATMs in the future?

Call centre – the focus of activity for telephone-based service providers. Bank call centres provide customers with banking information or a range of banking services. Call centres are buildings full of specially trained staff who deal with thousands of banking enquiries over the telephone so that customers can get information without needing to go to a branch of their bank.

Telebanking

It is no longer necessary for customers to go into their banks to carry out financial transactions or to ask for financial advice. Many of these services are now provided over the phone by banks offering their customers 24-hour access to specially trained staff working from **call centres**. When a customer calls the centre, certain code words will be requested to confirm the identity of the caller. This is referred to as 'telebanking'.

The call centre staff can tell account holders how much money they have in their account and what payments or receipts have been made. Customers can also transfer money between their accounts, obtain financial advice, make payments or even apply for loans or mortgages by telephone.

Internet banking

The Internet has allowed banks to offer more advanced services to their customers. Many banks now offer Internet banking services, enabling customers to look at their accounts online, 24 hours a day. After they have provided a password to confirm their identity, the Internet service gives account holders access to their bank balances, the interest rates they are being paid, or are paying, and details of their transactions without the customer having to use the phone or go to a branch of their bank. The use of Internet banking has improved access to information and the level of customer service provided.

Summary of main points from Unit 13

- A bank is an institution or company that provides banking services to organisations and private customers for a profit. Banks make their profits from charging money for each financial service or transaction they provide and from the interest they charge on money they have lent to organisations and private customers.
- Banking services include receiving money from organisations and private customers in the form of deposits to keep secure, lending money to organisations and private customers for a wide number of uses including buying property, vehicles or investing in the growth of a company, and commercial transactions such as sales made by credit or debit cards in retail outlets. Many banks also offer a range of other financial services such as business or personal insurances or investment packages.
- Every organisation and probably almost every person will have a bank account. Banks offer different accounts for different purposes. You will need to understand the purpose and use of current accounts and deposit/savings accounts. You may be asked in the exam questions about the documents and forms used by account holders to deposit money or withdraw funds from their account.
- Interest is the amount of money received by an account holder from the bank for letting them use their money while it is in the bank's care. The bank will pay an agreed interest rate which is the same for all savings account holders.
- There are many ways in which traders can make payments to suppliers including paying by cash or setting up standing orders. In the exam you may be asked to identify and describe a range of payment methods and suggest suitable methods for given circumstances.

Test your knowledge

Practice multiple choice exam questions

The diagram below shows a cheque. Look at it and answer question 1 below.

1) On which date will this cheque become out of date?

20 April 2006 70-56-64

MODERN BANK OF MAURITIUS

Pay *F Patel* Or Order

The sum of *One hundred and fifty dollars* *$150*

John Chang

a) 20th February 2007
b) 20th January 2007
c) 20th October 2006
d) 20th December 2006

2) The words 'Account Payee only' are regularly written as part of a crossing on a cheque. This means:
a) It must be paid into the bank account of the named payee on the cheque.
b) It can be paid into any account at the bank named on the cheque.
c) It can be cashed by the named payee at any bank.
d) It can only be paid into an account at the bank on which it is drawn.

3) A banker's draft is:
a) A refusal from the bank to allow an overdraft on an account.
b) A request for a transfer of money from one account to another.
c) A cheque issued by the bank.
d) A cheque that can be bounced if there are insufficient funds.

4) You sign a finance agreement for $8000 to purchase a new car and authorise your bank to pay monthly instalments on your behalf from your bank account to the lending company's bank account. This is an example of:
a) A cheque
b) A credit transfer
c) A direct debit
d) An electronic transfer

5) Which of the following is a secure way of paying employee wages and salaries?
a) Cash
b) Credit transfer
c) Direct debit
d) Standing order

Test your knowledge *continued*

Practice stimulus response and structured exam questions

1) Commercial banks offer many services.
   a) Distinguish between deposit accounts and current accounts. (*4 marks*)
   b) Name a bank service which could be used in payment of wages to employees. Give a reason for its use. (*2 marks*)
   c) You could either use a standing order or direct debit to repay your mortgage. Which would you recommend? Give reasons for your choice. (*3 marks*)
   d) State and explain two trends in commercial banking as the result of advancing information technology. (*6 marks*)

(CIE Commerce Specimen Paper 2 2005)

2) A trader can be paid by cheque or banker's draft.
   a) State two features of a cheque. (*2 marks*)
   b) State two features of a banker's draft. (*2 marks*)
   c) Why might a trader be more willing to accept a bank draft rather than a cheque in payment for a debt? (*4 marks*)

(CIE Commerce Paper 1 May/Jun 2004)

3) Mrs Sibanda is a retailer who owns two small shops. Why may Mrs Sibanda need the following services from a bank?
   a) A current account (*4 marks*)
   b) A night safe? (*3 marks*)

(CIE Commerce Paper 1 May/Jun 2004)

4) Josaphine and Boniface own a shop.
   a. They accept debit cards but not credit cards as payment for goods.
      i. Explain why they have decided to accept debit cards and not credit cards. (*4 marks*)
      ii. State and explain one possible disadvantage to their business of not accepting credit cards. (*3 marks*)

(CIE Commerce Paper Oct/Nov 2002)

5) Explain why retailers will usually accept each of the following in payment of debts.
   a) i. Cash (*3 marks*)
      ii. Cheques (*4 marks*)
      iii. Credit cards (*4 marks*)
   b) Distinguish between a credit card and a debit card. (*4 marks*)
   c) You wish to pay $500,000 for a consignment of goods you have imported. What method of payment would you recommend? Give reasons for your answer. (*5 marks*)

(CIE Commerce Paper 1 Oct/Nov 2003)

Question 5b asks you to 'distinguish' between two types of card. Here you are expected to clearly describe the features of each type of card and then explain the differences between them.

14 The business unit

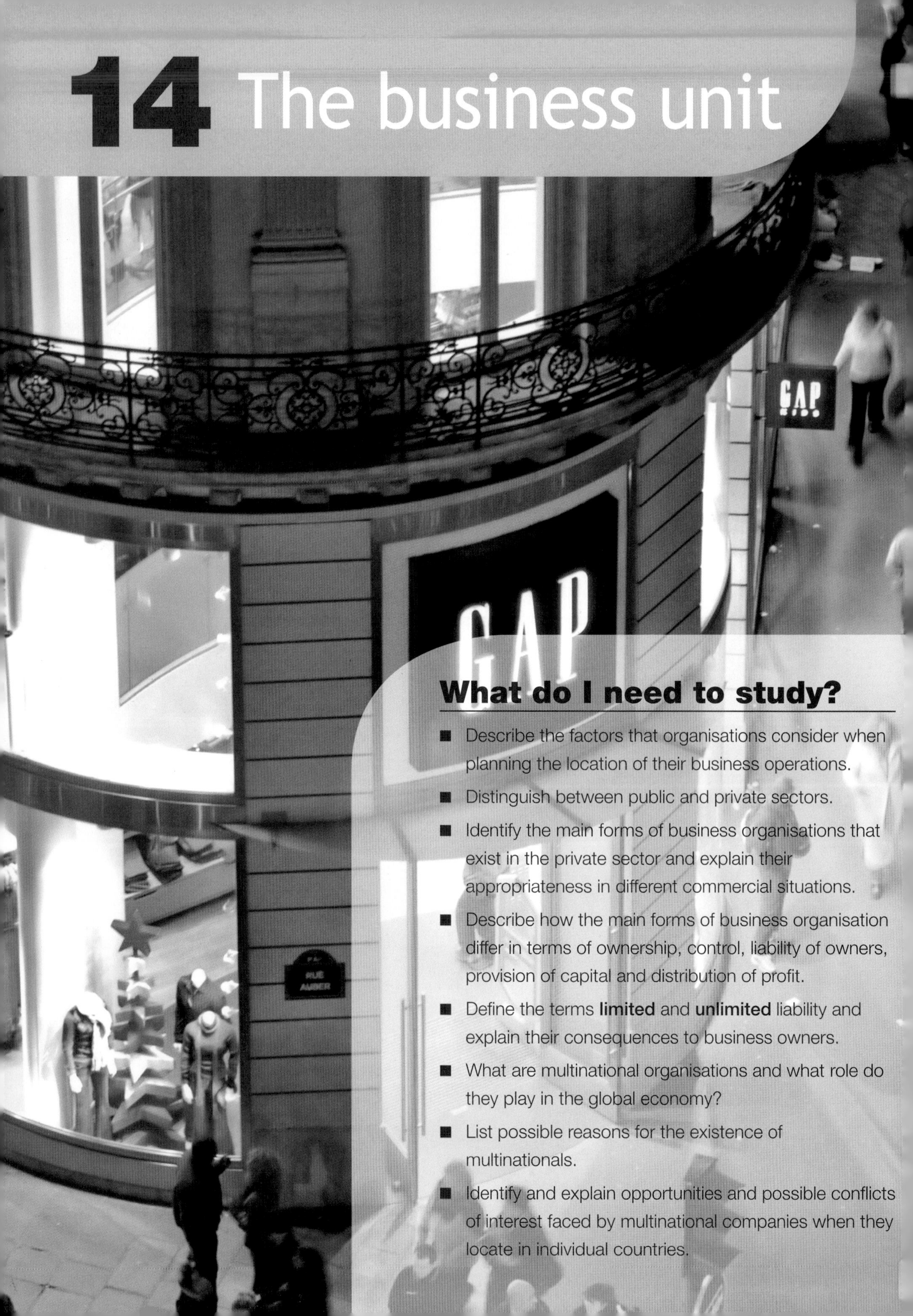

What do I need to study?

- Describe the factors that organisations consider when planning the location of their business operations.
- Distinguish between public and private sectors.
- Identify the main forms of business organisations that exist in the private sector and explain their appropriateness in different commercial situations.
- Describe how the main forms of business organisation differ in terms of ownership, control, liability of owners, provision of capital and distribution of profit.
- Define the terms **limited** and **unlimited** liability and explain their consequences to business owners.
- What are multinational organisations and what role do they play in the global economy?
- List possible reasons for the existence of multinationals.
- Identify and explain opportunities and possible conflicts of interest faced by multinational companies when they locate in individual countries.

Introduction

So far in this text book we have looked at many aspects of commerce and trade. This unit looks at the many different types of company that exist in our economies. By the end of this unit you will be able to classify organisations as belonging to either the **public** or **private sector** and understand the aims and objectives of organisations in each.

We will look closely at the many forms of private sector organisation that exist and how these forms change as organisations grow and develop. In addition, this unit will give you an understanding of the basic decisions that concern a company from the first phase of setting up and at each stage in its development or growth, including decisions such as where to get the capital to invest in a business and where the best place to locate business activities is.

Public sector – This sector includes all the enterprises run or operated by a country's government. These enterprises exist to provide free services to the public using money raised by taxing the public. Examples are national health services and national security services, including the military.

Private sector – This sector includes most commercial or profit-oriented organisations that are privately owned by one or many people. They include your small local grocery store that is likely to be owned and run by one person.

■ *The National Health Service in the UK is an example of a public sector organisation*

14.1 Location of a business

All businesses, new ones and businesses that have been operating for many years, have to find the best location for their business to do well, as we saw in the introduction.

Businesses will attempt to find a location that satisfies a number of basic requirements:

- It is cheap to purchase or rent
- It helps to minimise the costs of production and distribution
- It is near and/or accessible to suppliers for raw materials
- It is near and/or accessible to customers (wholesalers, retailers and/or the general public)
- It is convenient for skilled employees
- It is located far enough away from direct competitors.

Things that organisations consider when deciding on the location of a business include the following:

1. Supply of skilled labour – All businesses need skilled and experienced employees. Whether the business is a service like a bank, or manufacturing based, it will need to be located near to centres of population that will provide a workforce with the skills and qualities it needs. This is one of the reasons why you find similar organisations operating in the same regions. For example, a newspaper printing company might set up its production facility near other printing companies because they know there is an availability of skilled labour. However, the problem with this is the increased competition for skilled and experienced workers. Companies may have to offer very attractive pay to attract and keep high-quality staff from competitors.

2. Transport systems and networks – We investigated different transport systems (air, land and sea) used by business in detail in Unit 10. Companies will often choose a location near to established road networks, ports or railway terminals, depending on the raw materials and the goods and services they provide. For instance, car manufacturing organisations are usually located in the centre of a country, so that it is easy and cheap to distribute finished cars to retailers. They will also choose a location near other car manufacturers because there is a guaranteed supply of skilled employees. And their location will be near to steel suppliers so that these heavy raw materials do not have to be transported too far. Finally, they will want to be near an established road network so that employees can come from a wide distance in an acceptable length of travel time. As you can see, the location decisions made by organisations will rely on the types of activities they perform and their specific needs.

3. Nearness to raw materials – Businesses that are in the 'primary sector', extracting minerals from the earth, fishing or utilising the land in agriculture, have a limited choice of location and have to be near where these natural resources can found. Manufacturers that rely on bulky and heavy raw materials in huge quantities will usually put their factories near to constant and reliable sources of these materials. However, organisations that use raw materials that can easily be transported over long distances are not so limited in their choice of location.

4. Nearness to suitable utilities and other services
In the same way that it is important for some organisations to be close to sources of raw materials, some organisations may only be able to operate if they have access to utilities such as a supply of energy like electricity or gas. Other services such as, for example, waste management services may be particularly important if your business produces harmful waste products that need to be disposed of by professionals.

5. Nearness to markets
Just as it is important be close to populated areas for a source of employees, some organisations, particularly those offering services, like hairdressers and convenience stores, also need to be near where people live. It is in populated areas that they will find their target customers and where the demand for their products or services exists.

14.2 Public and private sector

Most commercial or profit-oriented organisations are privately owned. They are said to belong within the **private sector**. In some countries a wide variety of enterprises are run or operated by their governments. These enterprises exist to provide services to the public using money raised by taxing the public. They are said to belong within the **public sector**. Most countries have a mixed ownership or economy where many different types of private and public sector organisations exist.

Public sector

All the organisations or enterprises that exist in this sector are operated and managed by governments. For example, in some countries schools are publicly run so that every member of the public has the right to school and education services. If only private sector enterprises offered education and schooling, they would want to make a profit and charge prices that not everyone in the country could afford to pay. But keeping schools and education in the public sector means that governments can use taxes paid by the public to ensure access to education for everyone, not just those who can afford it. Enterprises in the public sector share the following features:

- They supply services such as defence or healthcare which would be difficult to supply profitably by privately run enterprises without having to charge very high prices or collect money from every member of society, which is impossible for private sector enterprises.
- They provide services which are essential to the well-being of the whole population of a country, such as healthcare, street lighting or defence.

Examples of public enterprises include:

- The National Health Service (NHS) in the UK, which was created to provide a range of free health and medical services for everyone in the UK.
- Electricité de France (EDF), which was created by France's Nationalisation Law to provide an efficient national electricity service to the entire population of France.

Private sector

All the enterprises that exist in this sector aim to supply goods and services needed and desired by their targeted customers, normally to make a profit. They will use pricing, promotion, new cost-efficient machinery, research and product development, and customer services to sell more of their goods and services than their competitors, and therefore secure a good share of the market. They are privately owned and run by people who have invested in them to earn money.

Examples of private enterprises include:

- Privately funded schools where parents pay fees every year their child attends school. These fees are used to pay staff wages, purchase resources for use in lessons, to maintain school buildings and facilities, and then what remains after all the costs are paid is profit for the owners.
- Manchester United, a world famous football team from England which was floated on the stock exchange. This means that anyone can buy shares in it and be rewarded financially with returns, called 'dividends', each year if the business performs well. Dividends are a share of the company's profits that a shareholder will receive depending on how many shares they own.

Consider the range of industries and organisations that exist in your country. In small groups make a list of five public and five private enterprises.

Other types of enterprise

There are some other enterprises that cannot be classified as public or private and you need to be aware of these. Not all enterprises aim to provide a national service or make a profit; some exist to make the world a better place. These are charities. They are non-profit oriented enterprises which actually aim to raise money to use to help people, animals or other causes.

14.3 The main forms of business organisation in the private sector

In section 14.2 we introduced you to the public and private sectors. We will now investigate in more detail the variety of different business enterprises that exist within the private sector.

Sole traders

Sole traders are people who set up a business on their own, usually selling goods or providing services. They invest the money that is needed to start the business. This is referred to as start-up capital. Sole traders generally work on their own but will occasionally pay for staff to assist them. Sometimes they are assisted by members of their family who usually do not require payment. These businesses are small in scale and often aim to provide a personal service to their customers, for example mobile hairdressing, plumbing, decorating etc. The sole trader has to work hard attracting and keeping customers, usually working long hours and risking all their private savings. Their reward is independence and receiving all the profits of the business.

Advantages of being a sole trader

- It is very easy to set up as a sole trader. There are no complicated forms to fill in or send off. As long as you have the right skills, equipment and, if needed, premises and stock, you can start trading almost straight away.
- Setting up as a sole trader can be inexpensive, requiring little capital investment. A window cleaner, for example, only needs a sponge, bucket, ladder and water; although many sole traders will certainly require more expensive equipment than this. Some governments may even provide small businesses with financial support and free guidance when setting up in business.
- If you make a profit, you can keep all that remains after paying taxes, or reinvest it in the business to fund growth.
- You are your own boss and you make all the decisions. You are independent – which for some people can be very satisfying. The sole trader has flexibility to decide what days or hours they work and when to have time off.
- Sole traders are able to get to know their customers well and provide a more personalised service than many larger organisations.

Disadvantages of being a sole trader

- The reality of being a sole trader is that they usually have to work very long hours to set up and establish the company.

- If the sole trader goes on holiday or is ill there maybe nobody to run the company and therefore no income. And if they die, this may cause financial problems for their family.
- A lot of small businesses fail in their first few years of trading, so banks are sometimes very reluctant to loan them money. Sole traders may, therefore, find it difficult to get the start-up capital they need.
- Small sole traders will not receive useful discounts when purchasing materials or goods for resale because, unlike larger organisations, they cannot buy in large enough quantities.
- A lot of sole traders may lack essential business skills like budgeting, good communication or keeping financial records.
- The sole trader may have used their own savings or secured loans on the value of their own homes to fund their business. If they want to expand they will need to ensure the business is highly profitable.
- Sole traders have unlimited liability. This means that if the company has debts then the sole trader who owns it is liable (responsible) for them. If a company fails to succeed or is declared bankrupt, the owner may be required to sell all their personal possessions (house, car etc.) to pay the debts up to an unlimited amount. Starting your own business using bank loans can be very risky.

Partnerships

If a sole trader's business becomes more successful and begins to grow, it will probably need more investment in equipment, machinery, vehicles, premises (buildings) and so on. This will involve even greater financial investment and risk, money which a sole trader may not be able to get. Some sole traders may choose to take on one or more partners in order to gain additional financial capital investment for the growing business so that machinery, premises and equipment can be bought to cope with the growing demand for products and services.

A partnership is defined as the union of two or more people who agree to work together and provide capital (investment money) to make profits. Partnerships are quite easy to set up. Each partner must sign a 'deed of partnership': a legal agreement that details the relationship between the partners. The deed is very important, particularly if there were to be a disagreement between partners at a later date. The deed will include the following information:

- What each partner will receive as a salary
- What each partner has invested in the company
- What share of the profits (return) each partner will receive, depending on the amount invested by each partner and how losses will be distributed.

Most partners will take an active role in the running of the company, but there are occasions when someone may wish to invest their money for a return yet have nothing to do with the day-to-day running of the business. This person is usually called a 'sleeping partner'. Partnerships are very common amongst professions such as doctors, dentists and solicitors.

Advantages of partnerships

- More investment capital is available to fund the growth of a business.
- Responsibility for business decisions and daily problems can be shared by all the partners, reducing the pressure on the original owner.
- New ideas, approaches, skills, qualities and even customers may be introduced to the company. Partners may have specialist skills which the company or original owner did not possess. (This is similar to the benefits of 'division of labour' discussed in Unit 1.)
- If a partner is ill or goes on holiday there is still someone available to keep the company operating.
- Partnerships are relatively easy to set up with very little legal documentation involved.
- Partners can start trading almost immediately.

Disadvantages of partnerships

- The partners have unlimited liability, with each partner being liable for a share of the business's debts if it becomes bankrupt or stops trading. This may result in the loss of personal possessions.
- Profits have to be shared between the partners in the ratio (proportion) to which they have invested in the company.
- Any disagreements between partners about how the company is managed could lead to very difficult working relationships.
- Partners can only introduce a certain amount of capital investment, so growth or development of the company further could still be limited.
- Partnerships end when a partner resigns or dies. If a partner died or became disabled their family members might inherit their share of the company but not possess the skills required to run it successfully. Existing partners in a company may not welcome this kind of new partner.

Private and public limited companies

Businesses that wish to grow will need ever-increasing amounts of investment capital. Some of this may come from profits retained (kept) within the business but more often this is achieved by forming a limited company.

Limited companies have a legal identity separate from that of their owners. The business, and not the owners, is responsible for the assets and enters into contractual relationships with customers and suppliers. Owners of the company benefit from limited liability and will only be liable for their original investment and not any further debts that the company may have.

Instead of partners, limited companies are made up of shareholders who each own part of the company. These shareholders become joint owners of the company and have a right to vote on how it should be run. The proportion they own is made up of 'shares'. The more shares that a shareholder has in the company, the more power and influence they have over the management of the company.

A limited company is run by a 'board' of directors elected by the shareholders of the company and led by a 'chairperson'. The shareholders will want good and effective directors because the better they are at their job the better the company's profits are likely to be, and therefore the better the return in investments received by shareholders. Their share of the profits is based on the number of shares in the business they own and is paid to them in the form of **dividends**.

Dividends – payments made to shareholders as a reward for investing their own money in a business. Dividends are paid out of the business's earnings or profits. A dividend is stated in dollar amounts. For example, a dividend may be $3 a share, so if you own 100 shares, you would receive $300 in dividends. Dividends are usually paid twice a year. The first payment is known as the 'interim payment', and the second is known as the 'final payment'.

Limited companies are more difficult to set up than sole traders or partnerships. Two documents need to be created:

1. **Memorandum of Association** – This contains the company details such as the name of the company, its registered address, the business's activities, the liability of the shareholders, the number of shares in the company issued and the amount of capital raised by the sale of shares.
2. **Articles of Association** – This describes how the company will be run and the rights of shareholders, how directors will be appointed, what the responsibilities of directors will be, how often directors will be re-elected and how the accounts of the company will be checked to ensure they are true and fair.

If a company's application to become a limited company is successful then it will receive a 'Certificate of Incorporation' which gives the company limited status.

There are two types of limited company, private limited and public limited companies.

Private Limited Company (Ltd)

Limited or Ltd companies are privately owned businesses whose name ends in 'Ltd', showing customers or suppliers that they are dealing with a company with its own legal identity. Such companies are usually larger than partnerships but can vary a lot in size. Private limited companies are often family owned, where each family member or close friend owns a particular share of the company. For example, three brothers who are shareholders of a construction company may hold an equal share in the business, giving them an ownership of exactly a third of the business each. These are usually smaller companies where family members or friends carry out the roles as company directors. As organisations grow there is more financial risk and an increased need for investment capital. Manufacturing and construction organisations that are growing may become private limited companies and in the event of the business failing they will only lose the money they have invested and no more (limited liability).

Advantages of private limited companies

- Shareholders benefit from limited liability.
- The minimum number of shareholders a private limited company can have is 1 and the maximum number is limited to 50. Companies can access the extra capital (money) they need to grow and develop their activities by introducing additional shareholders. But that does mean potential profits made have to be shared between more people.
- New shares can be issued and sold to new shareholders only if all the other shareholders agree. This means the company is not put at risk of being taken over by outsiders.
- Having a number of shareholders makes it possible for the company to continue even if one shareholder cannot work or dies.
- The larger the company becomes the more cost-effective it can become by taking advantage of bulk buying discounts offered by suppliers and the cost efficiencies of high-volume manufacturing.

Disadvantages of private limited companies

- If shares can only be sold to family or friends with the agreement of all the shareholders it is likely that additional investment capital made through the sale of shares will be limited.
- Profits generated by the company may have to be shared between increasingly large numbers of shareholders.
- Because of detailed and complicated legal requirements it is difficult and sometimes expensive to set up as a private limited company.
- Accounts detailing the financial performance of the company have to be produced and audited (checked) by firms of accountants, which can be expensive.
- The accounts have to be filed with the Registrar of Companies where the company's financial information can be accessed, even by competitors.
- It is difficult to sell your shares and leave the company because any buyers have to be approved by the remaining shareholders.

Can you think of two reasons why changing to a private limited company could help a partnership to grow?

Public Limited Company (Plc)

Public limited companies or Plcs tend to be a lot larger than private limited companies. Investors (organisations and members of the public) from around the world can buy or sell shares in a Plc on the **stock exchange**. They call this 'going public' and it is a very important stage in the growth and development of companies. For example, when Cadbury and Schweppes merged (became one company) and became a Plc as a result of floating on the London stock exchange, they were able to raise huge amounts of capital which they used to purchase competing firms such as Trebor Bassett and to grow the company even further.

Advantages of public limited companies

- All shareholders have limited liability and are protected.
- As the company grows it benefits more from economies of scale and is able to become even more dominant in the market.
- Huge amounts of money can be raised by selling shares to the general public to fund the expansion of the company.
- Shares can be treated as investments which can be traded on the stock exchange.
- When a shareholder dies, the activities of the business are able to continue.

Disadvantages of public limited companies

- Forming a Plc is a very complicated and long process.
- As shares are traded on the stock exchange it is possible for competitors to buy significant quantities of shares until they have enough to have a 'controlling share'.
- A wide range of accounts and financial information has to be sent to the Registrar and can therefore be viewed and used by competitors.
- Plcs can be impersonal because of their size, making it difficult for them to create a feeling of personal service for their customers.

■ *The trading floor of a London exchange*

Stock exchange – a marketplace where stock brokers and share dealers meet to buy and sell **stocks** (these are certificates of ownership in a corporation and are the same as shares) of publicly traded companies on behalf of investors; for example, the New York Stock Exchange (NYSE) in America. The NYSE is where most of the largest, most actively traded companies in the United States, such as General Motors and General Electric, are **listed**. A listed company is one which has permission for its shares to be admitted to a stock exchange's 'Official List', so that shares in it can be openly traded (bought and sold). Many countries have stock exchanges where shares of companies in that country are traded, such as the London Stock Exchange in the UK, the Tokyo Stock Exchange in Japan and the Frankfurt Stock Exchange in Germany.

Franchises

A franchise is the name given to a business run by someone who purchases the right to use or sell the products or techniques of a well-known international or national company. The owner of the franchise company will sell those products under the national or international company name. Companies that expand their business by offering others the opportunity to do business under their name are known as franchisors. The people or companies purchasing the right to do business under that company name are known as franchisees. There are many very famous international franchising companies, including The Body Shop, Subway, McDonald's, KFC and Burger King.

Franchising offers investors a ready-made business opportunity. They can operate under a well-known brand name, selling recognisable products and services in exchange for a lump-sum payment and a regular share of the company's profits.

Advantages of operating a franchise

- The franchise business is based on an idea that has already been proved, with an existing record of success. Investors can check how successful other franchisees have been before committing their capital.
- The brand name, logos and trademarks are recognisable to customers and franchisees will benefit from any advertising or promotional activities carried out by the franchisor.
- The franchisor offers support to the franchisees in the form of training, help with setting up the business, process manuals and ongoing advice services.
- Franchisees can sometimes negotiate exclusive rights in a certain geographical area, or 'territory', so they can guarantee that other franchisees do not set up in competition with them.
- Banks may be more willing to lend money to a franchise with an existing reputation, making it easier to raise investment capital.

Disadvantages of operating a franchise

- As well as the initial costs of buying the franchise, franchisees are required to pay continuing portions of their profits. They may also be committed to buying products and materials directly from the franchisor, rather than sourcing their own, cheaper alternatives.
- The franchise agreement usually includes restrictions on how franchisees are to run the business. This could even include the choice of furniture or layout of the premises.
- If the franchisor goes out of business or receives bad publicity, the success of the franchisees may be affected. Recent bad press about the negative effects on health caused by eating McDonald's products meant that many of the franchisees experienced a drop in sales.
- It can be difficult to sell a franchise as they can frequently only be sold to someone approved by the franchisor.

14.4 Multinationals

Some large public limited companies (Plcs) are known as multinationals. This word highlights the fact that the activity of their organisation takes place in a number of different countries or 'nations'. It is used to refer to companies that base their headquarters in one country, but have manufacturing and retail operations in a range of other countries around the world. For example, Nike produces footwear, clothing, equipment and accessory products for the sports and athletic market and is currently the largest seller of such products in the world. It sells to approximately 140 countries around the world. Most of its products are manufactured by contractors, with many being manufactured in developing countries. The company manufactures in China, Taiwan, Korea, Mexico, the USA and Italy. Nike is truly a 'multinational' organisation.

Multinationals in the global economy

There are many reasons that support or explain the growth of multinational organisations. Basically, they all support the argument that multinationals help to improve the global economy by distributing earning opportunities in developing countries where most multinationals set up production facilities.

- **Employment opportunities** – Multinationals offer employment opportunities to local workers when they set up manufacturing plants. Some chosen areas may be suffering from high levels of unemployment or poverty and new employment prospects could help some of the poorest parts of the world to improve their standard of living.
- **Development of skills** – Employment can lead to the development of new skills, acquired by training provided by the multinationals. These skills are sometimes passed on to local industries and organisations.
- **Economic stability** – Multinationals can create a flow of money into the host country, thereby providing a greater amount of economic stability.
- **Peaceful international relationships** – Setting up multinational companies involves a great deal of negotiation and relationship building. This can help to promote good relationships between countries and create a sense of community across international borders.
- **New technology** – Multinationals regularly bring with them new technology and technical knowledge which can benefit the local community and industry.

Opportunities offered to multinationals

There are a number of significant reasons why many multinationals decide to set up manufacturing facilities and businesses in other countries (including developing nations):

- To produce goods designed specifically for customers in that region whose tastes may vary from that of other markets. This can increase sales in that region.
- To benefit from lower labour costs in less developed countries. This allows the multinationals to reduce their overall manufacturing costs, which has two main benefits. The first is that they will experience increased profits and the second is that the companies may be able to offer their products at reduced prices and become far more competitive in their pricing.
- Governments will try to attract multinationals for many of the reasons explained in the previous section by offering them incentives such as:
  - i. Zero or reduced tax rates on profits.
  - ii. Subsidies (money) offered to multinationals who choose to set up new operations in certain countries.
  - iii. Reduced-rate loans as an incentive for multinationals who decide to manufacture in one country rather than another. These are large but inexpensive loans of money that multinationals will need to set up operations in another country. The rate of interest they will pay will be very low but the governments of developing countries will gladly do without high interest payments if a multinational provides their communities with employment, skills training and better economic prosperity.

Arguments against multinationals

Recently the media has been reporting a great deal of criticism of the effects of multinationals setting up their companies and manufacturing plants in developing countries. This is because the interests of multinationals and the interests of the countries in which they locate are not always the same. Some people argue that multinationals:

- May possibly ruin or put into decline the local and traditional industries of countries, because workers leave them to work in what they believe to be higher paid jobs.
- May lead to a loss of cultural and traditional practices because multinational businesses expect their workforce to behave in the same way as their employees in other countries.
- Multinationals can be described as too big and have little interest in the individuals who work for them. Some very famous multinational organisations have received a great deal of criticism for allegedly using extremely cheap child labour in their factories.

- Multinationals can become very powerful in some countries because of the economic prosperity they bring to the country. They have even been known to try to influence political decisions so that they will be beneficial to them.
- Multinationals can create economic instability. They may withdraw their production facilities if it becomes too expensive to manufacture in a particular country or if the goods manufactured are no longer demanded. Countries may then struggle with high unemployment etc.
- Some feel that multinationals encourage materialistic values (values to do with money and profit) in the workforce of countries which were previously led by traditional values.

Summary of main points from Unit 14

- When locating an organisation, things which must be considered include the supply of suitably skilled labour, how developed transport systems and networks are, nearness to raw materials and suppliers, access to utilities and other services and nearness to their own markets.
- The public sector includes all the enterprises run or operated by a country's government. These enterprises exist to provide free services to the public using money raised by taxing the public. Examples are national health services and national security services, including the military.
- The private sector includes most commercial or profit-oriented organisations that are privately owned by one or many people. They include your small local grocery store that is likely to be owned and run by one person, and the multinational organisation Microsoft, in which almost anyone can buy a small share.
- Sole traders are usually individuals who set up in business on their own selling goods or providing services. They are small in scale. Setting up as a sole trader has certain advantages and disadvantages that you must be aware of for the exam.
- Partnerships are unions of two or more people who agree to work together and who invest capital to generate profits that are to be shared between them. Again, setting up a business as a partnership has certain advantages and disadvantages that you must be aware of for the exam.
- Private limited companies (Ltd) are privately owned businesses with their own legal identity. They can vary a lot in size. They are usually family owned businesses where members of the family own a certain share of the business. Again, setting up a business as a private limited company has certain advantages and disadvantages that you must be aware of for the exam.
- Public limited companies (Plcs) are much larger than private limited companies. Anyone can own shares in Plcs because they are sold publicly by the stock exchange. Again, setting up a business as a Plc has certain advantages and disadvantages that you must be aware of for the exam.

- The stock exchange is a marketplace where stock brokers and share dealers meet to buy and sell stocks (these are certificates of ownership in a corporation and are the same as shares) of publicly traded companies on behalf of investors.
- Franchises are businesses run by owners who have purchased the right to use or sell the products or techniques of a well-known international or national company. The owner of the franchise company will sell those products under the national or international company name. The company which expands its business by offering others the opportunity to do business under its name is known as the franchisor. The people or companies purchasing the right to do business under that company name are known as franchisees. Again, setting up a business as a franchisee has certain advantages and disadvantages that you must be aware of for the exam.
- Multinationals are usually Plcs that operate in a number of different countries. They offer many benefits to developing countries where they set up manufacturing plants and distribution networks, but some people feel that they take advantage of developing countries and abuse their power for profit. You may be asked questions on this topic in the exam.

Test your knowledge

Practice multiple choice exam questions

1) Which of the following four factors would be the **most** important when considering the location of a small business selling fresh food (which is perishable and has a short shelf life, meaning it only stays fresh for a short period of time) such as bread, milk and dairy products?
   a) Availability of labour
   b) Availability of transport
   c) Nearness to customers
   d) Nearness to suppliers
2) What happens when an organisation decides to become a Plc (public limited company)?
   a) All the profits made are given back to tax payers.
   b) It becomes part of the public sector.
   c) Another partner is invited into the business.
   d) It offers shares for sale to the general public through a stock exchange.
3) The limited liability status of a private limited company protects who?
   a) Employees
   b) Debenture holders (long-term lenders of finance)
   c) Company directors
   d) Shareholders
4) Which of the following types of business organisation would be the most suitable for a young person wanting to start their own shoe cleaning business from a van located in the middle of a city centre?
   a) Partnership
   b) Private limited company
   c) Public limited company
   d) Sole trader

Test your knowledge *continued*

5) A public corporation is defined as:
   a) A partnership between two members of the public
   b) A public limited company
   c) A publicly owned organisation
   d) A private limited business

Practice stimulus response and structured exam questions

1) Mosman Enterprises is a large multinational boatbuilding business. It was started by Jim Mosman who worked as a sole trader and developed the business, first into a partnership, then a private limited company and finally a public limited company.
   a) Identify one characteristic of each of the four types of business organisation. (*4 marks*)
   b) Explain advantages of making the following changes:
      (i) Sole trader to partnership.
      (ii) Partnership to private limited company.
      (iii) Private limited company to public limited company. (*6 marks*)
   c) What are the benefits to Mosman Enterprises of being a multinational boatbuilding business? (*4 marks*) *(CIE Commerce Paper 1 May/Jun 2004)*

2) Kobla Enterprises is a Plc making china and pottery tableware to sell at home and abroad. State four features of a Plc. (*4 marks*)

3) Premier Holdings is a multinational corporation wishing to expand its operations in Australia.
   a) What is a multinational corporation? (*4 marks*)
   b) State and explain two ways in which a multinational corporation differs from a public corporation. (*4 marks*) *(CIE Commerce Paper May/Jun 2000)*

4) Tinashe and Dambudzo are in partnership selling computers. They are considering changing their business into a private limited company.
   a) State four features of a partnership. (*4 marks*)
   b) What are the advantages to them of changing from a partnership to a private limited company? (*6 marks*) *(CIE Commerce Paper 1 May/Jun 2003)*

5) Fabrice, Charlene and Joseph own a printing business. They are in partnership.
   a. Explain two advantages of operating as a partnership. (*4 marks*)
   Fabrice, Charlene and Joseph share profits in the ratio of 7:3:2. Total profits for the year are $120,000.
      (i) Calculate how much each receives, showing your workings (*3 marks*)
      (ii) Suggest possible reasons why Fabrice gets a larger share than the others (*2 marks*)
   b. They are thinking of expanding their business. There are three options available. Look for a sleeping partner, apply for a loan from the bank or change the business into a private limited company.
      (i) Discuss advantages and disadvantages of each of the three options. (*9 marks*)
      (ii) Which one would you recommend? Give reasons for your choice. (*2 marks*)
   (CIE Commerce Paper 1 Oct/Nov 2004)

In Question 5b (i) remember to discuss both advantages and disadvantages for all three options available: sleeping partner, bank loan and private limited company.

15 Business finance

What do I need to study?

- List the short- and long-term sources of finance used by organisations in various commercial situations.
- Describe the methods of self-financing used by companies.
- Explain the importance of business finance and the meaning, calculation and importance of capital (fixed and working), turnover and gross and net profit.
- Suggest ways in which companies can improve their turnover and profits.
- Suggest financial choices in commercial situations and explain the suitability of your choice.

Introduction

In Unit 14 we discussed the various forms of organisations that exist in the private sector. We looked at how a small business can grow and develop from a sole trader into a partnership, then into a private limited company and finally into a public limited company. Whether the business is just starting up or it is growing, it will need money, and this is referred to in business as **finance**. In a great many cases this money will come from financial institutions like banks which we discussed in great detail in Unit 13.

Finance is needed to invest in buildings, equipment and machinery (regarded as the 'fixed assets' of the organisation) and is referred to as 'fixed capital'. In addition, finance is needed to buy the raw materials and pay for the daily expenses of producing goods, providing services or buying goods for resale.

Finance – Finance refers to the way in which individuals, companies and organisations raise and use sources of money over time, usually to achieve certain aims. For instance a company may finance the purchase of very expensive, new, high-tech machinery so that it can produce and sell more of its products in a shorter period of time than it did before.

Before organisations can start to make any money they need to obtain finance for buildings, equipment, machinery and the daily costs of doing business. The aim of this unit is to explain what sources of finance are available, their main features and when each one is most suitable to use. For example, we will examine the sources of finance available to organisations from external sources, such as banks, which a company may pay back quickly, over a short term, or pay back over a much longer time because the amount is so great. We will also examine internal sources of finance within an organisation such as the profits made from trading that are retained for investing in new machinery or buildings.

We will also learn how finance is used within the company to generate more money, thus making more profits that can be returned to the owners, or shareholders, or even reinvested in the company for further growth.

15.1 Sources of finance

Finance can be obtained from a variety of sources; the most common sources are shown in the diagram below. We will investigate each source in detail throughout the unit.

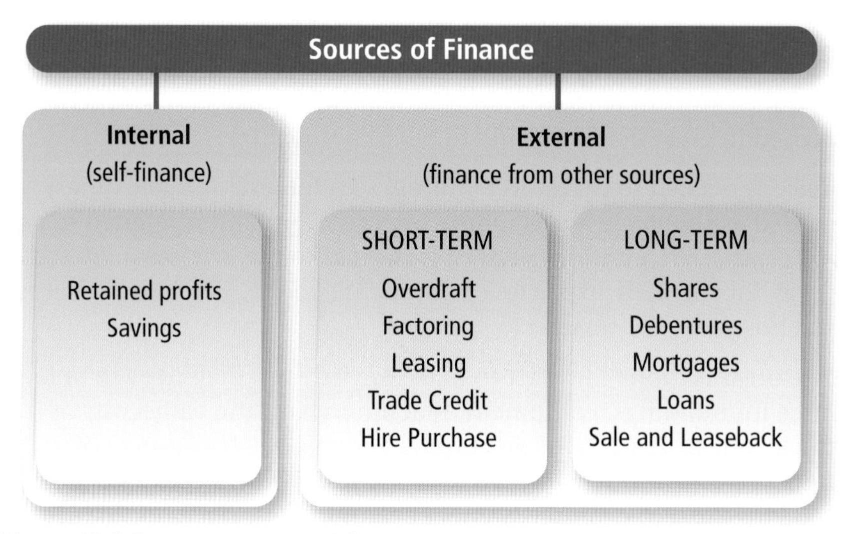

■ **Figure 15.1** *Common sources of finance*

Internal sources of finance

These are sources of finance that come from within the organisation itself and these are forms of self-financing. They include savings and retained profits.

Savings

As we learned in Unit 14 new businesses find it very difficult to find sources of finance because it is seen as very risky to invest in new businesses due to their high chance of failure. The most common source of capital for new businesses is from the savings of their owners. Many new businesses are started up using an inheritance or redundancy money.

Retained profits

Organisations receive money or income from selling goods or services. Any money that remains after paying the costs and expenses of selling those goods or services is 'profit'. Profit is the reward to owners of a company for risking money and time in their business. Some owners retain their profits, reinvesting them in the business to finance the purchase of more fixed assets so that it can grow and sell more goods or offer more services.

External sources of finance

These are sources of finance that come from outside the business. They can be grouped into one of two categories, long-term (needed for 5 years or more) and short-term (needed for up to 5 years). The source of finance chosen will depend on the amount of money borrowed and how long it may take to pay it back.

Long-term sources of finance

Loans

These are formal arrangements between an organisation and a bank that has agreed to loan an amount of money at a preset (set in advance) or variable rate of interest. The bank will decide the size and frequency of each repayment and the length of the loan period. Loans are often used for financing expensive fixed assets like machinery and equipment.

Advantages of loans

- The company knows the terms of the loan (cost and repayment terms) that they have committed to.
- Often quite quick and simple for the company to obtain.
- Terms can be changed and renegotiated. Companies may wish to repay their loans over shorter or longer periods of time.

Disadvantages of loans

- Loans that are paid for over a long period of time can cost the company a lot in interest payments.
- If the loan is paid off early the company may have to pay additional charges.
- Some banks may insist on having the loan secured, for example, on the owner's property.

Shares

Organisations wishing to grow may choose to become private or public limited companies (as discussed in the last unit). Public limited companies (Plcs) may choose to **float** their businesses on the stock exchange and sell shares in them.

Organisations that have already floated may choose to issue new shares to raise further finances. Shares are offered for sale to the general public at a **nominal value** (usually $1) which is their face value when first issued. As they are traded on the stock market they may increase or decrease in value depending on how successful the businesses are.

There are two types of shares:

- Ordinary shares – Ordinary shareholders are entitled to receive a share of the organisation's profits. The payment received is called a **dividend**.

Float – This is the term given to the process where a company offers its shares to the public and lists itself on a stock exchange.

Nominal value – This is the value given to each new share when it is first authorised and issued by a company. The nominal value of a share does not reflect the true market value of the share. This value will be established once they are bought and sold on the stock exchange.

Dividend – This is a portion of a company's profit paid out to holders of shares. The amount is decided on by the company's board of directors. A dividend may be in the form of cash payments or, in some cases, additional stock or shares in a company may be given.

Dividends can vary from one year to the next, depending on how much profit has been made, how much the company's management has decided to pay its shareholders and how much money it wants to keep within the business. In a year when business is bad ordinary shareholders may risk receiving no dividends at all.

- Preference shares – Preference shareholders have the benefit of a fixed dividend rate. They will get the same return or dividend on their shares no matter how high the company's profits are in a particular year. However, a company does not have to pay preference shareholders any dividends if it lacks the financial ability to do so (has made a loss, for example).

Advantages of shares

- Shares allow companies to acquire very large amounts of finance. Money received from selling share issues can be used to buy out competitors or invest in fixed capital expenditure. In addition, share issue money can be spent on conducting research and development of new products.

Disadvantages of shares

- Companies need to keep their existing and new shareholders happy by giving them a steady flow of good dividend payments. If shareholders are not satisfied with their dividend payments they may lose confidence in the business and start to sell their shares. This may force down the stock market value of shares.
- The need for the services of lawyers and bankers etc. makes it expensive for a company to become a Plc and offer shares on the stock market.

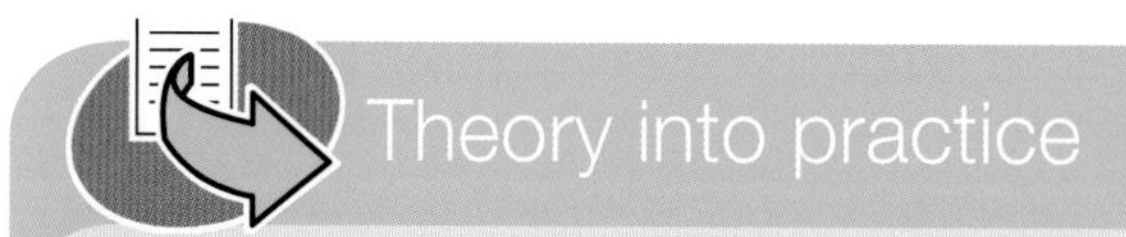

Theory into practice

Richard Damson has just bought 100,000 ordinary shares in a Plc. What are ordinary shares and how do they differ from preference shares?

Debentures

These long-term loans are a source of finance for very large Plcs and normally have a loan period of between 5 and 25 years. Plcs borrow stocks, bonds and even currency from debenture holders. They are used by organisations to finance very expensive assets such as buildings and machinery over long periods of time.

Advantages of debentures

- If a debenture is fixed then the company has agreed a date by which it will be repaid. It is aware how much the loan will cost over a fixed period of time so it can plan its future finances.

- They make expensive property and equipment affordable to companies because they can repay the loan over long periods of time.

Disadvantages of debentures

- Debenture holders have a legal interest in any assets that are purchased with their loans. The company will be unable to sell the property unless they agree and the outstanding amount of the loan is cleared.
- Debenture repayments have a very high priority. When a company goes into **liquidation** (which means it is forced to close down and its assets are sold to generate the cash needed to pay its outstanding debts), debenture loans will be repaid before any of the shareholders or suppliers of the business are paid.

Mortgages

These are long-term loans, usually for the purchase of buildings or land, which make the property affordable to organisations because of the long repayment period. Organisations that own property or land may also take out a mortgage on their property. We say that the property is used as security or 'collateral' as a guarantee against loss. This enables the organisation to release money tied up in their buildings to reinvest in machinery or other assets to help the business grow.

Advantages of mortgages

- A mortgage allows a company to raise money in a way that avoids selling shares in it and therefore avoids having to share the profits and the risk of losing control over how the company is run.
- Mortgage repayments are relatively small compared to the size of the finance obtained because the loan is paid for over a long period of time. This means that the repayments do not have a negative influence on the amount of cash flowing out of the company.
- As long as companies keep up regular repayments, at the end of the loan period they own the assets (property or land).

Disadvantages of mortgages

- The company can't sell the building or property unless the outstanding amount on the mortgage is settled. Companies that do this may have to pay very high early completion penalties.
- Companies have to pledge or secure the mortgage on the property or land purchased. If the company defaults on (fails to make) its repayments then the lender (bank) will be able to force the company to sell the secured property in order to pay the outstanding debt or even take ownership of the property themselves.
- In periods when interest rates rise, a company may find that their mortgage payments could increase so greatly that they may not even be able to meet their regular monthly payments. In this case, the mortgage provider will say the company has defaulted on their mortgage and will seize the property and sell it so that they can get their money back.

Sale and leaseback

This is an arrangement used by organisations that own high-value property, equipment or machinery. They release cash for the organisation by selling these assets to a buyer, and then automatically lease them back from the buyer for an agreed extended period of time. The organisation will make regular lease payments (similar to rental fees) to the company that owns the asset.

Advantages of sale and leaseback

- It is a useful way to access cash that is invested or tied up in assets without losing their use. This money can then be used for other investments to improve the business performance.

Disadvantages of sale and leaseback

- By selling assets and leasing them back, a business's worth will be reduced.
- Companies may be locked into a long-term lease agreement (often hard to get out of), during which time the machinery or equipment may become unnecessary.
- The machinery or equipment may become out of date but the organisation leasing it cannot change or adapt it.

Short-term sources of finance

Bank overdrafts

All companies have a current bank account through which payments made by, and to, the company will be made. This account provides an overdraft facility, which allows the company to draw out (borrow) more money than it actually has in the account. It may only be able to draw up to an agreed limit called an overdraft limit. Overdrafts are very useful to companies that may experience low sales (and therefore incomes) at certain times of the year. For example, an ice-cream manufacturer will have to spend money all year around, maintaining a factory and building up stocks, but most of his sales revenues will be made only from sales over the summer months.

Advantages of overdrafts

- Money is borrowed only when the company needs it.
- Interest is only payable when the overdraft is in use, unlike a loan where companies have to pay interest throughout the whole period of the loan until it is paid.

Disadvantages of overdrafts

- Usually have very high rates of interest compared to short-term loans because of their convenience.
- An overdraft is usually repayable on demand. If a bank feels that a company is having trading problems, it may request that the whole overdraft amount be repaid. Most companies will not be able to do this and it may cause them to become bankrupt. This means that a

court declares them unable to pay. All their assets will be sold to repay their debtors.

- Borrowers may be charged a fee by the bank for setting up and using an overdraft facility.

Factoring

This is defined as the selling of a company's **accounts receivable** to a third party (a 'factor'), in order to obtain funding. It turns sales that a company has not actually received payment for, into cash. This can be important to smaller companies who need money to flow quickly around the business so they can afford to purchase and pay for materials, labour and other costs of running a business.

Accounts receivable – This is the money which is owed to a company by a customer for products and services that were provided to them on credit terms.

The factor will give them the value of what is outstanding, minus a percentage charge. The factoring organisation then has the responsibility of actually collecting the debt that they have bought. They hope that they have the expertise to collect all the outstanding accounts receivable, and to make money on the difference in the value of what they collected compared with what they paid the original organisation for the accounts receivable purchased.

Advantages of factoring

- Allows organisations to guarantee a high percentage payment of the money owed to them by customers, known as 'creditor balances', on a regular basis. This means fewer cash flow problems because it speeds up the flow of cash into the organisation.
- Reduces the time and money organisations have to spend on collecting debts.
- Reduces the risk of non-payment from new and overseas clients.

Disadvantages of factoring

- Factors may take over the running of an organisation's collection of payments but some customers may not want to deal with a factoring company.
- Factors may ask, for example, to approve new customers and impose lower credit limits on existing customers so that there is a reduced risk to them.
- Organisations may pay a high percentage of their sales to factors. Debt factoring is certainly a very expensive way of getting money into the organisation.

Leasing

When organisations need expensive machinery, equipment and vehicles they may choose either to purchase them or to lease them for an agreed period of time. For example, organisations may lease a photocopier for three years and a car for two years. Leasing is similar to renting as the property belongs to the leasing company.

Advantages of leasing

- Companies do not have to take out expensive long-term loans or use their retained profits. This money can be invested in research and development or marketing to improve business success.
- It is very easy to organise leases. The amount of paperwork is far less than when applying for a loan.
- Companies may be able to access more expensive and advanced equipment than they could afford to buy through loans.
- Leased equipment may be maintained and repaired by the leasing company, saving the company thousands of dollars on maintenance costs.
- Repayment costs are usually fixed for the entire term of the lease.
- Leasing agreements may allow companies to upgrade to newer equipment for a small additional cost.
- Companies avoid being left with out-of-date machinery and equipment.

Disadvantages of leasing

- The company will usually pay more over the term of the leasing agreement than the machinery or equipment originally cost.
- The company never owns the item so they cannot sell it and the organisation may have to pay lease payments even if it has stopped using the equipment.
- Companies may, depending on the agreement, be responsible for maintenance and repair costs.

Hire purchase (HP)

This is a source of finance to organisations who wish to purchase machinery, equipment or vehicles. Organisations make regular payments for an item over a period of time. Until the last payment is made the equipment remains the property of the hire purchase company. The last payment will change the ownership over to the organisation that hired the equipment.

Advantages of hire purchase

- Helps cash flow by spreading the cost of expensive assets over a long period with fixed costs throughout the period of the hire purchase.
- Frees up cash to be spent on activities like marketing and research and development (as discussed in leasing).
- Once all the hire purchase payments are made, the company owns the asset, which can be sold if it is no longer needed.

Disadvantages of hire purchase

- If regular payments are not made the hiring company may repossess (take back) the item.

- Companies have no opportunity to update the machinery or equipment (which is sometimes allowed with leasing).
- At the end of the hire purchase term a company may own an out-of-date piece of equipment which has no value to it.

Extended credit (or deferred payments)

This is a source of finance which is similar to hire purchase in that repayments for goods purchased are made by regular instalments. But unlike hire purchase, the goods become the property of the purchaser as soon as the credit agreement is signed and the initial payment or deposit is made. It is common for these types of credit agreements to defer (delay) payments of instalments for a period of time after the purchase, to allow the individual or company to 'buy now and pay later' – to enjoy the goods now and look for the money to pay for them after the purchase. During this time it is usual for interest not to be charged on the amount owed as an extra incentive for people to purchase the goods. If the company or person who purchased the goods fails to make the repayments, the goods cannot be repossessed (taken back). The money owed can only be recovered by taking the purchaser to court.

Advantages of extended credit

- Many extended credit or deferred payment agreements do not charge the purchaser interest as long as they make the agreed payments by the time agreed.
- Goods can be purchased and used by organisations to generate income before any payments for them have to be made.
- The goods become the property of the purchaser immediately.

Disadvantages of extended credit

- If regular payments are not made the seller will take court action in order to get back the money owed to them.
- Goods purchased this way tend to be more expensive than those purchased by other means.
- Some people say that buying goods on credit is so easy that it encourages many individuals and companies to have huge credit debt that they struggle to pay.

Trade credit

This is an arrangement between organisations and their suppliers to buy goods or services on account. This means they can receive goods and services but do not have to pay for them for an agreed period of time, which can be anything between 4 and 12 weeks (if a business has a very good relationship with its suppliers). This gives organisations the time to make sales *and* collect payments from their own customers.

Advantages of trade credit

- Goods and services are provided free for a period of time. Meanwhile they can be used to make money for the company. It is a temporary way of increasing the cash available to the company.

Disadvantages of trade credit

- Suppliers may give companies that pay quickly good discounts on their purchases, so trade credit could actually *cost* the businesses that use it.
- If the company owes too much or has reached its trade credit limit the supplier may refuse to supply any more goods or services until a payment has been made.

Choosing the right sources of finance

Companies need to consider carefully which source of finance will be most suitable for their needs. For instance, you would not finance a new vehicle with an overdraft because overdrafts have a very high percentage interest rate compared to a loan or purchasing the car on hire purchase.

Companies need to consider the following when selecting sources of finance:

1. **The type of business, its stage in development and the availability of finance**
   The availability of certain types of finance may be limited, depending on what type of ownership an organisation has. For example, a start-up business may find it difficult to obtain a loan or finance from banks unless it has property on which to secure the loan. The table below summarises the typical sources of finance accessed by different types of private sector businesses:

	Sole trader	Partnership	Private Ltd	Public Ltd Company
Savings	✓	✓		
Retained profits	✓	✓	✓	✓
Overdraft	✓	✓	✓	✓
Loan	✓ (if properly secured)	✓	✓	✓
Leasing and hire purchase	✓	✓	✓	✓
Long-term debentures/mortgages			✓	✓
Share issue			✓	✓

■ **Figure 15.2** *A summary of the typical sources of business finance*

2. **The intended use of the finance**
   If a company needs to purchase high-value equipment or property (fixed assets) it would normally seek long-term finance such as loans or mortgages or even share issues.

If there is a lack of money within the company (working capital) because it is struggling to get its customers to pay, then in order to continue to trade, it may need short-term sources of finance such as overdrafts or trade credit with suppliers in order to pay its daily costs.

3. **The cost to the business of the source of finance**
   A company may have access to a range of sources of finance for the same purpose and will need to decide which is least expensive in terms of interest or dividend costs. For instance, a car can be bought using a five-year loan, making repayments with interest added over this period. Or, the car could be funded using hire purchase, but it is likely that the sum of all the payments would then be much more than the original cost of the car.

   A company that needs to purchase a new factory may issue shares to raise the finance, but it has to accept the cost of this is payment of dividends to the shareholders. It may choose to buy the new factory using a mortgage – which can be costly over a long period of time. Therefore, companies need to select the source of finance that is least expensive to them.

4. **The risk associated with the source of finance**
   When companies take out loans, mortgages or debentures they run the risk of losing property that has been secured against them. The loan companies need to be certain that, if a company is unable to make its repayments, they will be able to sell the company's property to get their money back. Companies may choose share issues as a more secure source of finance as the company does not have to pay dividends to shareholders if it makes a loss.

15.2 Business finance

Capital – This is the money shareholders/owners have contributed or invested in the company.

Reserves – These are the profits earned and other financial resources received by the company that have been kept within the organisation for the benefit of it and its shareholders/owners.

The capital of a business

New and existing organisations will constantly look at their finances to measure how well they are performing. They want to know how much their company is worth and how much profit the company is making. Anyone who invests their savings will want to know if they have made the right decision. They will want to know if the return they get from their investment is better than keeping their money in a bank account. And they will want to know that their investment is growing in value.

In this part of the unit we will investigate two key financial documents that enable an investor to assess the performance of his or her investment. They are the balance sheet and profit and loss (or P&L) account.

The balance sheet

The balance sheet for a company shows the value of it at a given time. It details all the assets and liabilities of the company, which should balance with the **capital** and **reserves** of the company.

Balance Sheet for Wedding Bells Ltd
as at 31st December 2005

Fixed Assets				160,000
Premises, fixtures and fittings				**160,000**
Current Assets				
Stocks		25,000		
Debtors	10,000			
Cash at Bank		47,500		
		82,500		
Current Liabilities				
Creditors (falling due within one year)	**(42,500)**			
Net Current Assets				**40,000**
Total Assets Less Current Liabilities			**200,000**	
Long Term Liabilities				
Bank Loan		10,000		
Mortgage		55,000		
		65,000		
Net Assets				**135,000**
Capital & Reserves				
Share Capital		100,000		
Retained Profit	35,000			**135,000**

■ **Figure 15.3** *An example of a typical balance sheet*

Working capital

This is sometimes known as **net current assets** and is the capital within the organisation that is used for its day-to-day running.

Working capital = cash within the business
+ value of stocks
+ money owed to the business by its customers
– money owed to the bank within 12 months
– money owed to other businesses.

Working capital is the lifeblood of a company. It is constantly flowing around it. Money that comes into the company is used to pay for materials or workers' wages. The materials and workers in turn manufacture goods which are then sold to customers. Sometimes the money owed from customers takes a long time to arrive. If it takes too long the company may not be able to afford to pay suppliers and workers for the next batch of goods to be made. This is what is called a '*cash flow crisis*'. Organisations may have lots of customers and make thousands of dollars' worth of sales, but if they do not keep money flowing around the company it might stop business. The diagram below shows the flow of money around a business. It is called the '*working capital cycle*'.

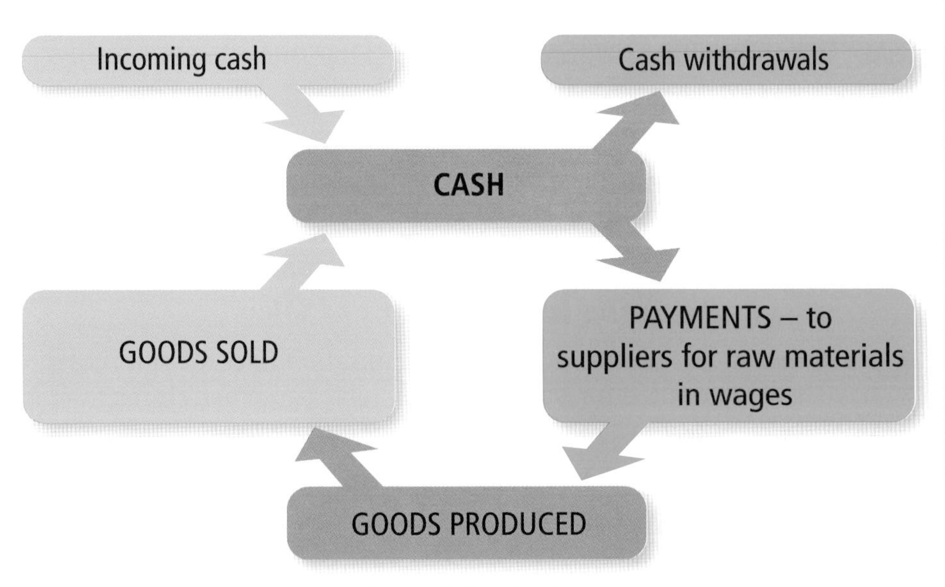

■ **Figure 15.4** *Typical working capital cycle in a business*

How do we calculate working capital or net current assets?

Organisations do not want too much or too little working capital in the business. If they have too much, it means they may have too much money tied up in stock doing very little and earning nothing. If they have too little working capital, then they may not have enough money to pay the daily expenses of business, which could actually lead to the company becoming bankrupt.

Net worth – This is sometimes also known as '**net assets**' and is the total assets of a company minus its total liabilities (money it owes to others such as the bank) so that an estimate of its value can be made.

Assets – There are two groups of assets. *Fixed assets* are usually made up from property (buildings and land), plant and equipment (machinery) and are usually tangible which means you can physically touch them. Fixed assets describe the types of property and equipment owned by a company that cannot easily or quickly be converted into cash by being sold. *Current assets* include the cash held on a company's premises or money in bank accounts. Current assets are described as liquid assets because in most cases they can be easily turned into cash for immediate use.

Fixed capital – This is the value of fixed or physical capital within the company which is not used up when a product is produced or a service is provided, for example, a factory building. A company that invests in fixed capital is investing its money in fixed assets so that profits can be made. The value of the fixed capital in Wedding Bells Ltd is $160,000 at 31st December 2005.

Debtors – These are the people or companies that owe money to the company. In Figure 15.3 Wedding Bells Ltd is owed $10,000 from its debtors.

Creditors – These are the people or companies that are owed money for goods or services that have been received. In Figure 15.3 Wedding Bells Ltd owes $42,500 to suppliers and other organisations and this amount will need to be paid within 12 months.

Net worth – The net worth of the company is $135,000, which means it is worth $35,000 more than when it was started. The company has kept the profits from the first year of trading within the business to fund growth.

Working capital – the value of cash and assets which can be easily turned into cash (such as stock) after the debts that are due from current liabilities (which include overdrafts and trade creditors).

Working capital is calculated as follows: (see also page 255)

net current assets = working capital = current assets (cash, debtors, stocks) – current liabilities (overdraft, creditors)

Most effective organisations will have current assets of about 1.5 to 2 times the value of their current liabilities. This means that the organisation will have enough cash to cope with unexpected bills – such as a creditor demanding payment of their account balance before they release any more stock to the company.

The way organisations work out whether they have enough working capital is to calculate a **current ratio**. The higher this ratio (figure) is the more working capital the company has available and the more secure it is.

The current ratio is calculated as follows:

$$\textbf{current ratio} = \frac{\textbf{current assets}}{\textbf{current liabilities}}$$

The profit and loss account

The profit and loss account allows the owners of companies to see how well they are trading and how successful they are. The profit and loss account is a statement of the revenues (money in) and costs (money out) of the company over a period of trading (usually one year). It shows the reader how well it has performed that year. It has the following details:

- **Sales turnover** – the value of sales or revenue made by the organisation in a trading period. It is usually calculated by:

  turnover = average price × quantity sold

- **Gross profit** – the profit made on sales before taking away the overheads of the organisation. It is usually calculated by:

  gross profit = sales turnover – cost of sales

- **Net profit** – the profit made by an organisation once all of its costs have been accounted for, such as wages, rent, equipment hire etc. It is usually calculated by:

  net profit = gross profit – operating expenses

- **Rate of turnover** – this is sometimes known as stock turnover rate and is the number of times a firm sells its average stock per trading period. Depending on the type of goods that a company sells or the industry that it belongs to, the rate of stock turnover can vary. Some goods have very low rates of turnover, such as farming machinery which would only sell in small numbers but the supplier is likely to have a great deal of machinery kept in stock. The seller will want a good selection for their customers to choose from because they only buy high-value farming equipment very rarely.

  rate of turnover = cost of goods sold – cost of average stock

Profit & Loss Account for Wedding Bells Ltd
Year Ending 31st December 2005

Sales Turnover		252,000
– Cost of Sales		151,200
= GROSS PROFIT		**100,800**
– Operating Expenses		
Directors' Wages	50,000	
Salaries	10,000	
Other (loan repayments, gas, electricity)	5,800	
	65,800	
= NET PROFIT		**35,000**

■ **Figure 15.5** *An example of a typical profit and loss account*

Methods of improving turnover and profit

Organisations want to make more profit to reward their investors. There is a wide range of things they can do to try and improve their profits. These include the following:

- **Increasing the use of advertising and sales promotion** – This may lead to an increase in sales, but the increase needs to be high enough to cover the extra costs of advertising and sales promotion before they can make increasing turnover and profits.
- **Reducing prices of goods and services** – This may lead to an increase in demand for goods and services, but sales will have to rise to make up for the reduction in sales profit caused by reducing prices.
- **Improving credit terms offered to business customers** – This may encourage customers to buy in bulk quantities, thus raising sales turnover and possibly net profit.
- **Reducing costs of supplies and expenses** – This may raise gross and net profits because sale prices will be maintained at their original levels.
- **Offering a wider range of products or services** – This may attract more customers and their average expenditure (spending) may increase. This will improve sales turnover while keeping expenses the same, therefore increasing net profits.
- **Expanding business operations** – Companies may choose to open up an additional branch or retail outlet to serve more customers or make more of a particular product. This may lead to an increase in sales turnover, but all the additional costs need to be covered before profits can be made.

Consider the list of methods used by businesses to improve turnover and profit. Can you think of one possible disadvantage or limitation of five of the methods to a business that uses them?

Summary of main points from Unit 15

- Finance refers to the way in which individuals, companies and organisations raise and use sources of money over time, usually to achieve certain objectives.
- Finance can be sourced internally (from within the company) or externally (from other sources outside the company).
- Internal sources of finance include retained profits from a previous year's trading or the savings of owners.
- External sources of finance include short-term sources (such as overdrafts, debt factoring, leasing, trade credit and hire purchase) and long-term sources (such as share issues, debentures, mortgages, loans, sale and leaseback). For the exam you will need to know in what circumstances each type is used and their advantages and disadvantages.
- Organisations wishing to raise finance may choose to float their company on the stock exchange. Floating a company is the process where a company offers its shares to the public and lists itself on a stock exchange.
- There are two types of shares that can be purchased in a company, ordinary and preference shares. You will need to be able to distinguish between them and explain their uses.
- Dividends are the amount of a company's profit that is paid to each shareholder.
- Companies will consider a range of issues when deciding on the right source of finance for a given purpose. They will consider what sources are actually available to them and this will depend on their stage of development, what the finance will be used for, how much the finance will cost the company and the risks that go with the source.
- Balance sheets are one of a company's key financial statements. They usually show the worth of a company at one particular point in time.
- Working capital is also shown on balance sheets and is sometimes called 'net current assets'. It is a measure of the capital within the organisation that can be used to cover all the debt that may become due at short notice.
- The profit and loss account is another important financial statement. It summarises the financial performance of a company, showing revenue (money in) and costs (money out) for a period of time. We can see from the profit and loss account what profit or loss has been made in the period of time that the statement covers.
- Companies trying to increase their turnover and profits may use a number of techniques, including increasing expenditure on advertising and revenue, reducing prices of goods or services, improving credit terms offered to customers, sourcing cheaper suppliers, increasing the range of products/services offered and finally, growing the business's operations.

Test your knowledge

Practice multiple choice exam questions

1) Which of the following sources of finance would be considered as a long-term source?
   a) Factoring
   b) Trade credit
   c) Bank loan
   d) Overdraft

2) A growing company needs to purchase a new computer system to enable it to track all its transactions. Which of the four sources of finance would you feel is the most suitable for this purpose?
   a) Sale and leaseback
   b) Leasing
   c) Hire purchase
   d) Mortgage

3) A trader's gross profit is 30 per cent of turnover. If his turnover was $300,000, what would be his gross profit?
   a) $3000
   b) $30,000
   c) $90,000
   d) $100,000

4) A statement of a business's assets and liabilities on a particular day is called a:
   a) Profit and loss account
   b) Trade credit sheet
   c) Balance sheet
   d) Factor account

5) Which of the following would be fixed assets for a business?
   a) Cash at the bank
   b) Fixtures and fittings
   c) Trade creditors
   d) Trade debtors

Practice stimulus response and structured exam questions

1) The figure, right, shows several sources of finance.
   a) Distinguish between long-term and short-term sources of finance. (*4 marks*)
   b) Name one other source of long-term finance not shown in the diagram. (*1 mark*)
   c) Explain three differences between bank loans and bank overdrafts. (*6 marks*)

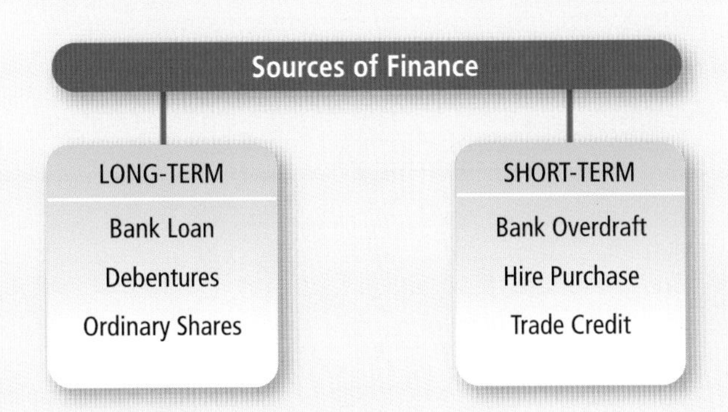

Test your knowledge *continued*

d) Giving reasons for each choice, recommend a source of finance given in the diagram that a limited company might use to:
  (i) Purchase a new factory. (*3 marks*)
  (ii) Pay for computer software. (*3 marks*)
  (iii) Make repairs to its office building. (*3 marks*)

(CIE Commerce Paper 1 May/Jun 2003)

When answering Question 1d, don't forget that the question asks for reasons for your answers. To get the full 3 marks, you must recommend a source of finance and provide a brief explanation of the reasons for your choice.

2) A retailer bought 100 shirts from a wholesaler for $25 each less 20 per cent trade discount.
  a) What is meant by trade discount and why does the wholesaler offer it to the retailer? (*4 marks*)
  b) Calculate how much profit the retailer will make if he sells each shirt for $35. Show your working. (*4 marks*)

(CIE Commerce Specimen Paper 2 2005)

3) a) What are the main characteristics of a bank loan? (*6 marks*)
  b) In what circumstances would a building company use a bank loan instead of a bank overdraft? (*4 marks*)
  c) The building company wishes to obtain a loan of $600,000.
    i. Imagine you are a bank manager. What information would you require before you decide whether or not to give the loan? (*5 marks*)
    ii. Interest rates are 6 per cent per annum. Calculate how much interest the building company will pay each year if it is given the $600,000 loan. Show your working. (*2 marks*)
  d) Explain why the building company might use its retained profits to finance a project. (*3 marks*)

(CIE Commerce Paper 1 May/Jun 2004)

4) The diagram shows the costs, including the retailer's profit, involved in producing and marketing a can of juice which sells for $2.
  a) Calculate the manufacturer's costs for producing the can of juice. Show your working. (*2 marks*)
  b) What percentage of the selling price is the manufacturer's profit? Show your working. (*2 marks*)
  c) If a retailer sells 1000 cans of juice, calculate how much profit he makes. Show your working. (*2 marks*)
  d) State and explain one reason why the retailer's profit is higher than the manufacturer's profit. (*3 marks*)

(CIE Commerce Paper May/Jun 2002)

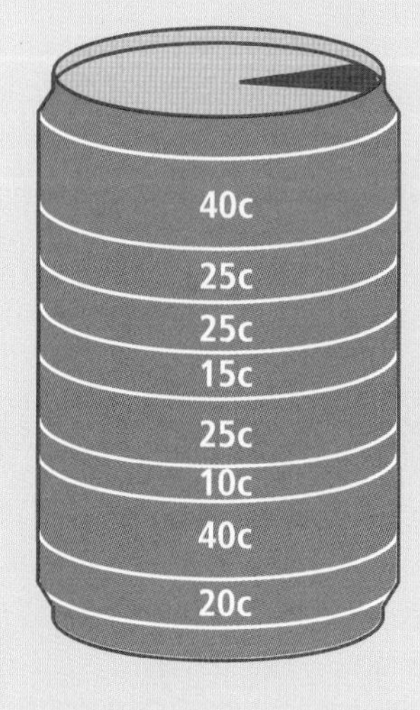

Retailer's profit
Retailer's costs
Tax
Transport costs
Advertising costs
Manufacturer's profit
Processing the juice
Cost of the can

Test your knowledge *continued*

5) The profit and loss account below is of a limited company called Penny Ping Enterprises Ltd.

PENNY PING ENTERPRISES LTD

PROFIT AND LOSS ACCOUNT AS AT 31/12/2001

			$m
Sales Revenue			500
less Cost of Goods sold			(a) (i)
			200
		$m	
Expenses	Labour	68	
	Rent	12	
	Power	10	
	Advertising	30	
			120
Net Profit			(a) (ii)

a) Calculate the cost of goods sold and net profit. (*2 marks*)
b) Explain the term 'sales revenue'. (*2 marks*)
c) Explain the term 'net profit' and show why it is important to the owners of the business. (*4 marks*)
d) Calculate net profit in relation to sales revenue as a percentage. (*2 marks*)
e) Explain two ways in which Penny Ping Enterprises Ltd might improve the company's net profit. (*4 marks*)

(CIE Commerce Paper Oct/Nov 2002)

- Make full use of the time given to you in exams. If you have any spare time, read through your answers, checking for any spelling or grammatical errors.
- Make sure you express yourself clearly and check that you have answered the question that is being asked.

Index

Note: Page numbers in **bold** indicate where definitions of key terms are to be found.

accident risks insurances 195
accounts receivable **249**
added value **3**
advertising 14, 115
  benefits of 117
  dangers of 118–19
  purpose of 116–17
  social aspects of 117–18
  types of 119–20
advice notes 85
after-sale services 32
AIDA model, advertising 119
aids to trade 13–14
air transport 165–6
air waybills 174
airports, additional services 175
annual percentage rates (APRs) 52
APR (Annual Percentage Rat) **52**
assets **255**
automatic teller machines (ATMs) 220

balance of payments 102–3
balance of trade 102
balance sheets 254–6
bank accounts 208–9
bank giro credits 215
bank overdrafts 208, 248–9
bank statements 211
banker's draft 219
banking 13, 206
  banking services 207
  documents, customer 210–12
  payment means 213–19
  trends in banking 220
  types of bank account 208–9
banks **206**
'barriers to trade' 106–7
bill of lading 173
bonded warehouses 105, 186
brand **31**
brand loyalty **115**
branding 31
brokers 76
business finance 13, 243
  capital of a business 256–7
  sources of 244–53
business reply service 156
business risks and insurances 195–6
business units 225
  location of a business 226–7
  main forms of 230–6
  multinationals 237–9
  public and private sector 228–9

call centres **220**
call routing 158
canal transport 168
capital of a business **254–7**
cash 213
cash and carry wholesalers 73, 187
cash discounts **90**
catalogues 83
cell phones 158
certificates of posting 156
chain of distribution **22**, 23–4
chain of production 3–7
cheques 213–14
chip and PIN **217–18**
codes of practice 61–2
cold-storage warehouses 186
collective advertising 120
commerce **11–12**
commercial transactions **80**
communications 14, 137
  electronic 149–54
  importance to global trade 138–9

methods 140–55
oral 141–3
the post office 156 7
telecoms 157–8
visual 148–9
written 143–7
'comparative advantage' 98–9
comparative advertising 120
compensation 191, 195, 197, 201
competitive advertising 120
computer technology 33–5
consequential loss insurance 194
consumer associations 64
consumer councils 64–5
consumer law 60–1
consumer protection 57
codes of practice 61–2
consumer law 60–1
organisations 63–6
reasons for 58–9
containerisation 171
contracts **155**
contractual agreements 84
contribution, insurance principle 197
credit **44**
credit cards 50–1, 216
credit notes 87–8
credit transfers 209, 215
creditors **256**
crossed cheques **213**
current (cheque) accounts 208–9
current ratio 256
customer credit 44
types of credit 48–53
use of credit 45–7
customer debt 45–6
customs authorities 104–5
customs duties, collection of 104, 186

debentures 246–7
debit cards 217–18
debt 103
debtors **256**
deferred payments 49, 251
deficit 103
delivery notes 85, 173
department stores 28
deposit accounts 209
direct debits (DDs) 215
direct services 15
directory enquiries 158
dividends **192**, 233, 245
division of labour **9**
documentary credits, banking 219
documents of trade 80
home trade 81–9
international transport 173–4
terms of payment 90–2
'duty of disclosure' 198

e-commerce 35–6
e-mail 150–1
e-tailing **35–6**
'economies of scale' 33
electronic communication 149–54
electronic data interchange (EDI) 35
electronic funds transfer at point of sale (EFTPOS) 35, 217
embargoes **106**
endorsing open cheques **213**
enquiry document 81
EPOS systems 34–5
export merchants 110
export tax 104
export trade 97
exporters 13
difficulties faced by 109–10
documentary credit 219
exports 102
extended credit 49, 251
external communication 140

face-to-face communication 141, 151–2
factoring 249
factors (agents) 76
faxes 150
finance *see* business finance
financial protection, insurance 191
fixed capital **255**
float **245**
flowcharts 148, 149
foreign trade *see* international trade

forwarding agents 76
franchises 236
free trade 106
freephone numbers 157
freepost 156

generic advertising 120
global trade *see* international trade
graphs 148, 149
gross profit 256

hire purchase (HP) 48, 250–1
home shopping 37–8
home trade 12
hypermarkets 28

import tax 104
import trade 97
importers 13
imports 101
'impulse buying' 32
indemnity, insurance principle 197
independent retailers 26–7
industry **3**
informative advertising 119
insurable interest 197–8
insurance 14, 190
  arranging cover 199–200
  insurable risks 194–6
  making a claim 201
  non-insurable risks 196
  pooling of risk 191–3
  principles of 197–8
  purpose of 191
insurance brokers **200**
insurance premiums 191
interdependence of organisations 15–16
interest **209**
internal communication 140
international and national consumer councils 64–5
international trade **13**, 97
  advantages of 100
  balance of payments 102–3
  customs authorities 104–5
  free trade and protectionism 106–7
  importance of 98–9
  importance of communications 138–9
  imports and exports 101
  trading blocs 108
  transport services 175
Internet 152–3
Internet banking 220
Internet shopping 37
intranet 153
invisible trade 101
invoices 85–6

large-scale retailing 39
leasing 249–50
letters 145–6
life assurance 196
limited companies 232–3
liquidation **247**
loans 245
local consumer advice centres 64
local environmental health organisations 64
local trading standards organisations 63
location of a business 226–7

mail order 37
marine risks and insurances 194–5
mark-up 92
'marketing mix' 116
marketing, role of 116–20
meetings, advantages of 141, 142–3
memos 144
merchants 76
'middlemen' 76
mobile phone communication 158
mortgages 247
multinationals 237–9
multiple chain retailers 29

natural disasters, insuring against 191, 194
needs **2**
net current assets, calculating 255–6
net profit 256

net worth (net assets) **255**
nominal value **245**
notices 146

open cheques **213**
oral communication methods 141–3
orders 83–4
overdrafts 208, 248–9

packaging 31
partnerships 231–2
paying-in slips 210
persuasive advertising 119
pipelines 168
pooling of risk 191–3
postal services 156–7
pressure groups 64
price lists 83
primary sector industries 4
private limited companies (Ltd) 233–4
private sector **225**
private sector enterprises 228–9
private warehouses 185
product promotion, methods of 116
production 2
  aids to trade 13–14
  commerce **11–12**
  industry, commerce and direct services link 15–17
  specialisation and division of labour **8–10**
  stages of 3–7
  trade **12–13**
profit and loss accounts 256–7
profit, methods of improving 257
protectionism 106–7
public limited companies (Plc) 234–5
public sector **225**
public sector enterprises 228
public warehouses 186–7

quality assurance **62**
quotas **106**
quotations 82, 192

radio paging 157
rail transport 164–5
rate of turnover 256
receipts 89
recorded delivery 156
regional distribution centres 185
registered service 157
reports 143–4
reserves **254**
retail trade 12, 22
  chains of distribution 23–4
  e-commerce 35–6
  home shopping 37–8
  large-scale retailing 39–40
  selling techniques 31–2
  trends in retailing 32–5
retail warehouses 185
retailers **22**
  functions of 24–5
  types of 26–30
retailing 12
retained profits 244
risks, insuring against 194–5
road transport 163–4

sale and leaseback 248
sales orders 83–4
sales turnover 256
savings 244
savings accounts 209
sea transport 167–8
seaports, additional services 175
seasonal demand for goods 183
secondary sector industries 4
self-service 32
self-service retailers 27
selling techniques 31–2
shareholders 233
shares 245–6
signs and symbols 148
small-scale retailers, survival of 39–40
sole traders 230–1
specialisation **8–10**
standards institutions 66
standing orders (SOs) 214
statement of account 88
stock exchange **235**
stockpiling 183

storage of goods *see* warehousing
store cards 52
subrogation, insurance principle 197
supermarkets 27
superstores 28

target audience **117**
tariffs **106**
telebanking 220
telecommunications (telecoms) 157–8
teleconferencing 141–2, 158
telephone communication 141–2
telesales 38
tertiary sector activities 4
trade **12–13**
trade credit **73**, **90**, 251–2
trade discounts **91**
trading blocs 108
trading statistics, collection by customs authorities 104
transport 14, 162
  benefits of having own 169–70
  containerisation 171
  documents 173–4
  factors affecting choice of 169
  importance of 163
  international 175
  methods of 163–8
  modern trends in 172
trends in retailing 32–5
turnover 256
  methods of improving 257
TV shopping 38

unit retailers 26–7
'utmost good faith', insurance principle 198

Value Added Tax (VAT) 104
videoconferencing 151–2
visible trade 101
visual communication methods 148–9

wants **2**
warehousing 14, 180
  advantages to trade 182
  functions of 182
  growth of 184
  main reasons for 183–4
  role of 181
  types of 185–7
wholesale trade 12, 70
  intermediaries 76
wholesalers **70**
  functions of 74–5
  role of 71–2
  types of 73
wholesaling 12
working capital, calculating 225–6
World Wide Web **153–4**
written communication methods 143–7